S/O mL
NO Inf

42371622

CIRIA C518

London, 1999

Safety in ports – ship-to-shore linkspans and walkways

A guide to procurement, operation and maintenance

R J E Marks

D
627.22
MAR

CIRIA *sharing knowledge ▪ building best practice*

6 Storey's Gate, Westminster, London SW1P 3AU
TELEPHONE 0171 222 8891   FAX 0171 222 1708
EMAIL enquiries@ciria.org.uk
WEBSITE www.ciria.org.uk

Summary

This report provides authoritative best-practice guidance on the procurement, operation and maintenance of ship-to-shore linkspans and walkways. It provides information about existing linkspans and walkways obtained from a comprehensive survey of ports, ship operators, designers and manufacturers. In particular, the book provides data on incidents and experiences with linkspans and walkways reported in the survey.

The book is divided into five chapters. Chapter 1 is a general introduction to linkspans and walkways, Chapter 2 looks at the legislation and technical standards, and Chapter 3 describes the procurement process and sets out the requirements essential for safe functioning of the facility. Emphasis is placed on the selection of competent individuals and organisations to carry out these functions, on the importance of carrying out independent design assessment and on the need for the owner to audit the procedures required by legislation to ensure safety. Chapter 4 is concerned with operating requirements and documentation. It describes a procedure for recording incidents and includes a pro-forma. Chapter 5 describes good maintenance practice and strategies for maintenance and documentation. The latter chapters both emphasise the need for adequate training of the staff involved in operating and maintaining linkspans and walkways. Appendices describe the research process, provide questionnaire survey data, discuss automation and electronic systems, and list British and European standards.

Chapters 2, 3, 4 and 5 include highlighted recommendations and conclude with important guidance arising out of the research, which is intended to enhance the safety of ship-to-shore linkspans and walkways.

R J E Marks

Safety in ports – ship-to-shore linkspans and walkways. A guide to procurement, operation and maintenance

Construction Industry Research and Information Association

Publication C518   © CIRIA 1999   ISBN 0 86017 518 9

Keywords		
Ferry terminal, linkspan, machinery, regulations, ro-ro terminal, safety, shore ramp, walkway		

Reader interest	**Classification**	
Port owners, ro-ro and/or ferry terminal owners, linkspan or walkway operators, ro-ro ship and/or ferry operators, naval architects, port engineers, port maintenance engineers, linkspan manufacturers, machinery suppliers, port consulting engineers, insurers, safety managers.	Availability	Unrestricted
	Content	Guidance, industry survey
	Status	Committee-guided
	User	Ports industry

Foreword

The need for this guide became apparent following the tragic collapse of the passenger walkway at the port of Ramsgate. The collapse was caused by faulty design, even though the port had employed experienced and highly reputable designers, constructors and third-party assessors. However, it has since become clear that a port in that situation still has responsibilities in respect of design and construction, as well as operation. This gave added stimulus to the provision of guidance on how ports should go about fulfilling these responsibilities.

Linkspans and walkways must not only fulfil the functions of a bridge; they must also accommodate movements due to tides, waves, the ship, and in some cases the movements of buoyant supports. They involve mechanical and electrical components in addition to the structure. The system is complex, and design should only be undertaken by organisations and individuals who are appropriately qualified and experienced. The structures are subject to machinery regulations as well as construction regulations. There are about 400 of these structures in the UK alone, and many more outside the UK. As this guide makes clear, there is also an urgent need for a design standard.

Ports must not only comply with mandatory procedures, but must also take and record all possible steps to ensure safety. Extreme diligence and vigilance are required at all times.

The objectives of this guide are to assist ports in the provision, operation and maintenance of linkspans and walkways that are safe, efficient, and reliable.

J C Chapman
Chairman, Project Steering Group
10 June 1999

Acknowledgements

Research contract

The research work and preparation of this guide were carried out by Posford Duvivier under a contract with CIRIA. The principal author was Richard Marks, who was assisted by the project co-ordinator Stephen Osborn, electrical adviser Joseph Tierney, and mechanical adviser Stephen Hopper. CIRIA's research managers for the project were Dr Ghazwa M Alwani-Starr and Mr Robert Dent.

Funding

The research project was funded by the ports industry through PSO (Technical Services) Ltd, the Health and Safety Executive, the TT Club, the Safety Assessment Federation Ltd (SAFed), Lloyd's Register of Shipping, and the Department of the Environment, Transport and the Regions (Ports Division).

Project steering group

The work was overseen by a steering group established by CIRIA to advise on the technical content of the guide. The steering group comprised:

J C Chapman (Chairman)	Chapman Associates
M A Banasik	SAFed/ACE Engineering Insurance
J R Batte	Lloyd's Register of Shipping
M L Compton	PSO Technical Services Ltd
R Cooper	Consultant – Port Ramsgate Limited
P J Gadd	Portsmouth Commercial Port
C Clark (replacing D Goodchild)	DETR
C R Hedges	Dover Harbour Board
J E Hood	HSE Docks National Interest Group
A C Meek	Stena Line Ltd
J Nicholls	The TT Club
P G Preston	Caledonian MacBrayne Ltd
N Qamar	Associated British Ports

The steering group was supplemented by the following corresponding members:

R N Appleton	Poole Harbour Commissioners
V Barback	Sir William Arrol
T J Bownes	Mersey Docks and Harbour Company
D F Evans	ICE Maritime Board
J M Felstead	HSE Regional Specialist Group
D P Galway	Larne Harbour Ltd
J R Plumb	The Institution of Civil Engineers
G R Steele	Port of Felixstowe

CIRIA and Posford Duvivier would like to express their thanks and appreciation to all the members of the project steering group for their helpful and useful comments and advice; to the members of the port industry who agreed to be interviewed in depth about their good practices; to the numerous individuals and organisations who contributed information to the extensive survey of linkspans and walkways; and to the organisations that provided photographs.

Photograph locations and acknowledgements

Cover	Ringsakiddy Ro Ro Terminal, Cork	Finbarr O'Connell
Figure 1.2	Dover Harbour	Dover Harbour Board
Figure 1.3	Victoria Terminal 1, Belfast	Belfast Harbour Commissioners
Figure 1.5	Sheerness	Medway Ports
Figure 1.6	Sandefjord, Norway	Nor-Ent
Figure 1.7	Elizabeth Harbour, Jersey	Posford Duvier
Figure 1.14b		FMT Aircraft Gate Support Systems AB
Figure 1.14c	Sheerness	Chorley and Handford
Figure 1.17	Dun Laoghaire	Peter Barrow
Figure 1.18	Ringsakiddy Ro Ro Terminal, Cork	Finbarr O'Connell
Figure 1.19	Portsmouth	Posford Duvivier
Figure 1.22a	Dover	Dover Harbour Board
Figure 1.22b	Ramsgate	Port Ramsgate
Figure 1.22c	Dun Laoghaire	Peter Barrow

Guidance overview

ABOUT THE PROJECT

The Ports' Safety Organisation (PSO) represents the health and safety interests of more than 200 ports. It approached CIRIA in August 1996 with a request to address its members' concerns about the safety of ship-to-shore linkspans and walkways following several recent incidents. These concerns were shared by the British Ports Association (BPA) and the HSE Docks National Interest Group. The ports industry indicated that research was urgent because of the need:

- to take into account the implications for the docks industry of the Construction (Design and Management) Regulations 1994 and the Docks Regulations 1988
- to establish industry best practice that would result in common standards being developed for the procurement, operation and maintenance of ship-to-shore linkspans and walkways within the UK and elsewhere.

The ports industry required that the research should address and resolve the differing needs of port owners, operators, engineers and health and safety advisers in order to enable all interested parties to benefit from the final output.

Key objectives

The general objective of the research project was:

To produce an authoritative best practice guide for procurement, operation and maintenance of linkspans and walkways, having regard to the Health and Safety at Work, etc Act and associated Regulations including, but not limited to, the Construction (Design and Management) Regulations, the Supply of Machinery (Safety) Regulations, the Provision and Use of Work Equipment Regulations, the Docks Regulations and to relevant standards.

The specific objectives were to promote improvements in the following aspects:

- safety
- minimising failure that could lead to danger
- operational efficiency
- reliability
- durability
- whole-life economy.

With these objectives in mind, the report was required to include guidance on:

- specification of functional requirements
- information to be provided by ports to designers and suppliers
- contractual options
- selection of designers and contractors
- good operational procedures
- good maintenance procedures.

Purpose and scope

This guide is intended to provide practical and user-friendly best-practice guidance on the procurement, operation and maintenance of ship-to-shore linkspans and walkways, covering all aspects of the process, including the safety regulations and requirements, but excluding design. It is principally aimed at members of the port and associated industries, and assumes some basic knowledge of operating vessels, the procurement of port facilities, and the operation of roll-on/roll-off terminals and ferry passenger terminals. It is also intended to be of use to designers, contractors, operators, and health and safety advisers involved in port facilities.

The guide covers the following procurement, operation and maintenance issues.

Procurement

- the types and common characteristics of ship-to-shore structures in the UK

- hazard identification and risk analysis

- obtaining and providing information: that is, information that needs to be given to the designer or specifier by the port operator or facility owner, and information that needs to be given to the port operator by the designer and contractor

- the selection of suitable designers and contractors

- understanding and assessing tenders

- understanding and selecting appropriate forms of contract.

Operation

- operating requirements

- recording and investigating incidents

- training

- documentation and instructions for use.

Maintenance

- understanding whole-life costs

- maintenance requirements

- identification of and access to areas requiring regular inspection and maintenance

- recording maintenance history

- recording and investigating recurrent problems.

Sources of information

The research was initiated by sending detailed survey questionnaires to ports, ship operators, designers and manufacturers. Information was obtained from an analysis of the questionnaire survey, from consultation meetings with four major UK ro-ro ports and one ferry operator, and from a review of incidents that have occurred. The conclusions of the research were presented and discussed at a workshop attended by invited specialists. Information has also been obtained from European Union directives, UK and Irish statutory instruments, and a number of official publications and approved codes of practice. In addition reference has been made to previous CIRIA and Construction Industry Board publications. The guidance is thus not simply based on current practice but has also considered the effects of legislative requirements and operational matters.

Exclusions

This guide is intended to cover the movable connection that gives access to allow the horizontal loading and unloading of vehicles, persons or animals on the hoof to ships from the dockside, quay or berth structures in a port or harbour. Such vehicles may be wheeled cargo or vehicles loaded or unloaded using roll-on/roll-off methods.

However, the scope of the investigation does not cover:

- ship ramps
- fixed shore ramps (non-adjustable)
- access towers, accommodation ladders, brows or gangways for ship's crew
- access to footbridges between floating and fixed offshore installations
- marina pontoons and connecting footbridges for recreational craft
- floating piers or landing stages and connecting footbridges for river buses
- fish farm pontoons and connecting footbridges
- pontoons and connecting footbridges in non-tidal waters
- fastenings to the ship
- ship's gear
- movable ramps and doors on the ship, such as internal tweendeck ramps
- ship bow ramps and ship stern ramps
- mobile appliances whose sole means of propulsion is by vehicle or manpower (manual effort).

Nevertheless, the principles set out in the guide would be generally applicable to the excluded facilities and supports.

CONTENTS OF THE GUIDE

The main best-practice guidance is found in the three central chapters on procurement, operation and maintenance – Chapters 3, 4 and 5 – each of which ends with a series of recommendations. Equally important are Chapters 1 and 2, which set the scene in terms of types of equipment and incidents, and the regulatory and legislative framework. The Appendices provide detailed information on the research process and the questionnaire survey results, plus a note on automation and programmable electronic systems. The Glossary provides terms and definitions, and the sources of information are given in the References section.

The chapters containing guidance include highlighted text that emphasises important information or recommendations, and each chapter concludes with recommendations for changes and improvements in current practice. These recommendations are primarily aimed at the UK ports industry, but will be generally applicable throughout the European Union and worldwide.

Setting the scene: linkspans and walkways

The detailed survey questionnaires provided information about the features of linkspans and walkways and typical incidents that had occurred. The incidents were analysed and compared with a number of features in order to identify any linkages. Various specialist terms have been defined in the guide.

The regulatory framework

Linkspans and walkways are hybrid and generally complex items of port equipment consisting of both fixed and movable elements. They are subject to the Health and Safety at Work Act and a variety of regulations covering docks, safety, construction, machinery and work equipment. A summary of the requirements of particularly relevant regulations is set out as Table 2.1 in Chapter 2.

Table 2.1 does not, however, cover all the regulations relating to linkspans and walkways, and a thorough study of the regulations and approved codes of practice should be made. It is essential that those legally responsible for the safety of these facilities should read and understand both the specific regulations and the guidance given in the approved codes of practice.

This section of the guide is required reading for those involved in the management of safety for these facilities. Its principal recommendation is that a port industry arrangement be set up to collect, monitor and promulgate information on incidents, accidents and failures.

Ship-to-shore linkspans and walkways must provide a properly maintained, safe means of access to the ship, and should not be used unless they are of adequate strength for the purpose required, of sound construction and properly maintained. This obligation is absolute.

A risk assessment must be carried out to identify the hazards that exist for the particular facility with reference to the essential health and safety requirements.

The client has specific duties under the CDM Regulations. These include appointing a planning supervisor and a principal contractor, and being reasonably satisfied of the competence of these appointees and of the adequacy of resources allocated by the appointees to perform their duties. The client must provide health and safety information about the project, must not permit construction work to start until an adequate construction health and safety plan is available, and must hold the health and safety file and make it available to others.

Procurement and implementation

While this section is intended to include preliminary design considerations from the initial identification of need and the identification and collection of basic design information, it does not provide guidance on detailed design.

Linkspans and walkways involve a mixture of construction, equipment, machinery and control systems and a variety of professional disciplines. There is no ideal standard form of contract, but civil engineering or electrical and mechanical supply forms can be adapted depending on the mixture of elements.

There are several approaches to procurement including:

- traditional designer-led method
- design and build method
- equipment purchase
- management contracting
- construction management.

The overall process is set out as Figure 3.1 at the beginning of Section 3.

It is important that the purchaser considers the type of approach at an early stage in the procurement process so that appropriate choices can be made about the appointment of advisers, the timing of design input, and the involvement of manufacturers. Several important roles need to be filled during the procurement process. Some of these roles depend on the method of procurement, but others are common and include:

- project adviser
- planning supervisor
- engineer
- principal contractor
- independent design assessor
- systems engineer
- responsible person
- project safety auditor.

The contractual arrangements between the supplier and the construction contractor need to take account of the various physical and regulatory interfaces between the machinery and the structural elements.

The implementation process should ensure that the following documentation is handed to the purchaser:

- training programmes
- technical file (prepared by manufacturer)
- health and safety file (prepared by principal contractor)
- operating manual
- maintenance manual.

The main contractor is normally appointed as the principal contractor under the CDM Regulations, but purchasers have a statutory duty to ensure that the contractor to be appointed is competent to carry out this duty. Therefore contractors should be requested to provide details of their experience in acting as principal contractor and examples of construction health and safety files prepared for previous developments. Purchasers should also request the names and CVs of the key staff who will be involved in health and safety issues and details of their experience in carrying out the duties of the principal contractor.

It is essential to carry out an independent verification rather than merely checking the calculations produced by the supplier's designer or the purchaser's designer. In some cases the design calculations have been incorrectly carried out and have been checked, yet major errors have been missed. The independence of the proposed procedure means that the original designer's conceptual thinking will not influence the assessor.

The provision of adequate and effective training for all personnel is not only a statutory obligation upon employers but also a necessary adjunct to the management of a commercially successful undertaking.

The supplier of any new facility should be required as a contractual obligation to provide high-quality input to a programme of training for all personnel who will take on responsibilities in connection with the new linkspan or walkway. This provision should be structured to suit all relevant personnel, and would probably include separate syllabuses and demonstrations for operating and maintenance personnel.

The questionnaire survey and consultation discovered that access for the purposes of operation of linkspans and walkways is relatively poor, and the design of access is an area that requires major improvement.

It is recommended that adequate thought be given to the operators' welfare requirements at the design stage. There should be sufficient communication between operating organisations and the specifiers or designers at an early stage in the procurement of a facility to ensure proper implementation of that facility's particular requirements.

The wording and layout of the instructions for use should cover the essential requirements and must take into account the level of knowledge and training that can be expected from operators of machinery.

Operating manuals should cover the safe starting-up, running and close-down of all systems. They should be written specifically for each facility. Generalised operating manuals are not acceptable for ship-to-shore linkspans and walkways.

It is important that those responsible for planning and implementing maintenance work are involved in the creation of the project brief and in the technical specification of the maintenance requirements for the linkspan or walkway when it is procured.

The role of the project safety auditor has not been formalised before, and should previously have been carried out by the purchaser. In order to provide evidence that the purchaser has taken all reasonably practical steps to ensure the safety of the facility it is strongly recommended that safety matters are properly audited and that this role is formally identified. The project safety auditor must be knowledgeable and competent in health and safety matters related to linkspans and walkways. The auditor should preferably be independent.

Operation

This chapter establishes that a clearly defined management system needs to be set up for the safe and reliable operation of a linkspan and walkway. Several key functions need to be fulfilled by various personnel, including:

Operator	Person specifically trained and authorised to operate the linkspan or walkway
Berth superintendent	Oversees operation of linkspan or walkway and mooring of ship
Port control duty manager	Issues instructions to ferry concerning berthing and unberthing and to berth superintendent (or operator)
Terminal manager	Has overall responsibility for traffic control and shore-based personnel
Harbour master	Controls all shipping movements in harbour and manages the port control duty managers.

At some small ports several or all of these functions will be combined.

The terminal manager prepares operating instructions, work instructions, training procedures and emergency plans based on information provided by the supplier. The instructions and plans should take into account the results of risk assessments, and should cover contingencies such as ship collision, structural failure of lifting equipment and extreme environmental conditions. They should state operational limitations including loading, geometry and environmental conditions.

A chain of communication and management should be established, and every person involved in the operation of ship-to-shore linkspans and walkways should understand the routes for communication, authorisation and reporting incidents.

The operator must be assessed to have a suitable level of competence and capability, be provided with appropriate training and given definite authorisation to operate a particular facility. Before each period of use, the operator or other competent person should carry out a routine inspection of the linkspan or walkway and complete an inspection record. The operator should check that no damage to the facility has occurred during berthing or unberthing. When the ship is berthed and safely moored the operator should only make the various connections to the ship after receiving authorisation from the port control duty manager, who must receive agreement from the ship's master. Authorisation should also be given for disconnection at the end of the period of use.

During operation the operator should monitor the functioning of the facility, should check that warning lights and alarms have not been triggered, and should observe any dangerous parts and the interface with the ship to ensure that the facility remains safe to operate. In the event of an exceptional occurrence, the emergency plan for the facility should be followed. The operator should complete a daily log for the facility, including the recording of any unusual incidents or damages. Safe access must be provided to control stations and safety critical parts requiring regular inspection.

Significant incidents, including near misses, should be reported on an incident record and appropriate further investigations carried out, including thorough examinations of the lifting equipment and surveys of structural damage. These reports should be used to plan repairs and to provide feedback into reviews of the operating instructions.

Operators of facilities should complete daily logs recording any significant occurrences.

Instructions on operational limitations should be known to operators and displayed at an appropriate location on the facility. These operational limitations would include loading, environmental conditions (wind speed, wave heights, tidal extremes) and other parameters that define the performance capacity of the facility. Such information should also, wherever practicable, be made known to the vessel's master, who will necessarily be involved in decision making about the berthing or unberthing of his vessel.

All incidents of damage, failure or faulty operation should be recorded in writing and investigated.

A "no blame" management culture needs to be established so that incidents are accurately and properly recorded at the time that they occur. Witnesses or record-keepers should not have to concern themselves with the attribution of blame, insurance matters, loss adjustment and possible legal proceedings. It is recommended that all operating organisations and facility owners introduce policies on the reporting of incidents, and that a much higher priority is given to the proper reporting of these incidents and to providing feedback to the ports industry.

Daily logs and incident records tend to refer to actual damage and failures. However, it is equally important that near misses are reported, as repeated near misses indicate a strong likelihood of an accident happening in future. These near misses should be reported and acted on in the same way as an incident that causes damage or failure.

Consideration should be given to setting up an industry-wide feedback system for passing on information about incidents involving ship-to-shore linkspans and walkways.

Maintenance

Linkspans and walkways are essential for the operation of ro-ro ships and passenger ferries. Because of this need for a high level of reliability, equipment needs to be designed ergonomically and for ease of maintenance. Whole-life costs should be taken into account in the design and supply of the facility. In order to maintain the facilities in an efficient and safe condition, a maintenance strategy needs to be developed so that the instructions in the maintenance manual can be implemented. There are several approaches that can be adopted, including a combination of the methods set out below.

1. **Breakdown maintenance**. Rectify faults or failures as and when they occur.

2. **Planned preventive maintenance**. Replace parts and make adjustments at pre-planned regular intervals at a frequency determined by risk assessments and experiences of previous breakdowns.

3. **Planned condition-based maintenance**. Monitor condition of safety-critical parts to detect trends in wear or failure, and plan maintenance to be carried out before breakdown occurs.

4. **Planned modifications**. Modify structure, lifting equipment or machinery to improve reliability based on records of previous breakdowns and condition monitoring.

5. **Periodic surveys**. Carry out annual or periodical survey of the condition of the structure or machinery and identify repairs required.

6. **Incident investigations**. Survey damage caused by ship impact or other incident.

Before any repairs, adjustments or examinations are planned or carried out, a safe system of work must be established and documented. A useful method is through a permit-to-work system. This requires a nominated person to isolate power sources and give written authorisation for the facility to undergo maintenance. On completion of maintenance, reinstatement and testing, the person carrying out the maintenance certifies that it is safe to be put back into use.

Maintenance teams need to have sufficient shared knowledge of the particular characteristics of each installation to ensure that all maintenance work is carried out efficiently and safely. Appropriate training in the maintenance of the various elements of the facility should be provided, and refresher courses should be arranged periodically. Training records should be kept, so that individual employees' competence can be assessed. Authorisation to carry out particular maintenance work should be given only to those who are properly trained.

Information about repetitive faults, defects or failures of structures, lifting equipment and machinery should be recorded by the maintenance organisation and used to determine whether improvements or replacements are required. Significant problems should be reported on an industry-wide basis to other maintenance organisations, designers and suppliers.

Recommended actions

1. **Prepare guidance on the design of linkspans and walkways.** This guidance should be provided urgently in a form that will cross-reference existing structural, mechanical, electrical and control system standards and classification rules related to linkspans and walkways. The guidance should provide authoritative design practice for those areas not covered by other specific standards, including the aspects listed in Section 2.5.5

2. **Produce a Type C standard for linkspans and a separate Type C standard for walkways** to facilitate compliance with the essential safety requirements of the EU directives relating to machinery. These standards would define as a minimum the functional, performance, and health and safety requirements for linkspans and walkways. It is expected that these standards would cover requirements for stability of the facility. They would also cover crushing, trapping and falling hazards due to movement of the facility and other essential health and safety requirements relating to the design and construction of the machinery and safety components.

3. **Produce a design code of practice**. There is also a need for design guidance to be codified, covering all necessary topics including those aspects listed in Section 2.5.5. This could be achieved by BS 6349: Part 8, or by an equivalent European standard, or both, depending on which is the most expeditious route.

4. **Set up a port industry arrangement to collect, monitor and promulgate information on near misses, incidents, accidents and failures.** Owners, operators and maintenance organisations should co-operate with the above arrangements by providing records of incidents, if necessary by direct, anonymous, confidential reporting.

Contents

FIGURES

TABLES

Abbreviations

ACoP	Approved Code of Practice (see Glossary)
AUWED	Amending Directive to the Use of Work Equipment Directive
BPIT	British Ports Industry Training
BTEC	Business and Technician Education Council
CDM	Construction (Design and Management), *as in CDM Regulations*
CE	Communauté Européenne
CEN	European Committee for Standardisation
CENELEC	European Committee for Electrotechnical Standardisation
DETR	Department of the Environment, Transport and the Regions (of the UK Government)
DTI	Department of Trade and Industry (of the UK Government)
EEA	European Economic Area
EN	Euronorm
EU	European Union
HSC	Health and Safety Commission
HSE	Health and Safety Executive
HSWA	Health and Safety at Work etc Act 1974
ICHCA	International Cargo Handling Co-ordination Association
ILO	International Labour Organisation
IMO	International Maritime Organisation
LOLER	Lifting Operations and Lifting Equipment Regulations 1998
LRS	Lloyd's Register of Shipping
MHSWR	Management of Health and Safety at Work Regulations 1992
NDT	non-destructive testing
NVQ	National Vocational Qualifications
PIANC	Permanent International Association of Navigation Congresses
PLC	programmable logic controller
PSO	Ports Safety Organisation
PUWER	Provision and Use of Work Equipment Regulations 1992
PUWER 98	Provision and Use of Work Equipment Regulations 1998
SCOTVEC	Scottish Vocational Education Council
SM(S)R	Supply of Machinery (Safety) Regulations 1992 and Amendments 1994
UWED	Use of Work Equipment Directive

Glossary

This section gives explanations of the specialised terms used in this guide. Where explanations have been extracted from existing documents or sections within this report, this has been noted.

abutment
A structure onto which the shore bearings of a linkspan, shore ramp or link bridge are seated, and which may also provide resistance against anchorage forces for the facility, often incorporating a relatively high retaining wall. See also **bankseat**.

access
Properly maintained safe means of entry/exit for any person and of adequate strength for the purpose required and of sound construction.   *(Docks Regulations)*

accident
Unplanned event giving rise to death, ill-health (made worse by working activity or environment), injury, damage or other loss.

adjustable shore ramp
The vertically adjustable **roadway**, usually hinged at the inshore end and supported independently of the ship near the outer end, that provides an intermediate connection between the shore and the ship, and on which the shore end of a **ship ramp** can rest.   *(BS MA 97)*

A **roadway** providing an intermediate connection between the shore and the ship, and on which the shore end of a **ship ramp** can rest. The **roadway** is suspended vertically, is adjustable, and is usually hinged at the inshore end and supported near the outer end independently of the ship.   *(ICHCA glossary)*

approved body
Appointed by an EU member state as a qualified person or organisation responsible for carrying out conformity assessment for Schedule 4 machinery (ie dangerous machinery posing special hazards) and who meets the minimum criteria set out in the Machinery Directive.

approved code of practice
Practical guidance on achieving compliance with regulations and aimed at maintaining or improving standards of health and safety.

authorised person
Person authorised by an employer to drive or operate equipment or vehicles under the Docks Regulations. In Regulation 10(6) it means the person who operates: (a) a ship's ramp or door associated with a ship's ramp; (b) a power-operated hatch covering; (c) a retractable car deck; or (d) a shore-based ramp. In Regulation 11(1) it means a person who is authorised to drive a powered vehicle or a powered lifting appliance.

Person authorised to carry out defined tasks under relevant regulations such as the Pressure Regulations and the Electrical Regulations.

ballast
Solid or liquid materials placed in internal tanks or compartments on ships, pontoons, floats or integral tanks to alter their trim, draught or stability.

bankseat
Structure onto which the shore bearings of a linkspan, shore ramp or link bridge are seated, and which may also provide resistance against anchorage forces for the facility; usually relatively shallow. See also **abutment**.

belting
Reinforced outstanding protective strip along the side of a ro-ro ship or ferry, usually at the level of the lower vehicle deck.

berthing superintendent
The shore-based person responsible for organising the mooring and unmooring of the ship through control of the mooring gang and also for overseeing the operation of the linkspan or walkway. *(Section 4.2.1)*

boarding pod
Platform that is mechanically (or buoyantly) lifted; allows pedestrian access to the ship via a brow or gangway, and is connected to the **hinged link**. *(Section 1.3.1)*

bollard
Shaped block of steel or cast iron secured to a dolphin, quay, dock, wharf or linkspan to secure mooring lines from ships.

bridgehead
Transitional area at the aircraft end of the **passenger boarding bridge** at airports. *(pr EN 12312-4)*

brow
Narrow platform placed between ship and shore for embarkation and disembarkation; sometimes called a **gangway**. *(Admiralty manual of seamanship)*

Bridge that is hinged onto the **boarding pod** or **telescopic end**, and which either rests on the coaming of the ship's passenger access door or opening, or is supported by cantilever action from the **boarding pod** or the **telescopic end**. *(Section 1.3.1)*

bus system
Electronic data connection system that carries several different electronic messages through a common path, which are then differentiated and suitably responded to by the devices to which they are addressed.

capstan
Shaped winch drum attached to a motor; usually used for pulling a mooring line from a ship to the shore.

CE mark
Mark applied to a machine that satisfies the requirement of the EU Machinery Directive (or the Supply of Machinery (Safety) Regulations in the United Kingdom), or any one or more of the New Approach or CE Marking Directives including, for example, the Low Voltage Directive and the Electromagnetic Compatibility Directive.

certificate of conformity
Document issued by an organisation designated by an EU member state certifying descriptions and conditions applicable to use for a construction product and the provisions to which the product conforms, including test results.

classification
The process of approval of the design and construction of ships, linkspans and walkways; carried out by **classification**

	societies. Includes periodic surveys of structural components, equipment and engineering systems. *(Section 3.8.3)*
classification society	National organisation set up under legislation to carry out faithful and accurate **classification.**
clevis	Pair of lug plates or U-shaped bar forming a fork on the female side of a male/female pinned joint, which fits either side of the male lug plate with a pin passing through all three lug plates to make the joint.
client	Any person for whom a project is carried out, whether carried out by another person or in-house. *(Regulation 2(1), CDM Regulations)*
coaming	High raised rim at the passenger entrance in the hull of a ship, or a raised edge along an open deck on a ship.
combined facility	Facility comprising both a linkspan and a ship-to-shore walkway.
commissioning	The process of taking an installation from static assembly to full dynamic working order, including setting it into motion and regulating it to adjust it to specified tolerances.
competence	Having the skills, knowledge, education, training, experience, systems and support necessary to carry out particular work.
competent person	Person, appointed by an employer, with sufficient training, experience, knowledge and other qualities to properly assist in ensuring compliance with the requirements and prohibitions of health and safety legislation.
	Some statutory regulations, eg the Electricity at Work Regulations 1989, give specific requirements for persons to be considered competent.
daily log	Daily record of activities; kept by the operator of a linkspan or walkway. *(Section 4.4.3)*
declaration of conformity	The document whereby the **responsible person** confirms that each item of relevant machinery complies with all the essential health and safety requirements, and specifies the standards used. *(Regulation 22 SM(S)R)*
declaration of incorporation	The document whereby the **responsible person** specifies that each item of machinery, or machinery parts for assembly into other machinery, must not be put into service until the machinery into which it is incorporated is in conformity. The declaration also states the standards used.
deployment and retrieval structure	Mechanically operated beam, frame or plate hinged to a **boarding pod, telescopic end** or **drawbridge** and cantilevering below a **brow, gangway** or **drawbridge** to lift them onto or over a ship's coaming for deployment, or to lift them off the coaming or passenger deck of the ship for retrieval. This structure is lowered after connection so that the brow, gangway or drawbridge can hinge freely with the movement of the ship. *(Section 1.3.1)*
design and construct	A method of procuring construction work in which the contractor is responsible for both the design and the construction of the facility.

designer	The person or organisation that carries out the design of a facility or part of a facility.
dock operations	The loading or unloading of goods on or from a ship…; the embarking and disembarking of passengers on or from a ship…; the movement of goods, passengers or vehicles. *(Docks Regulations)*
dolphin	Fixed marine structure for supporting fenders, mooring bollards, hoist towers or the restraint guides of buoyant linkspans. Usually of relatively small plan area in relation to the length of the berth.
downtime	The time during which a malfunction of machinery or environmental conditions make a berth unusable.
draught	Depth of the submerged part of a ship, pontoon or integral tank.
drawbridge	Liftable bridge section hinged at the shore end and supported by a strut/tie or rope system at the seaward end. *(Section 1.3.1)*
engineer	Qualified engineer or competent organisation, appointed by the client or purchaser, who fulfils the obligations of designing and supervising construction work under the terms of engineering conditions of contract.
engineer's representative	Competent engineer who is delegated specific powers by the engineer to perform certain duties under the contract. Typically, this person will be a resident engineer on a construction site or will visit workshops to test and examine plant.
essential health and safety requirements	Obligations under the EU Machinery Directive (or the Supply of Machinery (Safety) Regulations in the UK) that have to be addressed against a set of listed hazards for particular machinery. The list of hazards is set out in Annex 1 of the directive. *(Schedule 3 of the SM(S)R).*
essential requirements	Requirements that must be satisfied for a product to be suitable for construction work. The requirements are set out in Schedule 2 of the Construction Products Regulations.
facility maintenance engineer	Person responsible for managing the maintenance of the facility and for repairing it when it malfunctions. *(Section 4.2.1)*
fail safe	Concept that acknowledges that a person or system has a finite probability of failure and seeks to arrange that such failure will not lead to the occurrence of dangerous circumstances.
fender beam	Fender system in the form of a long horizontal beam supported by several fender energy-absorbing units so that ship impact loads can be withstood, normally separately from the linkspan.
ferry	Ship used to convey passengers with their baggage, road vehicles or railway carriages and wagons on regular schedules between ferry ports.
fixed shore ramp	Fixed incline between the normal quay surface and the outer face of the quay wall on which the shore end of a ship ramp can rest. *(BS MA 97).*

finger flap	Series of narrow steel bridging pieces, plates or structures attached to the end of a ship ramp, to some types of shore ramp, or to the ship end of some walkways.
fixed walkway	Walkway structure that has no moving parts. *(Section 1.3.1)*
flap	Extension, normally hinged to the ship or shore end of a shore ramp, to provide a transition between running surfaces.
float	Buoyant body or tank supporting the ship end of a semi-submersible linkspan.
freeboard	Vertical height between an open deck or a particular deck and the water line (or load line).
gangway	Narrow platform between ship and shore. See **brow**.
	Bridge structure to allow safe embarkation and disembarkation from ship to shore. *(BS MA 78).*
	Bridge that is hooked onto the coaming and supported on the **telescopic end**, **boarding pod** or **drawbridge**. *(Section 1.3.1)*
guide pile	Vertical pile used as a guide structure to restrain a pontoon/link bridge or semi-submersible or integral tank-type linkspan from floating away, but which allows it to move up and down with the rise and fall of the tide.
harbour master	Person in control of all shipping movements within a port. For day-to-day contact with specific berthing operations, he will delegate tasks to a port control duty manager. *(Section 4.2.1)*
hazard	Source of possible injury or damage to health. *(EN292-1)*
health and safety file	Record of information for the client (and others who need to see it) that focuses on health and safety. It alerts those who are responsible for the structure (and equipment in it) of the significant health and safety risks that will need to be dealt with during subsequent use, construction, maintenance, repair and cleaning work. *(Designing for health and safety in construction, HSE 1995)*
health and safety plan	Document required under the Construction (Design and Management) Regulations that contains information to assist with the management of health and safety during construction. It has two main stages, pre-tender and construction. The pre-tender health and safety plan (so named because it is normally prepared before the tendering process for the construction contract) brings together the health and safety information obtained from the purchaser (client) and designers. The construction health and safety plan details how the construction work will be managed on site to ensure health and safety.
heave	Translation movement of a ship in a vertical direction (eg due to waves).
hinge	Mechanical joint that allows rotation between two structures or structural members.
hinged link	Bridge between the ship or the **boarding pod** that is capable of rotating in the vertical plane to take up level differences between the terminal building and the ship. It may also rotate

in the horizontal plane. *(Section 1.3.1)*

hoist dolphin — Dolphin providing a foundation for the hoist tower.

hoist tower — Structure mounted on the shore or on a dolphin for supporting the lifting equipment of a mechanically lifted type of linkspan.

incident — Unexpected event resulting in a fault, failure, damage or loss of operation of the linkspan or walkway.

independent design assessor — Person or organisation engaged directly by the purchaser to verify the suitability and adequacy of the linkspan or walkway, including the technical and performance specifications, the design criteria stated in the project brief, and the technical specification, including environmental, geotechnical, loading criteria and dynamic behaviour. *(Section 3.1.3)*

interface — Boundary between the ship ramp, ship vehicle access opening or ship passenger access opening and the linkspan or passenger walkway. Sometimes the boundary between the mechanical, electrical, control, structural or foundation engineering systems or processes.

interface limit line — The line that defines the safe distance between the seaward end of the ship ramp landing area and the outer face of the shore ramp. *(ICHCA glossary)*

inter-ramp — Short ramp providing a smooth transition between telescoping tunnel floors or where a step might otherwise occur. *(pr EN 12312-4)*

lifting appliance — Work equipment for lifting loads. *(LOLER)*

lifting equipment — Work equipment for lifting or lowering loads; includes attachments used for anchoring, fixing or supporting it. *(LOLER)*

lifting frame — Fixed or carriage-mounted frame that supports the lifting equipment. *(Section 1.3.1)*

lifting operation — Operation concerned with lifting or lowering of a load. *(LOLER)*

lifting plant — Any lifting appliance or lifting gear *(Docks Regulations)*

Any stationary or mobile appliance… used… for the purpose of suspending, raising or lowering loads or moving them from one position to another whilst suspended. *(Docks Regulations)*

link bridge — Bridge connecting a pontoon to the shore.

linkspan — Generic term for a bridge ramp on which the ship ramp rests and which connects the ship to the quay or shore with the ship end on a floating pontoon. *(ICHCA glossary)*

Marine-type installation that provides a loading/unloading facility between ship and shore, and derives support from buoyancy forces and/or seabed, ship and shore. *(LRS rules for classification of ships)*

Non-self-propelled marine facilities, sited at fixed locations within protected waters for the transfer of vehicles and/or pedestrians between the shore and ship or other craft. *(LRS rules for classification of linkspans)*

	In this guide this term is used generically to describe any ship-to-shore facility for the transfer of vehicles, capable of vertical adjustment. This generic term includes **shore ramps** and all other particular types of linkspan described in the text.
machinery	Assembly of linked parts or components, at least one of which moves, with the appropriate actuators, control and power circuits, etc, joined together for a specific application, in particular for the... moving... of a material. *(EN 292-1 and Machinery Regulations)*
maintenance log	Document to be filled in by person carrying out a maintenance operation on the linkspan in order to record any maintenance or repair work carried out or faults noted during the work; retained as a historical record.
master (of a ship)	Person responsible for the navigation and management of a merchant ship. Among other responsibilities, he completes the log book giving an account of all that happens during a voyage or in port.
mooring line	Cable, wire, rope or line to tie up a ship.
motorised carriage	Rail- or rubber-tyre-mounted bogie and carriage system that is motorised. *(Section 1.3.1)*
nesting fender	Fender system consisting of close-spaced vertical fender frames used in ro-ro berths adjacent to a linkspan or shore ramp, to protect the linkspan and also to guide and hold the bow or stern of the ship in position during loading and unloading operations. The ship's bow or stern should be shaped so that they fit closely to the nesting fender. This is usually achieved by providing a steel frame on the bow or shaping to the stern transom.
nomination	Process by which a specialist subcontractor is selected by the purchaser for appointment by another contractor under standard terms in a construction contract.
novation	Process by which a specialist subcontractor is selected by the purchaser for appointment by another contractor under negotiated terms in a construction contract.
operating manual	Document containing the operating instructions recommended by the supplier of the linkspan or walkway.
operator	Person specifically trained and authorised to operate a particular linkspan or walkway.
passenger boarding bridge (PBB)	Enclosed adjustable passenger walkway connecting the terminal building to the aircraft. *(pr EN 12312-4 for airport passenger bridges)*
pawl	Short bar that acts as a lockable lever to catch the teeth of a spragging frame. *(Figure 1.4)*
pedestrian walkway	Pedestrian access separated from roadways. *(Safety in docks)*
pennant	Rope to support the seaward end of a semi-submersible linkspan.

pitching (or **pitch**)	Rotational movement of a ship in profile causing downward and upward movement of a ship at the bow and stern.
planning supervisor	Person appointed by the purchaser (client) who is competent to ensure the design considerations give adequate regard to the need for foreseeable risks to be avoided, combatted at source or protected from; that the design includes adequate information on hazards to health and safety; that a health and safety plan is prepared and that a health and safety file is prepared, reviewed and delivered to the purchaser (client) on completion of construction work. *(Construction (Design and Management) Regulations)*
pontoon	Floating structure used as a buoyant support or landing stage. *(Admiralty manual of seamanship)* Floating structure of large plan area relative to its draught, used as a buoyant support for a link bridge to the shore and sometimes as a manoeuvring area for vehicle movement. The ship ramp rests on the ship end of the pontoon.
port control duty manager	Person who issues instructions to the masters of ships using the port, including the ro-ro or ferry berth, concerning berthing and unberthing procedures. Has direct contact with the person in authority at the berth. *(Section 4.2.1)*
principal contractor	Contractor appointed by the client who ensures co-operation between all contractors, compliance with health and safety plan, access to site only by authorised persons, display of notification of project, and the prompt provision of information to the planning supervisor. *(Construction (Design and Management) Regulations)*
project adviser	Person appointed by the client or purchaser to assist in the identification of options for procurement and in the preparation of the project brief. *(Section 3.1.3)*
project manager	Person appointed by the client or purchaser to co-ordinate and manage the procurement of the linkspan or walkway. *(Section 3.1.3)*
project safety auditor	Person appointed by the client or purchaser to review the documentation produced by the supplier and contractor under the various relevant regulations, particularly the CDM Regulations and SM(S)R. *(Section 3.1.3)*
proof load	Load to which lifting plant, tested by a competent person, exceeds the **safe working load** by a factor specified in the relevant British Standard or *Safety in Docks*. *(Safety in Docks)*
purchaser	Person or organisation procuring a linkspan or walkway.
ramp	Inclined road along which wheeled vehicles and trailers may pass. Loading bridge fitted to ro-ro vessels. *(ICHCA glossary)*
ranging (or **range**)	Horizontal movement of a ship in a direction along the longitudinal axis of the ship.
responsible person	The manufacturer or the importer into the EEA or a person nominated by the manufacturer or the importer. *(SM(S)R)*

restraint system	System or device for connecting a floating body to a guide pile or other mooring arrangements to hold it in position at all states of the tide.
risk	Combination of the probability and the degree of the possible injury or damage to health in a hazardous situation. *(EN 292-1)*
roadway	The part of the deck of a linkspan that carries vehicles.
roll-on/roll-off (ro-ro)	Mode of marine transport in which the cargo may be loaded into or unloaded from the ship by essentially horizontal movements, every cargo unit being moved on its own wheels or by a temporary mobile system. *(BS MA 97)*
ro-ro ramp	Bridging structure, which enables vehicles to pass between ro-ro ships' vehicle decks and the shore. *(BS 6349: Pt 2)*
ro-ro ship	Ship on which the method of horizontal access is used. Cargo is driven on board under its own power, or towed on roll trailers or by fork lift truck etc. *(ICHCA Glossary)*
safe working load	Maximum load that any lifting appliance is permitted to lift. *(ICHCA Glossary)* This load can be exceeded for the purpose of carrying out a test. *For a more detailed definition refer to Regulation 2(1) of the Docks Regulations 1988.*
scissor lift	Scissor-type lifting device to raise the **boarding pod**. *(Section 1.3.1)*
semi-submersible	Type of floating structure in which a platform or other structure is supported at an appropriate height above sea level by support legs or towers of small plan area, which are in turn supported on **floats** of a limited size that are always fully submerged.
sensor	Device that detects a particular physical condition, such as temperature, magnetic fields, angles, pressures, strains in materials, or the existence of a structure close to the sensor. Position sensors or proximity sensors are important and frequently used in linkspans and walkways.
sheave	Running wheel in a pulley block through which the rope passes.
ship ramp	The adjustable structure fitted to the ship that when lowered to and resting on the shore approach forms the connecting roadway between the ship and the shore ramp. *(BS MA 97)*
shore ramp	Roadway providing an intermediate connection between the shore and the ship, and on which the shore end of a ship ramp can rest. The roadway is usually hinged at the inshore end, and supported near the outer end independently of the ship. This term is used for ramps that are adjusted in height by lifting equipment. This is sometimes referred to as an **adjustable shore ramp** to distinguish it from a fixed shore ramp, which does not move. See generic term **linkspan**.
slave carriage	Rail- or rubber-tyre-mounted carriage that is not motorised but moves when pulled by the motorised carriage. *(Section 1.3.1)*

slave pod	Platform supported on the **slave carriage**. *(Section 1.3.1)*
sprag	Short pin or bar used to support a lifted platform or structure at a particular height on a spragging frame or beam so that the lifting equipment can be taken out of operation.
spragging	Descriptor associated with **sprag.** Used in terms such as spragging frame and spragging beam.
standard	Document agreed by producers, consumers and other partners in an industry, which defines testing regimes, qualities of materials or products, design parameters or workmanship, and is published by an authority such as the British Standards Institution, CEN or CENELEC.
structure	Any building, steel or reinforced concrete structure (not being a building), dock, harbour, …bridge, viaduct, … and any other structure similar to the foregoing. *(CDM Regulations)*
sway	Translation horizontal movement of a ship in a sideways (abeam) direction.
systems engineer	Person appointed by the contractor or supplier to carry out the co-ordination of the electrical and mechanical aspects of linkspan or walkway works, including design, manufacture, commissioning and handover. *(Section 3.1.3)*
telescopic end	Section at the end of a **hinged link** or **drawbridge** that is collinear with the **hinged link** or **drawbridge** and capable of being extended telescopically. *(Section 1.3.1)*
telescopic link	Intermediate section of bridge that is collinear with the **hinged link** and capable of being extended telescopically. *(Section 1.3.1)*
telescoping system	System used to extend or retract a **PBB**. *(pr EN 12312-4)*
terminal manager	The person who is in control of all aspects of the shore-side activities of the terminal, including responsibility for the operation of any linkspan or walkway within the terminal. *(Section 4.2.1)*
threshold height	Height of the vehicle deck above water at the ship end of the ramp at the stern or bow door opening. *(BS MA 97)*
transition	Specially shaped section of road surface or walking surface at the interface point between a **ship ramp** and **linkspan** or a **gangway** and **boarding pod** (or similar). It is smoothly shaped to allow vehicles or pedestrians to pass over them throughout the range of angles at which either structure may operate. The term also applies to the shape at the transition between two fixed slopes.
traversing drawbridge	Drawbridge that is able to traverse laterally in a **boarding pod** and hinge vertically. *(Section 1.3.1)*
tunnel	Enclosed walkway section on **PBB**. *(pr EN 12312-4)*
turnkey contract	Contract in which a client defines a project in general terms only and leaves the contractor to decide on all the necessary engineering parameters for the design and to manage the project independently of the client. The client ceases to have any influence on the conduct of the project until the facility

has been commissioned, and a completed and functioning facility has been handed over.

Type A standard   Harmonised standard supporting the Machinery Directive defining concepts and specifying general principles and techniques for achieving safety of machinery.   *(Section 4.4.7)*

Type B standard   Harmonised standard supporting the Machinery Directive interlinked with other type B standards and generally divided into B1 and B2 standards.

B1 standards apply to all machinery, and describe essential functional characteristics and principles of safety-related equipment and control systems and ergonomics aspects of machinery.

B2 standards are "apply when used" standards covering specific components and safety devices for ranges of machinery types.   *(Section 4.4.7)*

Type C standard   Harmonised standard supporting the Machinery Directive covering requirements for ranges of machinery types.
                                                              (Section 4.4.7)

walkway   Fixed structure providing pedestrian access.   *(BS 6349:Pt 2).*

In this guide the term is used generically to describe any ship-to-shore facility for the transfer of pedestrians, capable of vertical adjustment at the ship end and incorporating any fixed walkway.

well deck   Platform on a linkspan or pontoon set at a lower level than the vehicle roadway to accommodate lifting equipment and finger flaps or to allow sufficient depth for blunt-ended ship ramps to land and provide a smooth roadway

work equipment   Any equipment, machinery, appliance, apparatus, tool or installation for use at work.   *(LOLER)*

Any machinery, appliance, apparatus or tool and any assembly of components... arranged and controlled so that they function as a whole.   *(PUWER)*

yaw   Rotational movement of a ship in plan where the bow and stern of a ship move sideways relative to each other.

1   Setting the scene: linkspans and walkways

1.1   GENERAL

1.1.1   Introduction

The purpose of this chapter is to describe linkspans and walkways in order to set the context for the guidance. The chapter also briefly describes typical types of accidents and incidents that have occurred to linkspans and walkways. The reader is referred to Appendix B, which sets out most of the statistics derived from the questionnaire survey and presents an analysis of the information.

Because of the significant differences in the types of facility, this chapter is divided into the following sections:

1.2	Ship-to-shore linkspans
1.3	Ship-to-shore walkways
1.4	Combined facilities
1.5	Key points from the research process.

1.1.2   Definitions used in this chapter

The definitions used in the guide are given in the Glossary. However, some specialist terms associated with walkways are also defined in the relevant chapters, as these terms have not previously been defined by the industry and therefore may not be familiar, even to specialist readers.

1.1.3   General features of ship-to-shore facilities

Ship-to-shore facilities provide an intermediate connection between the port facilities on the shore and the ro-ro ship or ferry. The shore-end support is solid, stationary and fixed; ro-ro ships and ferries are large structures that float, and are subject to all the movements that a floating body can experience. Therefore ship-to-shore facilities have to tolerate a situation where their support is stationary at the shore end but the ship end is continuously moving. The ship movements can arise because of:

- fluctuations in water level due to tidal variations, and surges caused by atmospheric pressure causing total vertical movements of up to 11 m in United Kingdom waters but no more than 0.3 m in parts of the Mediterranean. Such movements are relatively slow, occurring over about 6¼ hours.

- change in ship's draught and trim caused by the loading or unloading of the ro-ro cargo and movements of ballast. Such movements are also relatively slow, occurring over several minutes.

- pitch, roll, heave and range motions of the ship under wave loads. Pitching movements at the bow or stern can easily exceed 0.5 m in circumstances where the wave lengths are long and the waves are fairly high, but may not be large if the waves are comparatively short but equally high. Such movements are relatively quick, and will often change from one extreme to the other in a few seconds.

- sway, yaw, range and roll motions of the ship under wind loads. The period of the movement depends on the size of the ship and the elasticity of the mooring lines, but is likely to be more than 10 seconds.

- movements caused by loads moving about within the ship. As a loaded vehicle moves about the vehicle deck of a ro-ro ship, the change in position of the load causes the ship to roll or pitch. These movements can be more than 0.3 m upwards or downwards on either side of the ship. The rate of change of movement depends on how fast the load moves around inside the ship, but it could easily move from one extreme to the other in less than 10 seconds.

The ship-to-shore vehicle and passenger access systems must be able to accommodate these movements without causing an unsafe situation to arise. The movements can either be accommodated by powered or buoyant movement of the structural part of the ship-to-shore facility, or twisting movements might be absorbed by the flexibility available within the structure. The alternative methods of accommodating movements are discussed and explained in the following subsections.

The research shows that facility owners generally regard their facilities as critical (Section B2.4 in Appendix B). Indeed, the criticality of a linkspan to the operation of a port can most easily be compared with that of a dockside crane or similar item of port equipment. If a linkspan fails, the berth is unavailable to handle ro-ro cargo. It may be possible to move a ship to another berth, but in effect the economic advantage of being able to use the length of quayside adjacent to the linkspan is lost for a period of time. However, in most ports there is more than one dockside crane on a berth, and this means that if one crane fails, the berth can still be used, but with a lower level of productivity.

1.2 SHIP-TO-SHORE LINKSPANS

1.2.1 Types of structure

Figure 1.1 illustrates some typical ship-to-shore linkspans.

The link from ship to shore usually consists of two elements. The first is a ramp from the shore to some point near the ship. The ramp is designed to move up and down with the tide and with major changes in draught of the ship.

The second element makes the final connection from the ramp to the ship. It is usually, but not always, designed to accommodate the smaller but usually faster movements caused by the ship's motion, particularly rolling or pitching. Usually this second element will be the ship ramp, which is hinged on the ship and lowered onto the shore ramp. It is provided with finger flaps to form a smooth transition for the roadway. Some types of ship ramp are not provided with finger flaps, in which case the ship ramp is supported on a well deck or step in the ship end of the shore ramp. Finger flaps hinged on the shore ramp are then lowered onto the ship ramp to form a smooth transition for the roadway.

However, there are facilities where the opposite approach is used, and finger flaps (long, narrow hinged bridging pieces) are hinged on the ship end of the shore ramp and lowered directly onto the ship's vehicle deck. This arrangement is particularly common for the upper decks of double-deck ro-ro linkspan facilities.

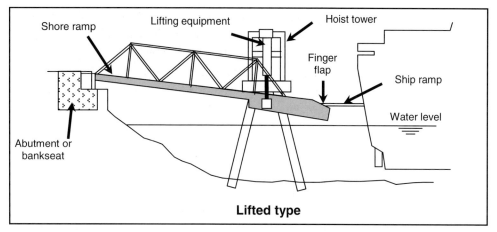

Lifted type

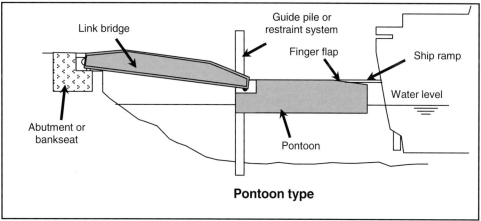

Pontoon type

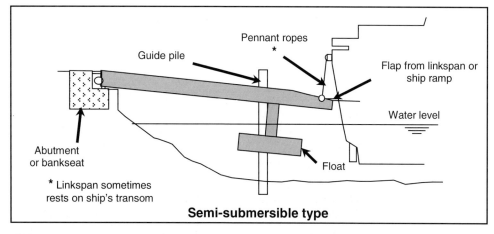

Semi-submersible type

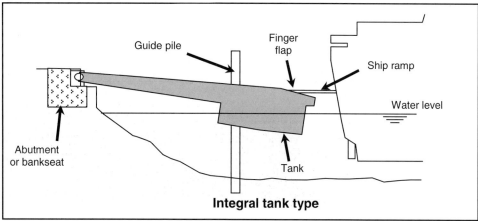

Integral tank type

Figure 1.1 *Generic types of linkspan*

This guide does not include ship ramps, but finger flaps attached to the ship-to-shore linkspan, which are lowered onto the ship, are included.

There are also linkspans that form a single element between shore and ship, and rest directly on the ship's transom or are supported by pennants on the ship.

Information on the different types of linkspan identified by the questionnaire survey are given in Appendix B.

Types of lifted facility

The most common type of linkspan has a lifted shore ramp. The two main types of lifting equipment are:

- rope winch hoist systems
- hydraulic cylinders.

These are illustrated in Figures 1.2 and 1.3.

Figure 1.2 *Lifted shore ramp, using rope winch lifting equipment*

Figure 1.3   *Lifted shore ramp, using hydraulic cylinder lifting equipment*

Some installations use ropes and hydraulic cylinders in a combined configuration. Such a combined configuration can be the result of two separate requirements:

- a need to position the hydraulic cylinders horizontally in a location that is convenient for maintenance. In this case the rope is passed over pulley wheels to allow the ramp to be lifted vertically

- a desire to reduce the stroke length of the piston. This is achieved by reeving the rope through a pulley attached to the end of the cylinder and a pulley attached to the ramp. A small movement of the piston then causes a much larger vertical movement of the ramp.

The power could also be provided through a rack and pinion system or scissor lift. The questionnaire survey asked whether such facilities existed, but the research revealed only one example of a linkspan lifted by a rack and pinion system and no examples of a linkspan operated by scissor lift.

Lifting systems require some means of controlling the movements on both sides of the ramp so that the ramp can be lifted level and not twisted. There are two ways of providing this control; occasionally both are used.

1. Linked drive systems control both sets of lifting equipment so that they move synchronously. With rope winch lifting equipment this may be achieved by driving the winch drums from the same winch motor. For hydraulic systems special pumps can be used to deliver equal quantities of oil from the fluid reservoir via flow controllers or proportional valves to the lifting equipment, which is powered either by hydraulic cylinders or by independent, hydraulic motor-driven winches supporting each side of the ramp.

2. A sensing system detects when the ramp is going out of level (twisting). One such system measures the number of rotations of the winch drums, and detects when one has rotated more than the other. Another type measures the extension of the hydraulic pistons on each side of the ramp and detects when one is extended more than the other. A third system simply measures the transverse twist on the ramp using a sensor that is, in effect, an electronic spirit level. Any of these systems can feed electronic signals to the control devices on the lifting equipment. The control

system might raise an alarm, which demands that the operating personnel take action to level the ramp. Alternatively it might send electronic instructions to the lifting equipment to level the ramp automatically. Where automatic correction is used there is nearly always an extreme limit beyond which the lifting equipment will not make an automatic correction, but will cease movement and raise an alarm.

Some types of lifting system operate in conjunction with a system of additional supports so that the linkspan is supported on a fixed structure rather than on the lifting equipment itself. A typical system may comprise a hanging plate with holes or slots at modular positions on either side of the ramp into which hydraulically operated pins (or pawls) are inserted when the ramp is at the appropriate height. Figure 1.4 illustrates the principle. There are many ways in which this type of system can be detailed.

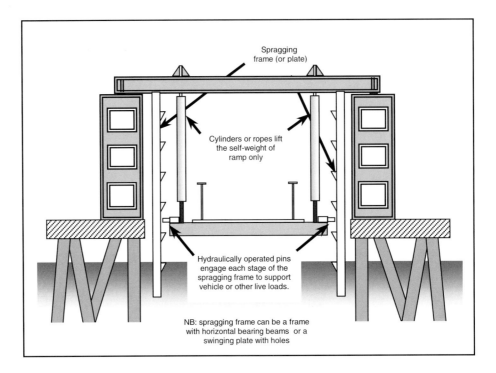

Figure 1.4   *Modular independent support systems*

If the linkspan is narrow, it may be possible to control the level of the ramp visually, as the operator can see whether or not the ramp is going out of level. For instance, a painted ruler mark on either side of the linkspan could be used. The lifting equipment can then be adjusted manually to level the ramp, by use of hydraulic control valves, for example.

Types of floating facility

There are three main types of floating facility:

1. **Pontoon type.** A pontoon is moored offshore and a link bridge spans the gap from the pontoon to the shore. These can operate without any additional support provided they are correctly sized. Examples of this type are the pontoon berths at Ramsgate, Harwich, Felixstowe and Pembroke Dock, and three berths at Sheerness. Figure 1.5 shows a typical example.

Figure 1.5 *Pontoon-type facility*

2. **Semi-submersible types**. The semi-submersible float supports only the self-weight of the linkspan. Additional support is required from the ship to support the seaward end of the linkspan under vehicle and other loads because the small size of the support legs passing through the water surface is such that the linkspan must move down a long way before sufficient additional buoyancy is developed to withstand the applied loads.

    The additional support could be provided by a shelf on the ship's bow or stern or by a pennant rope suspension system. There are several examples of this type, but a significant recent example is the linkspan for the Stena Line HSS 1500 high-speed ferry. Figure 1.6 shows a typical example.

Figure 1.6 *Semi-submersible type of linkspan*

3. **Integral tank types**. A tank is similar to a pontoon attached rigidly to the link bridge. It is self-supporting against twisting movements, but the water plane area is relatively small compared with that of a pontoon-type linkspan, so it is usually necessary to accommodate larger "dunking" (vertical displacement) movements as loads roll across the linkspan. Figure 1.7 shows a typical example.

Figure 1.7   *Integral tank type of linkspan*

All types of floating facility require the freeboard of the flotation system to be adjusted to suit the ship vehicle-door threshold height. This adjustment can be made by various methods including:

- permanent or semi-permanent ballast, where the freeboard does not need to be frequently adjusted

- pumping or compressed-air systems to displace ballast water, where periodic adjustment is required

- mechanically adjusted flaps attached to the floating structure, where rapid changes in freeboard are required (to counteract "dunking" movements).

Bridge structures

For mechanically lifted shore ramps, the bridge structures are usually made of steel. Steel provides a relatively high strength-to-weight factor, so that the weight to be lifted can be minimised. A heavier bridge will lead to more expensive lifting equipment. There are some older structures in which the bridge deck is made of concrete, but these were constructed at a time when the cost of concrete construction was much lower than that of steel fabrication.

Examples of different types of bridge structure are illustrated in Figure 1.8.

Plate girder bridges, of the type illustrated in the figure, have a comparatively small resistance to twisting (low torsional stiffness). Should the lifting equipment on one side fail, the bridge cannot be satisfactorily supported solely on the other side.

Truss bridges can be designed to be flexible or stiff when twisted depending on whether or not there is bracing between the two truss frames, and on the exact layout of such bracing. In either case, if one cylinder or rope fails or extends, the truss structure is unlikely to have sufficient torsional strength to prevent the bridge from twisting, since the size of members needed to achieve this will probably lead to an uneconomic structure. If the support on one side fails, the bridge is unlikely to be strong enough to be supported on the other side only.

Box girder bridges have high resistance to twisting forces. They can easily be designed to survive failure of one support provided that the shore bearings are designed not to lift. Shore bearings will need to be designed to resist larger loads than would be experienced with more flexible structures. If the lifting equipment does not lift the structure evenly, it will generate large bearing loads, and it is possible that one lifting point may experience a much higher load than would be calculated if the loads were assumed to be evenly distributed. To mitigate this problem, some box-type bridges include a length of plate girder construction to reduce the torsional stiffness sufficiently to achieve an acceptable bearing load. In other cases, the bridge is supported on a central shore bearing so that the bridge is free to rotate by a limited amount at the shore end.

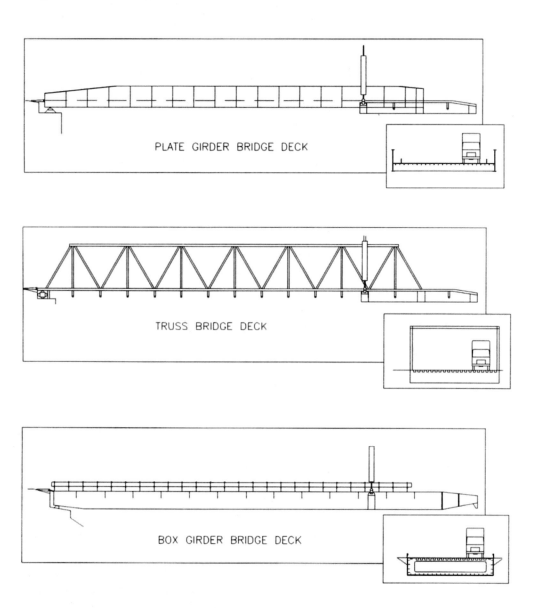

Figure 1.8   *Types of bridge structure*

The main purpose of discussing the bridge structure and deck types is to emphasise the importance of considering the structure and lifting equipment as a whole. Different structural approaches require different bearing design strategies. Decisions taken for one reason may have unexpected effects elsewhere. Failure of the lifting system must be taken into account when designing the system, the bridge and the bearings.

Ship impact

Linkspans sometimes have to resist ship collision impacts, and are provided with fenders fitted either at the ship end of the linkspan or at the shoreward end. Some linkspans are able to absorb berthing energy by swinging on their lifting systems with the shore bearings able to roll up on inclined channel. Where fenders are not provided it is considered prudent to design the berth so that the ship can be reliably brought to rest before approaching too close to the facility. In most cases this can be achieved by providing additional length to the berth, for instance by using an additional berthing dolphin. Some linkspans have separate fender beams or nesting fenders on dolphins to protect the facility.

Connection between ship and linkspan

The arrangements at the ship end of the linkspan require careful consideration. There are many types of ship ramp with different shapes and profiles, most of which are provided with their own finger flaps. These require a suitably profiled landing surface on the ship end of the linkspan so that vehicles can run across safely without grounding.

However, some ships that operate on important ferry crossings incorporate blunt-ended ship ramps. Such ramps have to land on a recess or shelf on the ship end of the linkspan sometimes known as a well deck, so that the roadway level on the ship ramp is the same as that on the shore ramp. If different types of ship ramp with either finger flaps or blunt ends are to be accommodated on the same linkspan, the shape of the ship end of the linkspan can be complicated. There is often a need to fill in the well deck with deck or flap sections that can be lifted manually or by forklift truck. Alternatively finger flaps that are hydraulically moved into or out of position can be used. Where such flexibility is required, it can have a significant cost impact. It can also add to the complexity of the control systems, with consequently higher maintenance costs.

Upper decks of double-deck facilities

The upper decks of double-deck facilities present some of the greatest design problems. Provided that there is sufficient load-carrying capacity in the lifting or flotation system, upper decks can be added to most types of linkspan. The upper deck nearly always has a series of finger flaps that are lowered onto the ship's upper vehicle deck, because there are very few ships that have ship ramps on their upper deck.

Upper decks are at their most complex when connecting with facilities that must receive the bow of a ferry. The bow stem usually has a substantial overhang relative to the main vehicle deck. For the ship to be able to berth without fouling the upper deck it is necessary to have either very long finger flaps or a system that allows the upper bridge deck to be rolled back clear of the bow of the ship during berthing and then returned to an operating position after the ship is moored. Similarly it is often necessary to adjust the vertical spacing between the upper and lower roadway decks of a double-deck facility to accommodate the different deck levels of various ships. It may also be necessary to slew the upper deck to suit the varying beams of ships.

As a consequence, the geometry is often complex, and there is a need for very careful design of interface profiles, transition flaps, bearings and lifting equipment. Figure 1.9 demonstrates some of the geometrical problems to be solved.

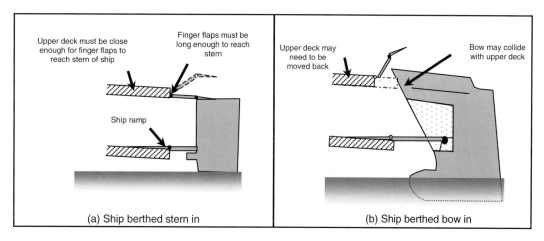

Figure 1.9 *Geometrical problems of double-deck linkspans*

If the double-deck facility is constructed on a pontoon or other floating linkspan very careful attention should be paid to the movements that will occur as a load rolls over the facility. The change in flotation attitude can cause angular movements, which can lead to substantial horizontal movements at the upper deck level. Clearly the bearings of such floating double-deck linkspans need particular attention if the upper deck is to be prevented from sliding off its supports and falling.

1.2.2 Construction incidents

The survey has not revealed any incidents that have occurred to these facilities during construction. However, the installation process is risky and needs careful planning. Installation often involves sophisticated heavy-lift operations using some of the largest floating cranes in Europe, so the contractors that carry out such work usually take considerable care with its planning and execution.

Nevertheless, there have been some incidents that have not been reported in the questionnaire responses. Generally these have involved the construction of floating facilities, particularly semi-submersible ones. Here the low level of the centre of buoyancy can create a risk of the structure becoming unstable and capsizing unless great care is taken in the management of the installation or removal operations.

The joining together of two heavy suspended or floating structures is an operation that also needs careful planning. Large heavy structures cannot be easily controlled, and there is a considerable risk of injury where personnel are required to work near the interface between the two.

Although there have been some significant construction incidents associated with linkspans, only one incident is known to have resulted in a fatality. However, it is believed that this apparently good record of safety is more likely to be due to the care taken by competent marine installation contractors than to the suitability of the design of linkspans for installation.

1.2.3 Operational incidents

The industry has offered information relating to a sample of 125 linkspans. Of these, it was stated that 77 facilities had suffered no significant incidents and 43 had experienced incidents leading to significant problems. Figure 1.10 shows the percentages of structures that experienced no incidents, one incident, two incidents and three incidents.

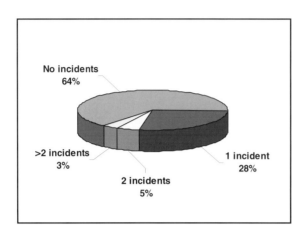

Figure 1.10   *Pie chart showing the percentages of structures that had experienced incidents (from the questionnaire survey)*

Figure 1.11 shows the results of some typical types of incident that have occurred to linkspans. A discussion of the disruption caused by accidents and incidents is included in Appendix B.

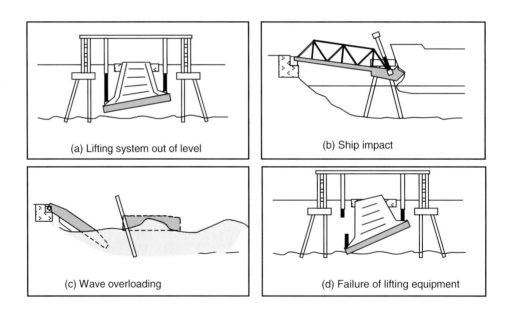

Figure 1.11   *Typical types of incident to linkspans*

Figure 1.12 shows the percentage of different causes of incident that occurred, and which are described below. In this diagram the percentage of incidents is the percentage of reported incidents, not the percentage of the linkspans for which information was provided.

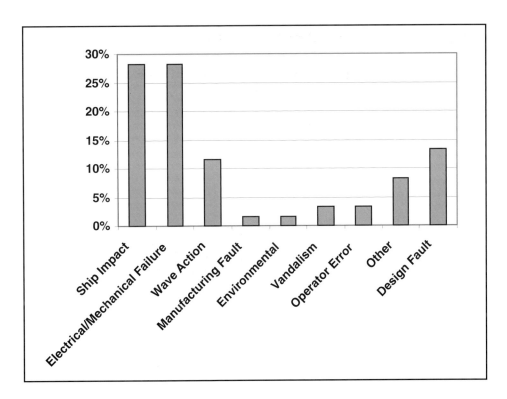

Figure 1.12   *Histogram showing the percentages of different causes of incidents reported*

- **Ship impact**: where a ship hits the linkspan or causes damage to the linkspan, either on approach to the berth, on departure from the berth, or as a result of mooring failure while on the berth.

- **Electrical/mechanical failure**: often caused by a failure of the control system or by leakage in a hydraulic circuit. Structural failure of elements of the mechanical system is also possible.

- **Wave action:** typically where waves cause the restraint systems of buoyant linkspans to fail. However, there have also been problems caused by buoyant forces on lifted linkspans, which can cause failures of shore bearings or lifting systems as indicated in Figure 1.13.

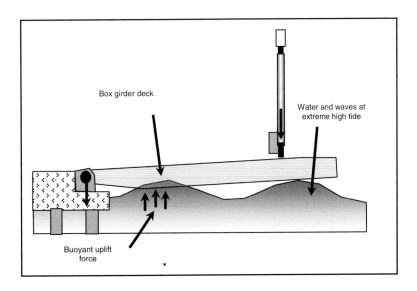

Figure 1.13 *Buoyant uplift on bearings*

There is evidence from some incident records that too little attention was given to making a realistic assessment of the wave climate at a berth before the design of a linkspan. Ro-ro ships are often of such a size that they can safely remain on the berth in quite severe conditions. When conditions become too severe, the ship can depart and seek shelter elsewhere. The linkspan, will remain and must be designed to withstand all the forces generated by its environment. Even in harbours with breakwaters or other protection from waves there can be certain wind directions that cause large waves inside the harbour, even though for the majority of the time the wind directions are such that the harbour is well protected.

- It is likely that more new ro-ro berths will be planned in locations that are not well sheltered, and a proper assessment of the wave regime must be undertaken.

- Of the other remaining causes of incidents, operator error and design faults have been the most difficult to identify. For the first this is because witness reports can be unreliable (often originating from the operator), and for the second because the respondents did not make clear why a particular problem was believed to result from a design fault.

1.2.4　　　　Other information

Appendix B includes a detailed discussion of the following subjects:

- the importance that the facility owners place on their individual linkspans – that is, how critical the reliable operation of the linkspan is to the operation of the port

- the frequency with which incidents occur to different classes of linkspan, and indicating a need to take particular care in the design of integral tank and semi-submersible linkspans

- the reliability of the facilities and the extent to which they are subject to repetitive operating malfunctions

- information about the types of control system for linkspans and how they have been used

- information about factors where operators considered that improvements in operational facilities were desirable

- information about the convenience of maintenance facilities, indicating a need for considerable improvement in maintenance access and facilities in linkspans.

1.3   SHIP-TO-SHORE WALKWAYS

1.3.1   Types of structure

Principles

Ship-to-shore walkways are generally of a very different nature from linkspans and
shore ramps. Indeed, the whole approach to design is radically different.

The design of walkway structures has developed considerably over the last 20 years,
partly because of the increased height in passenger decks on ferries and partly in
response to the improvements in the travel environment expected by passengers, largely
led by the air travel industry. Figure 1.14 shows photographs of three facilities. The first
is a simple ship's gangway, which spans between ship and shore. The second is a
passenger boarding bridge used to board aircraft at modern airport terminals. The third
is a modern passenger walkway to a ferry.

The resemblance of the modern ship-to-shore passenger walkway to an aircraft
passenger boarding bridge is not very great. A ship-to-shore walkway has to follow the
large movements of the ship, whereas a passenger boarding bridge, once positioned,
remains almost stationary and is required to accommodate only the movements brought
about by very small alterations in aircraft suspension level due to changes of loading.
The movements that a ship might experience while it is on the berth have already been
described in Section 1.1.3. It is these large movements that cause there to be a radical
difference between ship-to-shore walkways and passenger boarding bridges for airports.

There are two walkway configurations:

- end loading onto the stern or bow of the ship (normally associated with a combined
  linkspan and walkway)
- side loading into a door or onto an open deck on the side of the ship.

Side-loading walkways often have to deal with significant variations in the levels of
passenger access points and the location of the doors or open deck along the side of
different ships. This results in long and high operating envelopes, leading to
complications in design.

Figure 1.15 shows three types of side-loading passenger walkways and the terminology
used in this report to describe the various parts.

(a)   A traditional ship's gangway

(b)   Passenger boarding bridge at an airport

(c)   Modern passenger walkway for a ferry

Figure 1.14   *Three types of walkway facility*

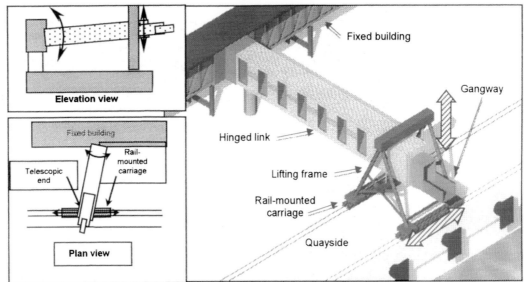

Type A – motorised carriage at ship entry, swivel at building

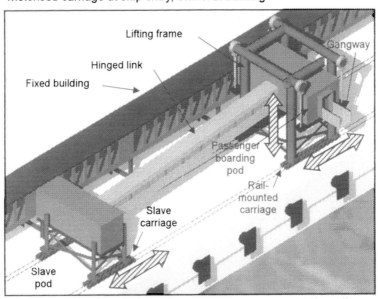

Type B – motorised carriage at ship entry plus slave carriage and pod

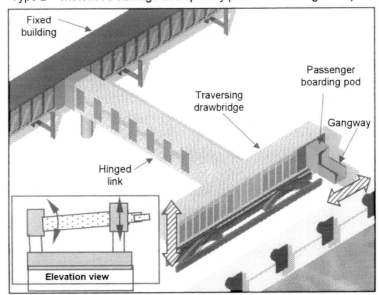

Type C – traversing drawbridge on boarding pod

Figure 1.15 *Types of side-loading passenger walkway*

Terminology

The various elements of a passenger walkway structure need definition, but this is believed to be the first time that an attempt has been made to define terms for many of them. This guide also gives specific meanings to certain terms (such as brow and gangway) that are in quite common usage but are usually given a more general meaning. For this reason the terms are listed below with the meanings used in this guide for the sake of easy reference. Figure 1.15 shows some of these items.

boarding pod	Platform that is mechanically (or buoyantly) lifted and allows access to the ship via a brow, gangway or drawbridge. It is connected to the hinged link.
brow	Bridge that is hinged onto the boarding pod or telescopic end and either rests on the coaming of the ship's passenger access door or opening, or is supported by cantilever action from the boarding pod or the telescopic end.
deployment and retrieval structure	Mechanically operated beam, frame or plate hinged to a boarding pod, telescopic end or drawbridge, and cantilevering below a brow, gangway or drawbridge to lift them onto or over a ship's coaming for deployment or to lift them off the coaming or passenger deck of the ship for retrieval. This structure is lowered after connection so that the brow, gangway or drawbridge can hinge freely with the movement of the ship.
drawbridge	Liftable bridge section that is hinged at the shore and supported by a strut/tie or rope system at the seaward end.
fixed walkway	Walkway structure that has no moving parts.
gangway	Bridge that is hooked onto the coaming and supported on the telescopic end, boarding pod or drawbridge.
hinged link	Bridge between the ship or the boarding pod and the fixed building or shore abutment, which is capable of rotating in the vertical plane to take up level differences between the terminal building and the ship. It may also rotate in the horizontal plane.
lifting frame	Fixed or carriage-mounted frame that supports the lifting equipment.
motorised carriage	Rail- or rubber-tyre-mounted bogie and carriage system that is motorised.
scissor lift	Scissor-type lifting device to raise the boarding pod.
slave carriage	Rail- or rubber-tyre-mounted carriage that is not motorised but moves when pulled by the motorised carriage.
slave pod	Platform supported on the slave carriage.

telescopic end	Section at the end of a hinged link or drawbridge that is collinear with the hinged link or drawbridge and capable of being extended telescopically.
telescopic link	Intermediate section of bridge that is collinear with the hinged link and capable of being extended telescopically
traversing drawbridge	Drawbridge that is able to traverse laterally in a boarding pod and to hinge vertically.

The fixed walkway and hinged link

The fixed walkway and hinged link are fairly conventional bridge structures. The architectural aspects of such structures can require as much consideration as the engineering design. The bearings of the hinged links are of critical importance and are subject to unusually large movements.

The most usual type of walkway structure is fully enclosed, and the structural forms are generally as shown in Figure 1.16:

- steel beam deck with light framing and cladding (Type 1)
- concrete beam deck with light framing and cladding (Type 2)
- steel truss with cladding round the truss (Type 3).

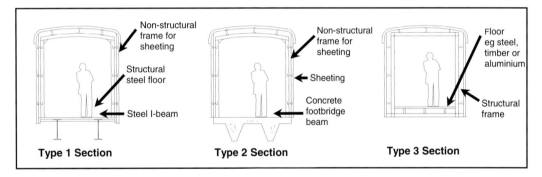

Figure 1.16 *Types of passenger walkway structure*

Of these, the truss option (Type 3) is the most common, with various types of cladding.

The main lifting structure

In order to accommodate tidal movements, changes in draught, and the different passenger access points on the ship, the walkway needs to have machinery or lifting equipment to lift and move it into the appropriate position.

The types of lifting structure can be grouped into the three main structural arrangements shown in Figure 1.15.

Examples of some actual walkways are shown in Figures 1.17 to 1.19.

Figure 1.17 *Passenger walkway accessing the stern of a ferry*

Figure 1.17 is an example of an end-loading walkway, in which the lifting frame is supported on a linkspan underneath.

Figure 1.18 shows an example of Type B in Figure 1.15.

Figure 1.18 *Passenger walkway with motorised and slave carriages*

Figure 1.19 shows a walkway similar to Type C, but with a range of travel of the traversing drawbridge that is relatively small.

Figure 1.19 *Passenger walkway with traversing drawbridge*

The arrangement of the passenger walkway and its bearings must take account of the movements that occur. Furthermore, account needs to be taken of possible twisting movements arising from malfunction of the lifting equipment, or extreme ship motion.

The gangway or brow

The connection to the ship is the key element in providing a safe ship-to-shore walkway that allows for movement of the ship. As explained in Section 1.1.3, some movements of the ship can be quite rapid. Most gangways connect with and are perpendicular to the ship's side. This makes it more difficult to accommodate the vessel ranging, and connection details have to be carefully considered to accommodate such movements.

The following options are available, which are illustrated in Figure 1.20:

(a) In this type the walkway has a gangway from the boarding pod or telescopic end with one end that rests on, and is hooked directly to, the coaming to the passenger door or access point.

(b) In this type the walkway has a brow from the boarding pod or telescopic end with one end that rests and slides over the coaming.

(c) In this type the telescopic link could rest directly on the coaming. The lifting equipment must be able to lift and extend the walkway into position and must then be able to release the lifting equipment once the bridge is supported by the ship.

(d) In this type the telescopic end projects into the doorway, which needs to be wide enough to allow a reasonable amount of vessel movement, and has a hinged finger flap forming a transition to the passenger deck.

(e) In this type there is a drawbridge in addition to a gangway in order to close a large gap between the facility and the berthing line.

Other options are possible, but require the use of sophisticated control systems.

(a) Simple gangway (with deployment and retrieval structure)

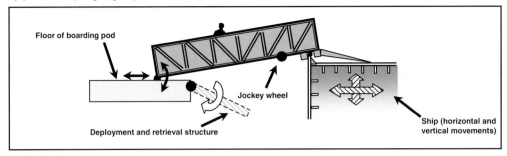

(b) Brow (with deployment and retrieval structure)

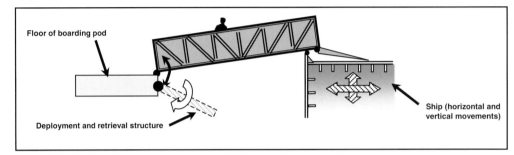

(c) Telescopic end

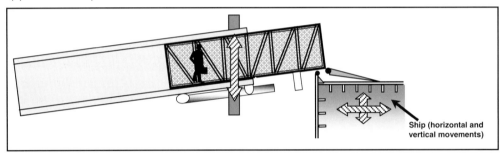

(d) Unsupported telescopic end

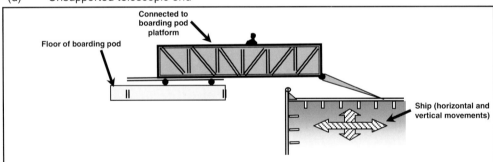

(e) Drawbridge and gangway

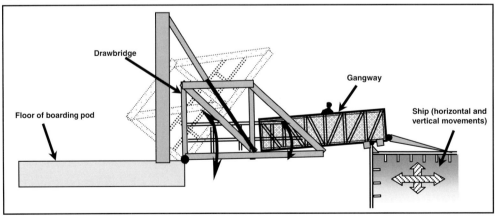

Figure 1.20 *Different types of final link or gangway*

The final link arrangements have received a great deal of attention in recent years, with particular reference to the problem of a ship drifting away from the berth while the passenger walkway is attached to the ship. With any final link arrangement involving a gangway or brow, it is clear that when the ship drifts too far away, the ship or shore end of the gangway will fall, unless preventive measures are taken. Ideally the final link has to remain supported horizontally if the ship drifts away. Design development has been high recently, but, despite this, the ideal solution to this problem has not yet been found.

1.3.2 Construction incidents

The survey did not reveal incidents that have endangered safety or caused damage during construction.

1.3.3 Operational incidents

Limited information has been received about operational incidents to walkways. Because of the small number of incidents it is possible to describe only the types of incident recorded. Figure 1.21 shows some typical examples of incidents.

1. The majority of incidents are caused by abnormal ship movements, resulting in either impact on the structure or movement of the ship outside the envelope of operational movement. The abnormal movements are caused by a failure in the moorings, or by a failure in communication between the ship and the shore at departure, so that the ship moves before the walkway has been disconnected.

2. There were incidents where wind funnelling between the boarding pod and the side of the ship had forced the gangway to move to one side, causing a minor injury in one case. For this reason, there has been a trend towards providing facilities that are entirely machine-driven up to the point at which the gangway is fully deployed.

3. There was an incident when a power cut occurred during operation. The ship continued to rise on the tide, and the gangway had almost jammed against the top of the lifted platform door opening when power was restored. There were no injuries.

4. There were incidents where a sophisticated electronic sensing system wrongly detected that the vessel was departing and initiated an automatic withdrawal procedure. There were no injuries.

There are some facilities intended for lifting into an operational location without personnel loading. In one case, the lifting operation was inadvertently carried out with personnel in the boarding pod. It was overloaded, but fortunately did not collapse.

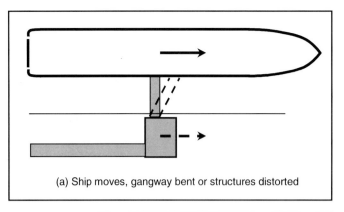

(a) Ship moves, gangway bent or structures distorted

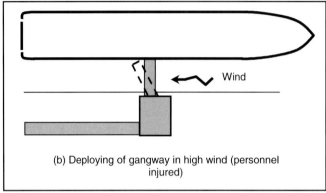

(b) Deploying of gangway in high wind (personnel injured)

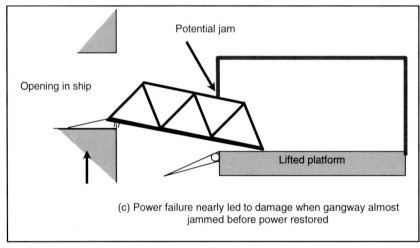

(c) Power failure nearly led to damage when gangway almost jammed before power restored

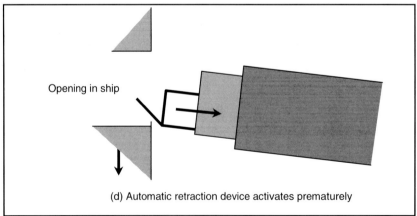

(d) Automatic retraction device activates prematurely

Figure 1.21 *Types of incident for walkways*

1.3.4   Other information

Appendix B includes detailed discussion of the following:

- the importance that the facility owners placed on their facility – that is, how critical it was to their operation
- the reliability of the facilities and the extent to which they are subject to repeated operating malfunctions
- information about the types of control system for linkspans and how they have been used.

There is no additional information about the convenience of walkways for maintenance in the questionnaire survey.

1.4   COMBINED FACILITIES

1.4.1   Types of structure

General principles

The term *combined facility* is used below to describe a combined linkspan and walkway. This section covers facilities where ship-to-shore walkways are combined with linkspans as a unified structure. The principles and structural arrangements required for such combined facilities are generally as already described in Sections 1.2.1 and 1.3.1.

The ship-to-shore walkway element of such a combined facility is usually light in terms of its construction and loading relative to the linkspan elements. Therefore the loading on the walkway element will contribute little to the movements and deflections of the combined structure.

In contrast, the movements of the linkspan elements are likely to be significant, particularly for a floating linkspan or pontoon. For instance, a heavy goods vehicle crossing a pontoon from one end to the other may generate considerable pitching and rolling movements. These movements are a major factor to be considered in the degree of movement to be accommodated by the walkway. Indeed, it was movements of a pontoon support that contributed to the collapse of the Ramsgate facility because they had not been taken into account in the design.

Therefore it is essential that the designer of such combined facilities, whether forming part of the original design or provided as an additional structure added to an existing linkspan, should be fully conversant with the forces and movements that can be induced by the supporting structure. It is essential that the purchaser does not assume that it is easy to add a walkway simply because the supporting structure has been operated successfully for some time.

(a) Dover

(b) Ramsgate

(c) Dun Laoghaire

Figure 1.22 *Examples of combined facilities*

Structural types

The structural types of linkspan and walkway have been discussed at length in Sections 1.2.1 and 1.3.1. Recent examples of combined facilities are shown in Figure 1.22:

(a) the combined linkspans and walkway facilities at Dover. Here the walkway is supported by the upper level of the linkspan through fixed portal structures. The linkspans are suspended by ropes from a lifting frame.

(b) the combined linkspan and walkway at Ramsgate. Here the walkway was supported by portal frames on heavy pillars on the pontoon and on the passenger building.

(c) the linkspans for the Stena Line HSS1500 high-speed ferry, such as those at Dun Laoghaire, Harwich, Holyhead and Stranraer. Here the passenger walkway acts as a principal structural tie/strut member that is a critical element in maintaining the flotational and structural stability of the facility.

1.4.2 Construction incidents

No specific incidents were reported for combined facilities during construction, but problems or incidents to the separate linkspan and walkway elements have been reported in the previous sections. Combined facilities are more difficult to install, and it is known that incidents have occurred during the installation of such facilities.

1.4.3 Operational incidents

The survey that was carried out did not reveal any operational incidents associated with combined facilities. However, this may have been due to a misunderstanding by the consultees of the categories offered in the questionnaires. In fact, the most significant incident of recent years was the collapse of the passenger walkway at Ramsgate in 1994, which was part of a combined facility.

1.4.4 Other information

There are no additional comments on the matters set out in Sections 1.2.4 and 1.3.4 that have not already been covered in Appendix B.

1.5 KEY POINTS FROM THE RESEARCH PROCESS

This is a summary of the key points that have arisen from this section of the guidance and Appendix B.

1. There are many more hoisted linkspans than there are floating types.

2. The data suggest that reliability of semi-submersible and integral tank linkspans is not as high as that of other types. Additional care is needed in the specification, construction and operation of such facilities.

3. The potential magnitude of wave forces must be assessed. Wave forces that might affect lifted structures must be considered.

4. There is a higher probability of a linkspan or walkway suffering an accident if it relies for support on the ship. This is because of the added possibility of excessive ship movement due to mooring failure.

5. Apart from the accident at Ramsgate in 1994, the research has not revealed any incidents that have led to fatalities arising from a failure of the linkspan or walkway structures or systems.

6.   Apart from Ramsgate, no cases of injuries to members of the public were reported, but two cases of injuries to dock workers were reported.

7.   It is essential that the designer of a walkway that is to be added to a linkspan should be fully aware of all aspects of the structural and mechanical behaviour of the supporting linkspan.

8.   Ports regard linkspans and walkways as operationally critical structures, linkspans more so than walkways. Generally, both linkspans and walkways are reliable, with very few instances of events that lead to incidents.

9.   Training of operating and maintenance personnel using simulated emergency situations will be beneficial.

10. There is evidence of a need for more refresher courses for operators and maintainers of facilities.

11. The design of facilities, for both operation and maintenance, has frequently been criticised. There is evidence that the design for maintenance access should be considerably improved.

12. There is no significant difference between the incident records of facilities procured by the various procurement routes.

13. The designs of 97 per cent of linkspans had been subject to an independent checking process but only 42 per cent of walkways were reported as either having had an independent check or having been classified, or both.

14. The understanding in the port industry of the relevant regulations is generally good.

2 The regulatory framework

2.1 INTRODUCTION

2.1.1 The regulatory framework

The activities of the construction, manufacturing, cargo-handling and related industries are controlled by a framework of legislation and regulations. These regulations and the related approved codes of practice, and the ways that the regulations are enforced, can assist in developing good practice.

This chapter outlines the regulatory requirements affecting the procurement, operation and maintenance of ship-to-shore linkspans and walkways. The regulatory framework is undergoing considerable change because of recent European Union directives and because new regulations on work equipment are coming into force.

The chapter highlights background information associated with the UK and European regulatory framework to give the reader a better understanding of the current requirements. However, the wide range of non-EU legislation on health and safety at work, supply of machinery, construction, and operation and maintenance of work equipment. is outside the scope of this guide.

2.1.2 History of development of UK regulations

The United Kingdom has a long history of legislation for safety. The Health and Safety at Work etc Act 1974 (HSWA) incorporated much of the experience gained under the earlier Factory Acts and other safety legislation. More recently a number of regulations have been introduced under HSWA. The safety aspects of ship-to-shore linkspans and walkways are covered by the Docks Regulations 1988 in Great Britain and the Docks Regulations (Northern Ireland) 1989 in Northern Ireland. Approved Codes of Practice entitled *Safety in docks* were published for each set of regulations, and came into effect in 1989. These regulations are based upon international standards set out in ILO Convention 152 *Health and safety in dockwork*.

In 1992 the Management of Health and Safety at Work Regulations were introduced and specify the concept of systematic risk assessments for work activities. The Approved Code of Practice gives guidance on the general principles of risk assessment. The Workplace (Health, Safety and Welfare) Regulations were also introduced in 1992; they cover requirements for cleanliness, maintenance, access and welfare facilities at work.

The Construction (Design and Management) Regulations came into effect in 1995; giving specific duties to the various parties involved in the construction process. The Approved Code of Practice provides guidance on the avoidance, elimination and minimisation of risk for construction and cleaning work. It also sets out specific information to be provided by the various parties to the construction process.

Further regulations associated with machinery and work equipment have been introduced to comply with European directives.

2.1.3   European directives

The European Commission issues directives that establish common minimum standards throughout the European Union in order to ensure that all industries in all member states have to operate under the same conditions, and to enable the member states to trade successfully across borders. The directives have required the introduction of specific legislation by the member states, and these are leading to new or revised practices and standards within industry.

Initially the European Commission proposed directives based on a unified approach to the production and supply of products and goods across Europe. However, these directives were prescriptive, and they were felt to be having a detrimental effect on innovation and invention. The Commission therefore started to introduce the New Approach directives (CE marking directives), which are not prescriptive, but lay down minimum criteria for compliance. These directives must also be introduced into the legislation of each member state, and this often necessitates amendments to existing legislation.

2.2   REGULATORY PROCESS

2.2.1   Legislative framework

This section outlines the legislative framework for the regulations. Figure 2.1 illustrates in a very simplified form the relationship between the legislature, legislation and the regulations enacted under the primary legislation.

Health and safety legislation in the UK goes back over many years through the Factories Acts and related legislation. A variety of health and safety legislation was brought together in the Health and Safety at Work etc Act 1974 (HSWA). This Act provides the legal structures for making many of the subsequent health and safety regulations and in particular for the Docks Regulations 1988, the Management of Health and Safety at Work Regulations 1992 (MHSWR), the Workplace (Health, Safety and Welfare) Regulations 1992, and the Construction (Design and Management) Regulations 1994 (CDM Regulations). These are all supported by individual Approved Codes of Practice, which provide a relatively brief amplification for each regulation and comprehensive guidance. Different regulations apply in Northern Ireland, although they usually contain the same provisions.

Other health and safety legislation originates with directives produced by the European Commission in order to assist member states to trade goods and services successfully across boundaries. In 1985 a New Approach to Technical Harmonisation and Standards was agreed with the purpose of introducing non-prescriptive directives that would set out essential requirements for compliance. The directives are introduced as regulations in the United Kingdom through two acts, the European Communities Act 1972 for products, and the Health and Safety at Work etc Act 1974 for health and safety. Regulations based on directives include the Construction Products Regulations 1991, the Construction Products (Amendment) Regulations 1994, and the Provision and Use of Work Equipment Regulations 1992 (now replaced by two new sets of Regulations). The Supply of Machinery (Safety) Regulations 1992 (SM(S)R) and the Supply of Machinery (Safety) (Amendment) Regulations 1994 implement the various Machinery Directives through the European Communities Act.

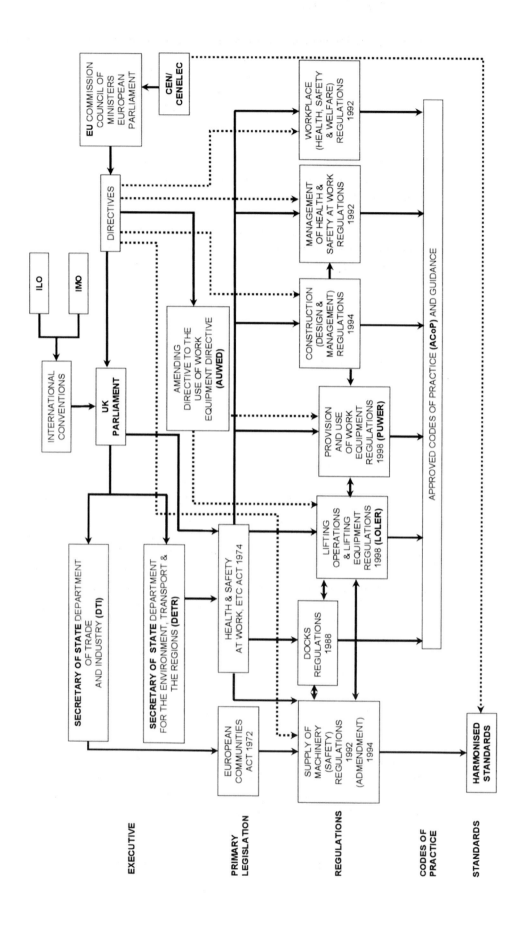

Figure 2.1 *Legislative framework for health and safety relevant to ship-to-shore linkspans and walkways in the United Kingdom*

More recently, in 1995, the Amending Directive to the Use of Work Equipment Directive was adopted by the European Council of Ministers. The requirements of this amending directive have been introduced under the Health and Safety at Work etc Act 1974 by the Provision and Use of Work Equipment Regulations 1998, which cover the general and non-lifting aspects of the Amending Directive, and by the Lifting Operations and Lifting Equipment Regulations 1998, which implement the lifting aspects of the amending directive. These new regulations, known as PUWER 98 and LOLER respectively, are supported by Approved Codes of Practice and guidance.

The EU Machinery Directives and the Supply of Machinery (Safety) Regulations require relevant machinery and safety components to satisfy the essential health and safety requirements that are annexed to the directives and regulations. The directives and regulations assume that harmonised European Standards will be produced for machinery and safety components, and that compliance with these harmonised standards will be presumed to provide compliance with the essential health and safety requirements.

The European Committees for Standardisation (CEN and CENELEC) have been contracted to produce a set of European Standards in support of the Machinery Directives. These standards take the form of Harmonised European Standards (having EN numbers), and are required to be adopted in all EU member countries. These countries are required to revoke any conflicting national standards. When national standards are generated that are identical in content to the European standards, they are known as transposed harmonised standards. In the UK transposed harmonised standards will have BSEN numbers.

2.2.2   Application and overlap of the regulations

There are relationships between the various regulations covering health and safety, construction, work equipment and machinery and the Docks Regulations. Some of these relationships are indicated in Figure 2.1 by arrows connecting the various regulations.

The Management of Health and Safety at Work Regulations lay down general requirements covering risk assessment, emergency procedures, co-operation, information for employees and training. These are complementary to the requirements of the Docks Regulations, Construction (Design and Management) Regulations 1994, PUWER 98 and LOLER.

The Docks Regulations 1988 need to be considered in conjunction with all the other relevant regulations including SM(S)R, PUWER 98 and LOLER. LOLER amends Regulation 13(4) and revokes Regulations 14, 15, part of 16 and all of 17 of the Docks Regulations 1988. The Docks Regulations will continue to cover the safe operation of lifting plant in docks. In general none of these regulations applies to operations carried out solely by a ship's crew, or to lifting equipment provided on board ships, as the equivalent requirements are covered by various merchant shipping regulations. However, they do apply where shore-based personnel operate aboard ships and where they use ship's gear. In this situation shore-based employers should collaborate with the ship's master in order to ensure that their duties under the respective regulations are properly discharged.

The adequacy and safety of the following types of on-board support are *not* covered by any of the above regulations but would be covered by the relevant merchant shipping regulations:

- semi-submersible linkspans
  - on the ship's stern transom
  - from pennants attached to eyes on the ship
- walkways
  - on the passenger deck of the ship
  - on the passenger access door coaming.

It is important that the safety of any supports or connections on the ship is verified by the operator's employer or other responsible person before the connections are relied on to support the linkspan or walkway. This verification should require the provision of reports of periodic thorough examinations, materials test certificates, confirmation of structural strength, and load test certificates for the connections.

Ship-to-shore linkspans and walkways are complex items of port equipment. They generally consist of both fixed and movable elements. Fixed structures include bridge abutments or bankseats, rail foundations, bridge piers and bases, guide piles, bearings, hoist frames or towers and their supporting walls or dolphins, and the foundations to these fixed structures. Movable structures include shore ramps, beam adjusters, bridges, link bridges, walkway tunnels, telescopic gangways, flaps and mobile gantries. Machinery of various types includes power sources, actuators, mobile gantries, lifting equipment, transition flaps, spragging equipment, slewing equipment, telescoping drives, control and power circuits, and floating or semi-submersible pontoons and tanks. Figure 2.2 shows a simplified diagram of these elements, and indicates the boundaries of the application of SM(S)R.

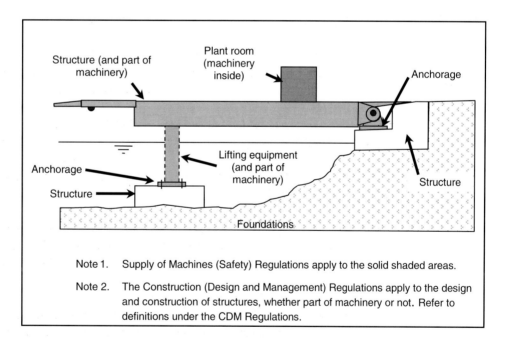

Note 1. Supply of Machines (Safety) Regulations apply to the solid shaded areas.

Note 2. The Construction (Design and Management) Regulations apply to the design and construction of structures, whether part of machinery or not. Refer to definitions under the CDM Regulations.

Figure 2.2 *Simplified diagram showing boundary of application of Supply of Machinery (Safety) Regulations*

The requirements of SM(S)R apply to the machinery and to those parts of the structure that are movable and form part of the machinery. The CDM Regulations apply to the design and construction of the fixed and movable structures, whether they form part of the machinery or not. The risk assessments required under both sets of regulations require consideration not only of the health and safety requirements for the design, supply or construction of the facilities, but also of the health and safety requirements during operation and maintenance (for the design and construction of machinery), and during cleaning, maintenance, repair and eventual dismantling or demolition (for the design of structures).

Floating pontoons, combined with their link bridges, and semi-submersible or integral tank linkspans move by tidal action or by ballasting and de-ballasting, and are considered to fall within the definition of machinery. The movements necessarily involve the risk of lack of stability and risk of contact with persons because of moving parts such as transition flaps and restraints. These risks should be assessed against the essential health and safety requirements relating to the design and construction of machinery included in SM(S)R.

There is a relationship between the application of the regulations and the stage in the process of procurement, operation and maintenance of the linkspans and walkways to which the various regulations apply. These stages are illustrated in Figure 2.3, and show that in general the CDM Regulations and SM(S)R apply to the supply stage for the facility, and the Docks Regulations, Workplace Regulations, and PUWER 98 and LOLER apply to the operation and maintenance stages for the facility. The MHSWR apply to all work activities throughout the process. However, many of the regulations have particular clauses that require reference to other stages of the process.

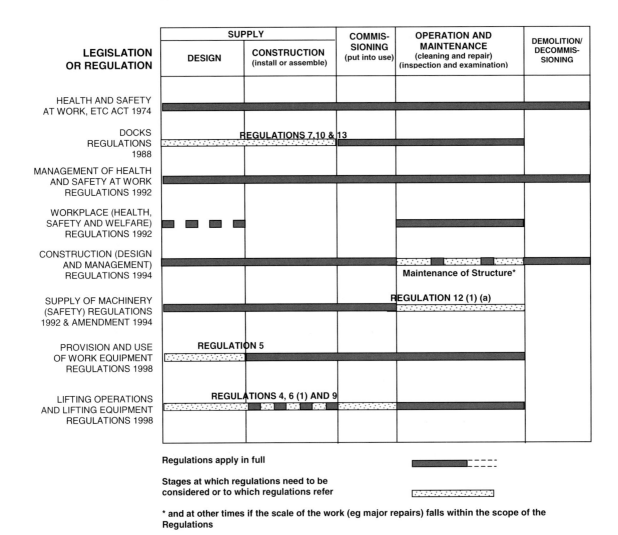

Figure 2.3 *Stages at which legislation applies either to work activities or to facilities*

For example, the regulations applying to operation and maintenance require suitable equipment to be supplied, and therefore have some influence on the supply stage of the process. In addition, the design and construction of the structure and machinery should take account of the need to clean and repair the structure, and to inspect and examine the machinery during operation and maintenance. The CDM Regulations also apply to the decommissioning and demolition stage of the process, and at any other time where the scale and nature of the work undertaken fall within the scope of the regulations.

The bar chart in Figure 2.3 shows simplified relationships between the stages and the various regulations, and readers should refer to the specific regulations and approved codes of practice for more detailed information.

2.2.3   Application of the regulations to second-hand, hired and leased equipment

The regulatory situation for second-hand equipment and machinery depends on the date of manufacture and supply, the country of origin, and the extent of refurbishment or modification of the equipment or machinery before it is brought back into use.

Machinery supplied or substantially refurbished and modified after 1 January 1993, particularly if these modifications alter the way it operates, must comply with all the requirements of SM(S)R. Machinery manufactured within the EEA and supplied since 1993 must comply with the EU Machinery Directives and have the appropriate documentation and, if supplied since 1995, should also be CE-marked. Machinery manufactured outside the EEA and imported since 1993 would have to comply with SM(S)R before being brought into use. Second-hand machinery that was first in use within the EEA before 1993 does not need to comply with SM(S)R.

However, all equipment and machinery must comply with PUWER 98 and with other regulations, such as the Electrical Equipment (Safety) Regulations 1994. For the purposes of PUWER 98, existing work equipment brought into use by another company or at a different port after 5 December 1998 becomes "new" equipment, even though it is second-hand. As such the equipment would have to comply with Regulations 11 to 24 and 31 to 39 of PUWER 98. Second-hand equipment imported from outside the EU must comply with all the requirements of PUWER 98, including the essential safety requirements of the appropriate product directive (generally SM(S)R in the case of linkspans and walkways).

There was a transitional period for "new" equipment up to 1 January 1995 and for "existing" equipment (pre-1993) up to 1 January 1997. Currently "existing" equipment (first brought into use before 5 December 1998) will need to meet all the requirements of Regulations 1 to 24 and 31 to 39 of PUWER 98, and therefore requires suitable and sufficient risk assessment. Each linkspan and walkway needs to be inspected and the hazards ranked, to determine whether or not it complies with PUWER 98. Those hazards with the highest non-compliant ranking should be rectified first, although all linkspans and walkways should be fully compliant, as the new regulations are similar to the original PUWER.

Hired and leased equipment should be treated in the same way as second-hand equipment. Existing equipment hired or leased to another company after 5 December 1998 is treated as "new" equipment, and would need to comply with PUWER 98 in the same way as similar second-hand equipment described above.

Most second-hand linkspans and walkways require new or substantially modified foundations, and these structures would need to be designed and constructed to comply with the CDM Regulations.

2.3 RISK ASSESSMENT

2.3.1 Regulatory requirements

There has been a legal requirement to undertake risk assessments for some years, although it has taken time for some sectors of the construction and manufacturing industries to understand the full meaning of the assessment process. Most professionals are now aware of the requirements but often less aware of how to actually measure risk.

Risk assessment is about identifying hazards, measuring risk and establishing acceptable safety standards. Such standards cannot be met solely on the strength of safe working practices. The European Union product directives recognise this and set down essential health and safety requirements. These requirements have to be assessed for particular products to ensure that the product complies.

The principle of risk assessment for work activities is specified in the Management of Health and Safety at Work Regulations 1992. These regulations require systematic assessment of all relevant risks and hazards in the workplace. Significant findings of the risk assessment must be recorded, and this record should include the measures taken to control the risk. The risk assessment should be reviewed and if necessary modified at intervals and where significant changes have been made.

The Construction (Design and Management) Regulations 1994 continue the principle of risk assessments, and require those involved in the design of a structure to avoid foreseeable risks, if practicable, or to reduce and control the effects of hazards. Information that affects the method of construction, maintenance, repair or demolition of the structure must be provided, and must set out the significant risks that have been identified.

The definition of *designer* in the CDM Regulations is very broad, and includes – among others – specifiers of materials or methods, cost consultants and, in some cases, clients themselves (that is, port operators and port owners).

The Supply of Machinery (Safety) Regulations 1992 require the preparation of a list of the essential health and safety requirements for a particular item of machinery, together with a description of the methods to be adopted to eliminate hazards. The regulations include a schedule setting out the essential health and safety requirements relating to the design and construction of machinery. The essential health and safety requirements are mandatory. However, when making assessments against the essential health and safety requirements for a particular item of machinery it should be borne in mind that the machinery being assessed may not incorporate a hazard against a specific essential health and safety requirement. Therefore all hazards must be considered, not only those relating to specific health and safety requirements.

The Approved Codes of Practice for the Provision and Use of Work Equipment Regulations 1998 (PUWER 98) and the Lifting Operations and Lifting Equipment Regulations 1998 (LOLER) give additional information about protection against specific hazards for work equipment and lifting equipment, and refer to risk assessments carried out under other regulations.

2.3.2 Risk assessment process

Books and reports giving detailed guidance on the risk assessment process are listed in the References.

The regulations all have slightly different wording about risk assessment, and refer to hazards that are particular to the subject covered by those regulations. However, because of the overlap of the various regulations and the professional disciplines involved in linkspans and walkways, it is recommended that a unified approach be adopted so that all the hazards related to linkspans and walkways are identified and dealt with in a single risk assessment. This approach will ensure that no hazards that occur at interfaces or that are caused by the effect of one element on another element will be missed.

2.3.3 Identification of hazards

The Supply of Machinery (Safety) Regulations set out essential health and safety requirements for machinery. Each one of the requirements identified in Schedule 3 of the Regulations should be considered, and if a hazard exists then this should be noted.

The Approved Code of Practice *Managing construction for health and safety* includes some guidance on hazards in construction. Information is also provided in the HSC's *A guide to managing health and safety in construction*, and in HSE information sheets on the pre-tender health and safety plan, and on the health and safety plan during construction. CIRIA has also published guidance documents for designers, planning supervisors and clients relating to the CDM Regulations.

2.3.4 Evaluation of risks

There are several systems for assessing the degree of risk from a particular hazard. However, common features of these evaluations are an assessment of the probability of occurrence of the hazard, the frequency of exposure of persons to the hazard, the degree of harm that can be caused to a person, and the number of persons at risk. For example these can range from a hazard that cannot happen under any circumstances to a hazard that occurs frequently and could lead to serious injury or fatality for many people. The latter risk would be unacceptable, and therefore the risk would have to be reduced or eliminated. Having assessed the various probabilities related to the hazard, most systems then multiply the probabilities together to produce a factor or combined probability. This is placed in a particular category or compared with a threshold value that determines whether precautions are required to control the risk from that hazard.

2.3.5 Precautions to control risk

There is an established hierarchy of actions to control risk. Attempts should be made to apply each of these in turn.

1. The best way to control the risk is to eliminate the hazard. This can be most effectively achieved as part of the design process.

2. If the hazard is such that it cannot be eliminated then the risk has to be reduced. This reduction might be achieved, for example, by reorganising work operations to reduce exposure to the hazard.

3. When the risk can be reduced no further, active control measures should be used. These should concentrate on protecting all workers or passengers from the hazard, for example by guarding or enclosing. The last resort is to provide specific protective equipment to those at risk.

The control of risks can be monitored by regularly inspecting work equipment and by carrying out periodic thorough examinations of lifting equipment. The possibility of control measures introducing new hazards and risks should not be overlooked.

> **Hazards must be identified and risks assessed at an early stage in the procurement of linkspans and walkways, so that methods of eliminating or reducing the risks from particular hazards can form an integral part of the development of the design of the machinery, lifting equipment and structure.**

2.3.6 Record of risk assessment

It is important that the risk assessment is carried out in a systematic way and that the significant hazards and precautions taken to control risks are set down in writing, so that they can be communicated to all concerned and an audit trail established. For linkspans and walkways the technical file for machinery and the health and safety file for completed structures provide a systematic method of recording the process. Risks arising during the construction process will be covered by the health and safety plan. However, the technical file is not available as of right to the purchaser unless specific contractual arrangements are put in place (see Section 3.10, Recommendation 12).

2.3.7 Review and revision of assessment

> **If changes are made to the design, construction or operation of a linkspan and walkway then it will be necessary to review the risk assessment and to revise the findings.**

Any changes should be systematically assessed and recorded. Alterations and repairs (and sometimes maintenance) inevitably change structures, lifting equipment and machinery, and should trigger a review of the risk assessment. The reason for a particular defect occurring needs to be considered, and if it is creating a hazard that has not been identified then a new risk assessment should be carried out.

2.4 RELEVANT LEGISLATION

2.4.1 Introduction

There are numerous regulations, in addition to those outlined above, that govern the supply, operation and maintenance of ship-to-shore linkspans and walkways. Many of these regulations apply to machinery and equipment, such as the various regulations covering electrical equipment, pneumatic equipment, pressure vessels and particular items of construction equipment, such as hoists. The following sections give brief details of the main requirements of a number of particularly relevant regulations. A summary of these requirements is also given in Table 2.1. However, **the commentary and guidance set out in this section are no substitute for a thorough study of the regulations and their associated approved codes of practice**.

> **All those involved in the procurement, operation and maintenance of ship-to-shore linkspans and walkways should be aware of all the applicable regulations and should know the requirements of the regulations that specifically apply to their own role in the process. However, those legally responsible for the safety of these facilities _must_ read and understand both the specific regulations and the guidance given in the associated approved code of practice. The person responsible under the relevant regulations is generally the managing director or chief executive officer of the employer, client (purchaser) or manufacturer. It is therefore essential that such persons have adequate knowledge of the requirements of the regulations and that they engage in the procurement, operation and maintenance of the facility only those who are competent.**

Brief details of the main requirements of the regulations that are particularly relevant to the procurement, operation and maintenance of ship-to-shore linkspans and walkways are given in the sections that follow. These regulations are enacted under the Health and Safety at Work etc Act 1974 unless noted otherwise.

Table 2.1   _Summary of UK regulations relating to ship-to-shore linkspans and walkways_

Person responsible*	Other regulatory appointments	Essential actions	Documentation
Docks Regulations 1988			
Employer	Authorised person (Regulation 10(6) and 11(1))	Plan work safely	Work plans
		Make obstacles and hazards conspicuous	Authorisations
		Provide and maintain safe access	Health records
		Assess competence of authorised person	Records of relevant training
		Assess fitness of authorised person	
		Provide appropriate training	
Management of Health and Safety at Work Regulations 1992			
Employer	Competent person (Regulation 6)	Suitable and sufficient risk assessment	Record of significant findings
		Review significant changes	
		Provide training	Information to employees on risks, protective measures and procedures
Workplace (Health, Safety and Welfare) Regulations 1992			
Employer		Maintain equipment and systems in efficient state and working order and in good repair	Records of maintenance
Person having control of workplace		Provide a system of maintenance	
		Provide suitable and sufficient lighting	
		Keep surfaces clean and remove waste	
		Protect workstation from adverse weather	
		Separate routes for vehicles and pedestrians	
		Provide welfare facilities	
Supply of Machinery (Safety) Regulations 1992 and Amendment 1994**			
Manufacturer or, if supplied from outside EU, importer of machinery	Responsible person (Authorised representative in Directive)	Mandatory risk assessment on essential health and safety requirements	EC Declaration of Conformity (or Declaration of Incorporation)
	Approved Body for Schedule 4 machinery	Draw up technical file	Technical file including:
		Affix CE Mark	• Drawings • Essential health and safety requirements • Harmonised standards and specifications • Instructions for machinery

Person responsible*	Other regulatory appointments	Essential actions	Documentation
Construction (Design and Management) Regulations 1994			
Person for whom construction is carried out (client)

Designer

Contractor/s | Planning supervisor

Principal contractor | Client or competent agent appoints planning supervisor and principal contractor

Carry out risk assessments on structure

Prepare health and safety plan | Health and safety plan

Health and safety file

Notice to HSE |
| **Provision and Use of Work Equipment Regulations 1998** | | | |
| Employer

Persons who control equipment

Persons who control use | | Where maintenance log exists keep up to date

Inspection after installation or reassembly by competent person

Provide record of result of inspection.

Provide adequate information on health and safety

Adequate training of operators and supervisors

Ensure stability of equipment

Automatic stopping of remote-controlled equipment | Inspection records

Record of significant findings of risk assessment

Maintenance log

Written instructions on use

Adequate health and safety information |
| **Lifting Operations and Lifting Equipment Regulations 1998** | | | |
| Employer

Controller of lifting equipment or of user of lifting equipment | | Risk assessment on suitability for purpose, health and safety of persons, and adequacy of strength and stability

Prepare plan of operation, supervise and carry out safely

Thorough examination by competent person and remedy defects

Competent person to decide whether to test, nature of test and method of testing | Safe working load mark

Thorough examination scheme

Notice of defects

Periodic thorough examination report |

* Note: Where the Regulations make more than one person responsible each may be required to carry out some or all of the essential actions.

** Regulations enacted under the European Communities Act 1972.

2.4.2   Health and Safety at Work Act

The Health and Safety at Work etc Act 1974 (HSWA) covers almost all work situations, and places general duties on employers to provide protection for all people at work and some protection to the general public. **HSWA is of over-riding importance, and its requirements should be considered before reference to other Acts and regulations that may also be applicable**. HSWA places a number of general duties on employers, including:

- the provision and maintenance of plant and systems of work that are safe

- the provision of information, instruction, training and supervision to ensure the safety of employees at work

- the maintenance of any place of work under the employer's control in a condition that is safe and without risk to health

- the provision of safe and risk-free access to and egress from any place of work under the employer's control

- ensuring that persons not in the employer's employment are not exposed to risks to their health and safety.

HSWA also requires the person who controls any premises to take reasonable measures to ensure that access to and egress from the premises and the premises themselves are safe. HSWA also places duties on employees to take reasonable care of their own and others' health and safety.

Section 6 of HSWA places duties on designers, manufacturers, suppliers, erectors and installers to ensure that articles are, so far as reasonably practicable, safe. They must also arrange any consequential tests and examinations, provide adequate information for safe use, and carry out necessary research to minimise risks to health and safety.

HSWA provides for health and safety regulations to be made under Section 15, and for practical guidance on health and safety to be provided in the form of approved codes of practice under Section 16.

> **Failure to observe the provisions of approved codes of practice without following effective and suitable alternative procedures can be taken as evidence of contravention in criminal prosecutions. This obligation is absolute.**

2.4.3 Docks Regulations

The Docks Regulations 1988 apply to all operations carried out in ports within Great Britain. The essentially identical Docks Regulations (Northern Ireland) 1989 apply in Northern Ireland. Approved codes of practice for each version of the Regulations entitled *Safety in docks* were published at the same time. The codes of practice include useful appendices giving details of other relevant legislation, HSE guidance publications and relevant British Standards, although some of the legislation, publications and standards referred to have been superseded by later documents. It is important to ensure that the latest versions of the relevant publications and standards are used.

The Docks Regulations cover the health and safety aspects of linkspans and walkways, and place duties on employers and employees, including vehicle drivers and equipment operators. Duties are also placed on owners of plant, but *not* on the master or crew of a ship when working on board without shore assistance, who are covered by a variety of merchant shipping regulations. However, operations involving ship's crew and dock workers working together are to comply with the Docks Regulations.

Operations must be planned and executed to ensure, so far as is reasonably practicable, that no person is exposed to danger. The term *reasonably practicable* requires risk assessment to be carried out and the level of risk to be weighed against the effort needed to introduce remedial measures. The term *practicable* means measures that are possible in the light of current knowledge and invention. Where more than one person controls operations, as in ro-ro operations involving ship's crew, stevedores and vehicle drivers, collaboration is required in setting up and agreeing strict procedures and systems of work. A reporting system is required for defects, so that timely repairs are carried out; the system of work should be reviewed and modified in the light of any defects.

The code of practice requires that appropriate arrangements are made for dealing with emergencies and other unexpected situations, and that appropriate instructions on these arrangements are given in advance.

Although the regulations do not apply specifically to ship's equipment, all dock operations are covered, and those making use of ship's equipment should be planned and executed safely and the safety of the equipment should be checked, including the inspection of certificates of test or thorough examination.

> **Ship-to-shore linkspans and walkways must provide a properly maintained, safe means of access to the ship, and should not be used unless they are of adequate strength for the purpose required, of sound construction and properly maintained. This obligation is absolute.**

Pedestrians should be segregated from vehicle roadways and moving plant.

Regulation 10(6) requires the operator of ship's ramps and shore-based ramps to be authorised by the person in control of the operation, and to be competent in that respect. The term *competent* means having the necessary theoretical and practical knowledge and experience to understand and take action to avoid dangers that might arise from the use of the equipment.

Regulation 11 deals with the authorisation, competence, training and fitness of drivers of powered vehicles and operators of powered lifting appliances such as linkspans and walkways. Authorisation is required either to drive or to operate the powered plant and to carry out operational maintenance of the plant. Authorisation should not be given unless the driver or operator is, and remains, fit and able to operate the plant. In order to assess fitness, periodic examination by a qualified medical practitioner will be required at an interval of not more than five years. The standard of fitness required will depend on the type of plant to be operated. Employees have a duty to report any change in their level of fitness to their employer. This includes the taking of medication that causes drowsiness or impairment caused by alcohol or other drugs. Authorisation should not be given unless the driver or operator is competent and appropriately trained. After training, a certificate should be issued to the operator clearly stating the vehicle or lifting appliance for which the operator has been tested. The employer must keep a written record of the training and testing of operators and the period of validity of the authorisation.

Regulation 12 requires roadways to be of adequate width and height clearance and clearly marked. Structures used by vehicles shall be sufficiently rigid and ramps should not be used by vehicles at a slope greater than 10 per cent, unless having sufficient grip and approved by a competent person. Traffic signals may be required to control vehicle movements. Suitable barriers must be provided to prevent vehicles from running over a dangerous edge, such as the end of the linkspan.

Regulation 13 requires lifting plant to be used only if it is of good design and construction, of adequate strength for the purpose required, of sound material and free from patent defect, properly installed or assembled, and properly maintained. It is implied that the lifting plant is provided in accordance with a relevant national or international standard and that it is subject to systematic preventive maintenance. Lifting plant should be subject to regular routine inspection by someone competent to assess its safety. The inspection should cover the operation of limit switches and overload indicators. In addition, lifting appliances should not be used in a manner likely to subject them to overturning, and lifting operations should be stopped when the wind exceeds the specified operating limit, and any additional braking system should then be brought into operation. A calibrated anemometer may need to be installed and an indicator or alarm fitted to warn the operator of excessive wind speeds. Rail-mounted walkways should provide the operator with a clear view of the area adjacent to the wheels, and the wheels should be fitted with guards.

The information provided in the approved code of practice is no longer up to date. New sets of regulations have been introduced that modify the Docks Regulations, and it is the responsibility of the user of the code of practice to ensure that the appropriate regulations and British or European standards are being used. It is understood that a substantial revision of the approved code of practice and guidance *Safety in docks* is intended.

2.4.4   Construction Products Regulations

The Construction Products Regulations 1991 and the Construction Products (Amendment) Regulations 1994 were prepared by the Department of the Environment under the European Communities Act 1972. These regulations require a construction product to satisfy the essential requirements and to comply with relevant national standards, European technical approval, national technical specification or harmonised specification. If they do not comply, they should be manufactured in conformity with relevant technical specifications, undergo the appropriate attestation procedures, be issued with a CE certificate or declaration of conformity and be CE-marked by the manufacturer or authorised representative or the first supplier into the Community. The essential requirements include mechanical properties, fire resistance, low energy, low construction noise and non-pollution of the environment.

2.4.5   Management of Health and Safety at Work Regulations

The Management of Health and Safety at Work Regulations 1992 (MHSWR) cover general matters of health and safety, and operate alongside many other regulations. Normally compliance with specific regulations will be sufficient to comply with those elements of MHSWR with which the specific regulations overlap. The regulations require every employer to assess the risks to employees and others who may be affected by the conduct of the undertaking, such as passengers or vehicle drivers embarking on or disembarking from a ship. A written record must be kept of the significant findings of the suitable and sufficient assessment of risks to health and safety. The significant findings should include hazards posing a serious risk, control measures and the extent that they control the risk, and groups affected by significant risks or hazards. The assessment must be reviewed where there has been a significant change.

Appropriate written procedures to be followed in the event of serious and imminent danger, and for danger areas, must be established. These procedures must be implemented by sufficiently competent persons. The procedures should include the requirements of specific regulations. Competent persons and employees must have sufficient training and experience or knowledge to implement the procedures. Employees must be provided with information on the risks to health and safety, the preventive and protective measures, the emergency procedures, and the identity of competent persons.

> **Where different employers share premises or workplaces they need to co-operate with each other and to co-ordinate their activities to ensure that they comply with the requirements of the regulations. Similarly, where employees of other employers, such as hauliers, work on the employer's premises, information about risks to their health and safety must be provided to the other employers.**

2.4.6   Workplace Regulations

The Workplace (Health, Safety and Welfare) Regulations 1992 took full effect for existing workplaces from the beginning of 1996. A workplace is any place within premises to which any employee has access, and includes all accessible parts of linkspans, and walkways, roadways and maintenance platforms, but not areas in or on a ship, nor construction sites. The requirements of the regulations apply to all employers and to every person who has, to any extent, control of a workplace.

> **The regulations require the workplace, equipment, devices and systems to be cleaned and maintained in an efficient state, in efficient working order, and in good repair. Equipment, devices and systems should have a suitable system of maintenance such that regular maintenance is carried out, defects are remedied and suitable records are kept. Enclosed workplaces should be properly ventilated, heated or cooled, and lit. Workplaces must be kept clean, and waste materials should not be allowed to accumulate. Special attention may need to be paid to providing non-absorbent and non-slip surfaces on linkspans and walkways. Floors and traffic routes should be suitably even, drained, slip-resistant and provided with handrails and barriers. Staircases and ladders must be provided where required for access to pits or tanks, and stepped changes in level should be marked conspicuously.**
>
> **Pedestrians and vehicles must be separated, and traffic routes must have sufficient width and headroom. Speed limits may be required on roadways. Where pedestrians and vehicle routes cross, barriers should be provided to prevent pedestrians from walking directly into a vehicle route. Crossing points should be segregated where traffic is heavy.**
>
> **The regulations also contain requirements for welfare facilities, including sanitary conveniences, washing facilities, drinking water, clothing lockers, changing rooms and canteen facilities.**

2.4.7   Supply of Machinery (Safety) Regulations

The Supply of Machinery (Safety) Regulations 1992 (SM(S)R) were enacted under the European Communities Act 1972 by the DTI in accordance with EU Directives 89/392/EEC and 91/368/EEC, and came into force in 1993. The Supply of Machinery (Safety) (Amendment) Regulations 1994 were enacted in accordance with EU Directives 93/44/EEC and 93/68/EEC, and came into force in 1994.

Unfortunately there is no approved code of practice for the SM(S)R. A guide was published by DTI in May 1995, *Product standards – Machinery – Guidance notes on UK regulations*, which gives background information, some information on compliance, and a useful annex on the essential health and safety requirements. However, it does not give clause-by-clause guidance on the regulations. An overview of the health and safety law applying to machinery is given in two leaflets recently published by HSE: INDG271, *Buying new machinery,* and INDG270, *Supplying new machinery.* Informed comments and answers to many potential questions arising from the application of the original European Machinery Directive are given in the document described in Section C1.3 of Appendix C.

The SM(S)R apply to machinery that is defined as:

an assembly of linked parts or components, at least one of which moves including, without prejudice to the generality of the foregoing, the appropriate actuators, control and power circuits, joined together for a specific application, in particular for the processing, treatment, moving or packaging of a material; an assembly of machines, that is to say, an assembly of items of machinery which, in order to achieve the same end, are arranged and controlled so that they function as an integral whole.

The regulations do not apply to machinery whose only source of power is directly applied manual effort unless it is a machine for lifting or lowering loads. This means that the regulations cover machinery where manual effort is accumulated in springs or accumulators, and lifting equipment such as hand winches, hoists and jacks. The regulations do not apply to electrical equipment where the risks to safety are mainly of electrical origin. Electrical equipment is covered by a number of specific regulations including the Electrical Equipment (Safety) Regulations 1994 and the Electromagnetic Compatibility Regulations 1992. In addition the regulations do not apply to equipment aboard sea-going vessels.

The Supply of Machinery (Safety) Regulations disapply parts of the Docks Regulations 1988 relevant to the provision of new machinery. In particular, Regulations 13(1)(a)(b) and (c) and the words "or assembled" in Regulations 13(1)(d), 13(2)(b)(c) and (d), 14(1)(a) and 16(7) are disapplied.

The regulations place duties on the supplier of the relevant machinery or relevant safety component, whether it is the manufacturer that put the machinery or safety equipment into service, or the importer of the relevant machinery or safety component from outside the European Economic Area (EEA).

> A prime requirement is for each manufacturer of each piece of relevant machinery to appoint a responsible person. For ship-to-shore linkspans and walkways the responsible person is likely to be the manufacturer of items of machinery forming the complete machinery, the assembler of the machinery (who could be a construction contractor), the authorised representative within the EU of a manufacturer, or the importer of the machinery.

In general, port owners and terminal operators will not be the responsible person unless they import the machinery themselves from outside the EEA or assemble and put the machinery into service themselves.

The regulations require that:

- the machinery satisfies the relevant essential health and safety requirements
- the machinery is in fact safe
- the responsible person draws up a technical file
- the responsible person issues either a declaration of conformity or a declaration of incorporation
- the responsible person affixes a CE mark.

The manufacturer is responsible for carrying out research and tests on components, fittings or the completed machine to determine that it is capable of being erected and put into service safely.

The technical file includes the following documents:

- drawings of the machinery and control circuits
- detailed drawings, calculations, test results and other data required to check that the machinery conforms with the essential health and safety requirements
- a list of the essential health and safety requirements, harmonised standards, standards and other technical specifications to which the machinery was designed
- a description of the methods used to eliminate hazards

- if necessary, a technical report from a competent body or laboratory confirming conformity with a harmonised standard
- a copy of the instructions for the machinery.

Where items of machinery are produced by a series manufacturing process, documentation must be provided to demonstrate the internal measures adopted to ensure continuing compliance with the Machinery Directive.

The responsible person draws up the declaration of conformity to confirm that the machinery supplied complies with all the essential health and safety requirements that apply to it. The declaration of conformity must include the following information:

- business name and full address of the responsible person and, if that person is not the manufacturer, of the manufacturer
- description of the machinery including its make, type and serial number
- all the relevant provisions with which the machinery complies
- harmonised standards used
- national standards or technical specifications used
- name of person authorised to sign on behalf of the responsible person.

Where items of machinery are to be assembled into other machinery to form the relevant machinery a declaration of incorporation is required. This declaration of incorporation must include the following information:

- name and address of the responsible person
- description of machinery
- harmonised standard used
- a statement that the part of the machinery must not be put into service until the relevant machinery has been declared to be in conformity with the Machinery Directive
- identity of the person signing the declaration of incorporation

The responsible person must retain the technical file for 10 years from the date on which the last unit of relevant machinery is produced. In the case of ship-to-shore linkspans and walkways this is the date on which the facility is brought into service.

> **It is good practice, although not mandatory, that copies of the technical file be issued to the owner, operator and maintenance organisation for the facility.**

Following the issue of a declaration of conformity, the responsible person shall affix a CE mark to the machinery.

The essential health and safety requirements are set out in Schedule 3 of the regulations as added to by the Amendment to the Regulations.

> **A risk assessment must be carried out to identify the hazards that exist for the particular machinery with reference to the essential health and safety requirements.**

These requirements include the following headings relevant to ship-to-shore linkspans and walkways:

- materials
- lighting
- control system and devices and stopping devices
- stability, moving parts and impact from falling objects (this probably includes vehicles and ships)
- overheating and fire
- reduction of noise
- containment of emissions of dust, gases, etc
- guards and protection devices
- safe access for maintenance and repair
- indicators, warning devices and instructions
- particular hazard due to lifting and moving persons.

Where a harmonised standard exists for a particular item of machinery, compliance with the harmonised standard will normally ensure that the essential health and safety requirements are met. The harmonised standards are provided in a hierarchy of three main groups as set out below:

Type A Standards. These apply to all machinery; they are essential reading for designers and manufacturers of machinery, and relate to general principles of wide application.

Type B Standards. These are laterally interlinked, and are generally divided into B1 and B2 standards.

- B1 Standards apply across broad categories of machinery, and are designed to promote the essential factors of safety
- B2 Standards are "apply when used" standards: if a particular safety device is chosen for a machine it must be manufactured and applied to the relevant standard.

Type C Standards. These will inform designers, manufacturers and users of specific safety precautions to be taken, and devices that are required to be used in particular applications.

The relationships between a selection of the currently available harmonised standards for machinery are shown in Figure 2.4.

With regard to the provision of ship-to-shore linkspans and walkways, all anticipated Type A standards now exist. Many Type B1 and B2 standards exist, but others are being prepared. Unfortunately there is no specific Type C standard for either linkspans or walkways. Therefore the essential health and safety requirements will need to be assessed for these specific types of machinery against the requirements in the Annex to the Regulations.

| 2.4.8 | **Construction (Design and Management) Regulations** |

The Construction (Design and Management) Regulations 1994, generally known as the CDM Regulations, came into force on 31 March 1995. An approved code of practice was also published in 1995. The regulations replace several older regulations and formalise requirements for risk assessment.

Every construction client is required to appoint one or more competent persons to assist him to fulfil the requirements of the regulations. A competent person can be either an employee or a specialist organisation. Such persons should be given sufficient time and resources to carry out their duties.

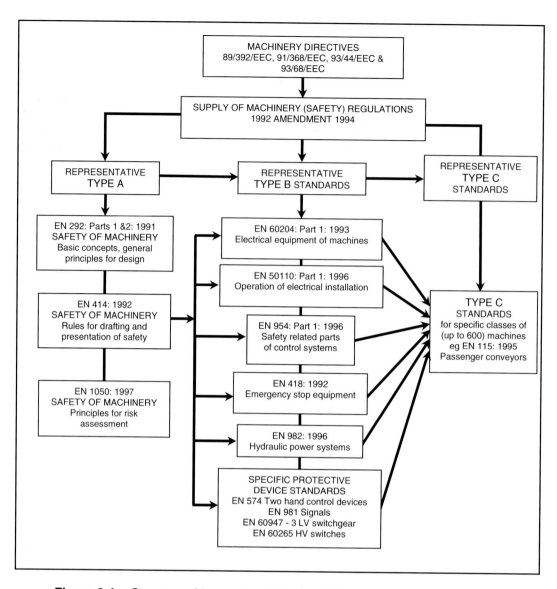

Figure 2.4 *Structure of harmonised standards for machinery.*

> **The appointment of these assistants does not absolve the construction client of his responsibilities under HSWA.**

The regulations apply to construction work, including building and civil engineering work and alteration, cleaning, repair, maintenance, demolition or dismantling of a structure; site clearance, site investigation, excavation and laying foundations for a structure. They also apply to the installation, commissioning, cleaning, maintenance and repair of mechanical, electrical, hydraulic or similar services normally fixed within or to a structure. For ship-to-shore linkspans and walkways a structure is any building, steel or reinforced concrete structure, dock, bridge or other similar structure; any formwork or scaffolding; and any fixed plant involving a risk of falling more than 2 m, but *only* in respect of installation, commissioning, decommissioning and dismantling.

The regulations place duties on the client, designer and contractor. A *client* means any person for whom a project is carried out. In the context of ship-to-shore linkspans and walkways, the term includes ship operators, port owners and terminal operators who procure or purchase a linkspan or walkway.

On appointment, a one of the designer's duties under the regulations is to advise clients of their duties.

> **The client has specific duties under the CDM Regulations, one of which is to appoint a planning supervisor and a principal contractor. The client must be reasonably satisfied with the competence of these appointees and with the adequacy of resources allocated by the appointees to perform their duties. The client must provide health and safety information about the project, not permit construction work to start until an adequate construction health and safety plan is available, and hold the health and safety file and make it available to others.**

A client may appoint an agent (or another client) to act in respect of the project provided that the client is reasonably satisfied that the agent has the competence to perform the duties imposed on a client by these regulations. The appointment must be notified by a written declaration to the Health and Safety Executive.

> **The client is responsible for providing information about the site. In the case of ship-to-shore linkspans and walkways this might include information on soil conditions, sea-bed levels, wave climate, ship operations and geometrical requirements.**

Titles that provide guidance on the CDM Regulations are listed in the References section. Particularly relevant guidance is provided in HSE Construction Sheet No 39 *The role of the client* and in CIRIA Report 172, *CDM Regulations – practical guidance for clients and clients' agents*.

2.4.9   Provision and Use of Work Equipment Regulations

The Provision and Use of Work Equipment Regulations 1992 (PUWER) implemented EU Directive 89/655/EEC (UWED) and covered health and safety requirements for the provision of safe work equipment and its safe use. The regulations came into effect in 1993, except for equipment that existed before this date, which were covered by a variety of old regulations. For existing equipment, the regulations came into effect in 1997. Existing work equipment sold second-hand since 1993 becomes "new" equipment for the purposes of the regulations, and the requirements of Regulations 11 to 24 apply retrospectively. However, it does not have to comply with the essential safety requirements. See Section 2.2.3 covering second-hand, leased and hired equipment.

Guidance on the regulations was published by HSE in 1992 in *Work equipment – guidance on regulations*. Many of the requirements of PUWER were already covered by earlier legislation and regulations, and several parallel regulations were enacted in 1992, such as MHSWR and the Workplace (Health, Safety and Welfare) Regulations. Where the various regulations set out duties that overlap, compliance with the more specific regulation will normally be sufficient to comply with the general requirement in other regulations.

EU Directive 95/63/EC, the Amending Directive to the Use of Work Equipment Directive (AUWED), lays down wide-ranging requirements for the provision, management and use of mobile, self-propelled and remote-controlled work equipment, inspection of work equipment, provision and use of lifting equipment, and the management of lifting operations.

PUWER was revoked by the Provision and Use of Work Equipment Regulations 1998 (PUWER 98), which came into force on 5 December 1998. They apply to all work equipment, including general requirements for lifting equipment, but will only implement the non-lifting requirements of AUWED.

The specific requirements for lifting equipment and lifting operations will be covered by LOLER, a separate but related set of regulations (see subsection 2.4.10)

PUWER 98 needs to be used in conjunction with MHSWR. The risk assessment procedure carried out under MHSWR will assist in the selection of equipment and assessment of its suitability for the particular task. The training requirements set out in the two sets of regulations are complementary. There is also considerable overlap with the requirements of SM(S)R, and equipment that satisfies these regulations will generally meet the requirements of PUWER 98.

The definition of *use* for work equipment is broad, and includes starting, stopping, programming, setting, transporting, repairing, modifying, maintaining, servicing and cleaning. *Work equipment* means any machinery, appliance, apparatus, tool or installation. The regulations do not apply to work equipment provided by the ship except where activities are carried out by shore-based contractors within territorial waters.

The primary duties under PUWER 98 rest on employers, but duties are also placed on the person who controls the work equipment and the person who controls the use of the work equipment.

Regulations numbers referred to below are for PUWER 98. The commentary takes account of the contents of the approved code of practice.

> **Regulation 5 requires that work equipment is maintained in efficient working order and that where any machinery has a maintenance log, the log is kept up to date. All linkspans and walkways should have maintenance logs. The frequency, extent and complexity of checking and maintenance will depend on the equipment and risks involved: it could be daily, weekly, monthly or at longer intervals. A maintenance management system is required.**

Regulation 6 requires installation of the work equipment to be inspected by a competent person where there is significant risk before being put into service or after assembly at a new location. This regulation also requires that work equipment that is subject to conditions causing deterioration, such as linkspans or walkways, is inspected at suitable regular intervals and following known or suspected serious damage. The level and thoroughness of the inspection will depend on the risk, but should be sufficient to detect deterioration of the work equipment, which must be remedied.

> **A competent person needs to have the necessary knowledge of the work equipment being inspected and of preventive protection, such as guards; where needed, appropriate training should be provided. The results of the inspection must be recorded.**

Regulation 7 requires the use of work equipment that involves a specific risk to health and safety to be restricted to persons who have been instructed and trained for its use. It further requires that repair, modifications, maintenance or servicing of the work equipment is restricted to designated persons who have received sufficient information, instruction and training.

Regulation 8 requires written information on the safe use of work equipment to be provided to operators, supervisors and managers, including information on the conditions in which the work equipment may be used and details of foreseeable abnormal situations and the actions to be taken in these situations.

Regulation 9 requires operators, supervisors and managers to receive adequate health and safety training concerning methods of operating and precautions to be taken against risks for the work equipment.

Under Regulation 10 work equipment must comply with the essential safety requirements of the relevant regulations listed in Schedule 1, which for linkspans and walkways would generally be the Supply of Machinery (Safety) Regulations. This regulation also provides that the extent to which Regulations 11 to 19 and 22 to 29 need to be considered is restricted to matters not covered by compliance with those essential safety requirements.

Regulation 11 covers measures to prevent access to dangerous parts and to stop the movement before any part of a person enters a danger zone; it covers the provision of information, instruction, training and supervision.

Regulation 12 covers protection against specific hazards related to the work equipment such as part of the equipment breaking or collapsing. These specific hazards should be identified by the risk assessment carried out under MHSWR. Risk-controlling measures should be provided as part of the equipment, where practicable.

Regulations 14 to 19 cover controls, control systems and isolation from energy sources. These controls should allow changes in operating conditions, including starting, stopping and access to danger zones to be safely controlled.

Regulation 20 covers stability of the work equipment, and requires additional measures to be taken in severe weather conditions, for example the provision of clamps or anchors for mobile walkways.

Regulation 22 requires the work equipment to be constructed or adapted to allow safe maintenance such as by remote lubrication points and interlocked guards on moving parts.

Regulations 23 and 24 cover the marking of work equipment with warnings or identifications of controls and the provision of warning devices such as audible alarms.

Regulations 25 to 30 cover risks from mobile work equipment including remote-controlled work equipment.

The provisions of PUWER 98 operate alongside the Dock Regulations 1988.

2.4.10   Lifting Operations and Lifting Equipment Regulations

The Lifting Operations and Lifting Equipment Regulations 1998 (LOLER) implement the specific lifting aspects of AUWED, and apply over and above the general requirements of PUWER 98 to cover specific risks arising from lifting loads. There were numerous existing regulations covering lifting equipment, of which the most relevant to linkspans and walkways were the Docks Regulations 1988 (Regulations 13 to 17) and the Lifting Plant and Equipment (Records of Test and Examination) Regulations 1992. The lifting equipment aspects of all these regulations are amended or revoked by LOLER. Regulation 14 amends Regulation 13(4) and revokes Regulations 14,15,16(3)(4)(5)(7) & (8) and 17 of the Docks Regulations 1988.

One problem of the various existing regulations is that they do not provide a common definition of lifting equipment. The ports industry generally adopts the definitions in the Docks Regulations. AUWED refers to "work equipment for lifting loads" but gives no definition. Throughout LOLER "lifting equipment" covers cranes and accessories, including slings, hooks and eyebolts.

LOLER generally cover the proper planning of lifting operations so that they can be carried out safely, the safe use of lifting equipment, and the thorough examination of lifting equipment at suitable intervals by a competent person. The regulations in LOLER are relatively concise, and in order to fully implement AUWED they have been amplified by an approved code of practice giving comprehensive guidance, which will also amplify relevant clauses in PUWER 98.

The Management of Health and Safety at Work Regulations already require risk assessments of work activities to be carried out to identify risks arising from the use of lifting equipment and the appropriate precautions required to deal with these risks. The level of precaution will depend on the degree of risk assessed, and should reduce the risk to as low a level as is reasonably practicable. Particular hazards to be considered are equipment striking a person or object and the consequences of equipment failing.

LOLER impose further requirements on employers, on persons controlling the lifting equipment, and on the operator of the lifting equipment or the method of operation of the lifting equipment.

LOLER define *lifting equipment* as work equipment for **lifting and lowering** loads. The enforcement agency has confirmed that LOLER will not be applicable to the majority of linkspans and walkways where the lifting machinery is an integral part of the installation and only adjusts the vertical location of one component of the machine rather than raising or lowering a separately identifiable load. The general exclusion of linkspans and walkways applies both to those that are adjusted to a level then "spragged" before vehicle or pedestrian loads are applied, and to those that are adjusted in level during use, because the primary function in both cases is not the lifting and lowering of loads.

All linkspans and walkways are considered to be *work equipment*, and are subject to the requirements of PUWER 98.

Where an identifiable and separate piece of *lifting equipment* such as a crane, hoist, jack or scissors lift is used to raise, lower or support a linkspan or walkway, or components such as ramps, bridges, gangways, brows or flaps, the requirements of LOLER will apply as follows:

- Regulation 4   Strength and stability
- Regulation 5   Lifting equipment for lifting persons
- Regulation 6   Positioning and installation
- Regulation 7   Marking of lifting equipment
- Regulation 8   Organisation of lifting operations
- Regulation 9   Thorough examination and inspection
- Regulation 10   Reports and defects
- Regulation 11   Keeping of information

> **All the above regulations are potentially important under relevant circumstances.**

Regulation 4 requires the employer to ensure that lifting equipment is not used unless it is of adequate strength and stability for the load. The ACoP gives guidance on forces to be considered, ductility of materials, mounting and fixing points, wind loads, bases and anchorage systems and testing of lifting points.

Regulation 5 requires that lifting equipment for lifting persons shall not be used unless it prevents people from being crushed, that the carrier is prevented from falling or has an enhanced safety coefficient for its suspension and prevents risk of the user falling from the carrier. The guidance gives examples of suitable devices to prevent the carrier from falling in the event of failure of the primary lifting system, including redundant safety systems, such as multiple suspension systems; and independent means of suspension. The guidance requires the carrier to have suitable edge protection, slip-resistant flooring, and secure inward-opening gates or doors.

Regulation 7 requires lifting equipment to be marked with its safe working load for each configuration of the equipment or that such information should be kept with the equipment. If it is not possible to provide the safe working load for all configurations, as is likely for a linkspan, then the employer should provide a statement of what should be done, such as contacting a manager.

Regulation 8 covers the planning and organisation of lifting operations, and is therefore relevant to ship-to-shore linkspans and walkways. Lifting operations involving lifting equipment must be properly planned by a competent person, appropriately supervised, and carried out in a safe manner. The plan needs to address the risks identified by the risk assessment, and to state the resources required, the procedures to be adopted and the responsibilities of persons involved. The competent person planning the operation should have adequate practical and theoretical knowledge and experience of planning similar lifting operations. The ACoP also refers to suitable measures to be taken to minimise risks to lifting equipment from its proximity to other objects. These risks include proximity to ships. The planning of the lifting operation should also include examples of potential defects that might be found by a trained user and the types of pre-use checks to be made by the user.

Regulation 9 requires that lifting equipment that could have a defect, be dangerous or have deteriorated, or which has just been installed, shall be thoroughly examined by a competent person before it is put back into service. Thorough examinations to determine potential deterioration should be carried out periodically. The competent person will decide whether a test is necessary, the nature of the test and the most appropriate method for carrying it out. In deciding what test to carry out, the competent person must take account of the manufacturer's instructions. Testing should take into account that some modern equipment is not designed to have an overload test. For complex lifting equipment the inspection may require different people to inspect particular parts.

Regulations 10 and 11 cover reports and records. Regulation 10 requires defects found during inspections to be notified to the employer and for a written and signed report of the inspection to be made. In circumstances where a defect could become a danger to persons, the report must be sent to the enforcing authority. The employer must not permit the lifting equipment to be used before the defect has been rectified. Regulation 11 requires the employer to keep the SM(S)R declaration of conformity or incorporation and all current inspection reports available for inspection by the enforcing authority.

The provisions of LOLER operate alongside the Docks Regulations 1988.

2.5 FUTURE DEVELOPMENTS

Some of the following subsections refer to detailed information in Section 2.4.

2.5.1 Docks Regulations

The Docks Regulations have been modified following the coming into force of PUWER 98 and LOLER during 1998. It is intended that the approved code of practice and guidance *Safety in docks* will be amended. There will need to be additional references to ship-to-shore linkspans and walkways and related matters, and to the effect of berthing and mooring ships on the safety of dock personnel and port equipment, particularly with regard to potential impacts between ship and dock premises or equipment.

2.5.2 Supply of Machinery (Safety) Regulations

The existing Machinery Directive is being revised, and a draft amendment has been issued for consultation. The amendment is intended to:

- strengthen surveillance of compliance with the directive
- clarify sections where the interpretation of the meaning is unclear
- list potential hazards under headings related to the various engineering disciplines.

It is envisaged that the amended directive will be published by 2003 with an amendment to SM(S)R coming into effect in 2004.

2.5.3 Specific machinery standards

Specific Type C standards are gradually being produced for machinery. The requirement for specific standards for linkspans and for walkways has not been acknowledged, and therefore work has not started.

It is strongly recommended that separate Type C standards should be produced for ship-to-shore linkspans and for ship-to-shore walkways. It may be that the Type C standard for linkspans could be developed from the draft Dutch Standard NEN 6786 *Rules for the design of movable bridges* and from the new German Standard DIN 19704 *Hydraulic steel structures* in conjunction with the following documents:

- supplement ZTV-W *Additional specification – water engineering* published by the German Federal Ministry of Transport
- Section 216/1 *Civil engineering aspects of water engineering* to DIN 18335 *Steel construction work.*

The Type C standards for walkways could be developed from the draft EN 12312-4 *Aircraft ground support equipment – specific requirements – Part 4: Passenger boarding bridges*.

Reference can also be made to the Lloyd's Register *Classification of linkspans* rules and regulations first published in January 1998, and including amendments by Notice No 2 published in October 1998. The rules and regulations are published in four parts covering: regulations; manufacture, testing and certification of materials; construction, design and testing requirements; and engineering systems.

The harmonised standards that have been listed in relation to the Machinery Directives were set out in Commission communication 98/C 183/02 published in the *Official Journal of the European Communities* dated 13 June 1998. Additional lists are published from time to time, and readers should obtain all relevant listings.

2.5.4 Canadian Standard

Transport Canada and other sponsors are developing a new standard for the design, operation, inspection and maintenance of ferry boarding facilities. The standard is divided into four parts. Parts 1 and 2, covering design and inspections, are in the form of codes, and Parts 3 and 4, covering operation and maintenance, provide guidelines and recommendations. The Canadian Standards Association intends to publish the standard in draft form in 1999 as Standard S826.

2.5.5 British Standards

Several existing British Standards are applicable, in part, to the design of linkspans and walkways. The most relevant of these are listed in Appendix D, and include loads, foundations, structure and machinery. However, some aspects of the design of linkspans and walkways are not satisfactorily covered in existing standards. These include:

- loadings due to ship or vehicle impact
- the ship-to-shore facility interface, particularly for walkways
- torsional behaviour
- connections between lifting equipment and structure
- accidental or emergency loadings from connections to ship
- extreme movements of the ship end of the structure due to ship motions and tidal changes or to wave action
- devices to prevent movement of structure in the event of failure of support bearings or suspension systems.

The existing standards do not satisfactorily cover the particular requirements of vehicle linkspans, such as:

- load factors suitable for relatively short design life
- load factors based on acceptability of minor overstressing of roadway deck
- specialist port vehicle characteristics (partly covered by BS 6349: Part 1)
- impact factors for lower vehicle speeds and solid wheels.

There has been an intention for some years to produce Part 8 to BS 6349 *Maritime structures*. It was proposed that Part 8 would be called *Design of ramps and walkways to ro-ro vessels*.

It had been hoped that work on the draft code would run in parallel to the production of this guide, and that there should be liaison between the research team and the BSI drafting committee. Work on Part 8 has not yet received funding.

If BS 6349 Part 8 was to include all necessary topics including those listed above, and if it could be drafted and published speedily, it would meet the need. It would also assist the production of a European standard.

2.6 RECOMMENDATIONS

The latest regulations provide a framework of requirements for the safe supply, construction, operation and maintenance of linkspans and walkways. Important matters have been highlighted in the earlier sections, and the following recommendations are made to enhance safety further.

1. **Prepare guidance on the design of linkspans and walkways.** This guidance should be provided urgently in a form that will cross-reference existing structural, mechanical, electrical and control system standards and classification rules related to linkspans and walkways. The guidance should provide authoritative design practice for those areas not covered by other specific standards, including the aspects listed in Section 2.5.5.

2. **Produce a Type C standard for linkspans and a separate Type C standard for walkways** to facilitate compliance with the essential safety requirements of the EU directives relating to machinery. These standards would define as a minimum the functional, performance, and health and safety requirements for linkspans and walkways. It is expected that these standards would also cover requirements for stability of the facility as well as crushing, trapping and falling hazards due to movement of the facility and other essential health and safety requirements relating to the design and construction of the machinery and safety components.

3. **Produce a design code of practice.** There is also a need for design guidance to be codified, covering all necessary topics including those aspects listed in Section 2.5.5. This could be achieved by BS 6349: Part 8, or by an equivalent European standard, or both, depending on which is the most expeditious route.

4. **Set up a port industry arrangement to collect, monitor and promulgate information on near misses, incidents, accidents and failures.** Owners, operators and maintenance organisations should co-operate with the above arrangements by providing records of incidents, if necessary by direct, anonymous, confidential reporting.

3 Procurement and implementation

3.1 INTRODUCTION

3.1.1 General

There are several reports and books on the procurement of design services, equipment and construction. The most relevant of these documents are listed in the References section. The guidance provided largely follows existing best practice (Figure 3.1).

Ship-to-shore linkspans and walkways are hybrid facilities, which may involve a mixture of civil engineering foundations and structures, movable bridge structures, floating structures, lifting equipment, machinery and control systems, and a variety of professional disciplines. The supply and construction costs of most mechanically lifted linkspans and walkways, excluding other shore and berth facilities, are generally divided almost equally between foundations and structural elements and mechanical, electrical and control system elements. Over the years there has been a trend towards equipment and machinery becoming more sophisticated and therefore forming a larger proportion of the total cost of linkspans and walkways. Mechanically lifted linkspans and walkways have generally involved civil, structural, mechanical and electrical engineering disciplines, and have usually been procured under various ICE forms of contract. Buoyant linkspans and walkways have generally involved naval architects and engineers, and have been procured under a wide variety of forms of contract, although more than half the buoyant linkspans and walkways were procured under the various ICE forms of contract. The remainder were supplied under standard Belgian, French and Swedish forms of contract or under manufacturers' equipment purchase contracts. Some guidance on appropriate forms of contract is given in Section 3.4, but **it is important that purchasers seek professional advice on the most appropriate form of contract for their particular facility.**

There are a variety of methods of procurement suitable for linkspans and walkways, and these are discussed in Section 3.3. Most port owners, terminal operators or other potential purchasers of linkspans and walkways will already have procurement procedures for infrastructure, structures and equipment. In addition, public contracting authorities must comply with the various public procurement regulations. The key roles in the procurement process are described below:

- purchaser, employer or client
- project adviser (client's representative)
- project manager
- designer
- planning supervisor
- engineer and engineer's representative
- independent design assessor
- systems engineer
- project safety auditor.

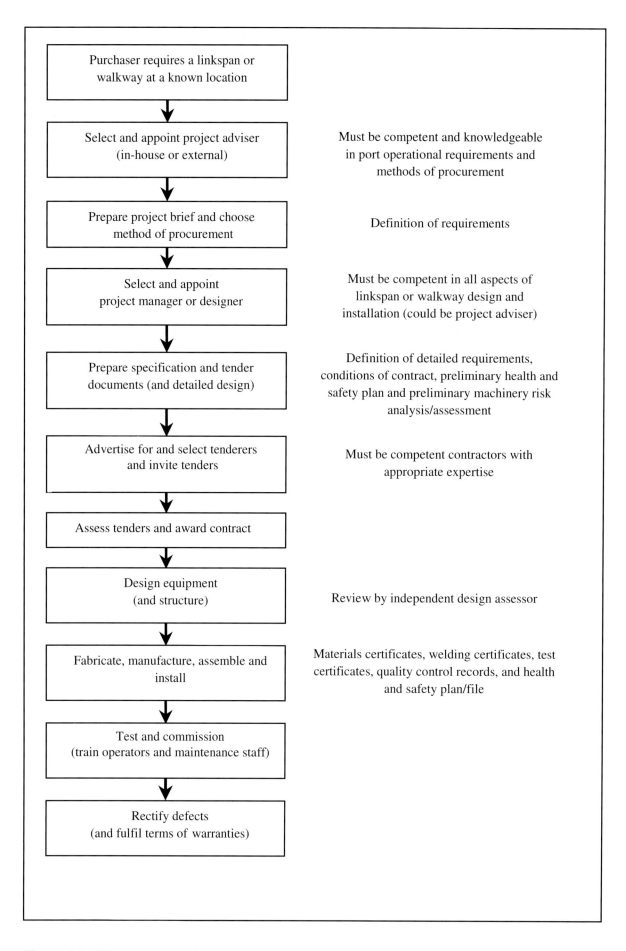

Figure 3.1   *The procurement process*

Although these designations may not be familiar to readers, the roles assigned cover tasks that are already carried out on well-run projects. **In defining these key roles, the intention is to ensure that all the tasks required to provide a safe facility that complies with the regulations, are properly undertaken.** Some roles may have different titles under some forms of contract, and some could be carried out by the same person or organisation. These definitions also help to ensure that **no tasks are omitted between the various parties to the procurement process, and that the purchaser, owner and employer can be reasonably certain that all reasonably practicable steps have been taken to ensure the safety of employees and users of the facility.**

3.1.2 The procurement routes

There are several procurement routes for construction and for the supply and erection of electrical, electronic and mechanical plant. Several publications give expert guidance on the procurement process, and it is not intended to repeat the detailed mechanics of the procurement process in this guide (see Section 3.3).

Ship-to-shore linkspans and walkways are procured through a variety of routes, and the routes available are increased by the hybrid nature of these facilities, which are neither entirely construction work nor entirely equipment. The procurement routes are influenced by:

- the procedures of the purchaser

- the significance of the linkspan or walkway in an overall development project

- the packaging of the construction and supply of the linkspan or walkway

- the allocation of design liability

- the initial definition of the requirements for the linkspan or walkway.

The procurement process starts when the purchaser decides that there is a requirement for a linkspan or walkway. At this time the detailed requirements for, and even the exact location of, the structure may not have been decided. However, for the purposes of this guide it is assumed that the feasibility and financial viability of the provision of a linkspan or walkway at a particular location have already been investigated. It is also assumed that the purchaser has a relatively firm view of the technical and operational requirements. The guide also assumes that the environmental constraints have been defined, that the local environmental regime has been investigated by means of field studies, soil investigations, wind and wave recording and analysis, and that any environmental impact assessment has been completed. These are standard matters of project planning, and are considered to be outside the scope of the guide.

It is essential that the purchaser considers the procurement options at a very early stage in the procurement process following the feasibility study, and decides on the appropriate procurement route. This early decision will enable appropriate choices to be made about the timing of design input and the involvement of the contractor. The options for the procurement route can be divided as follows:

- multi-contract procurement such as the traditional designer-led option
  – either with single-stage tendering by the contractor
  – or with two-stage tendering by the contractor

- management contracting

- construction management

- single contract options
  – design and construct
  – equipment purchase.

These options involve either the design being provided to the contractor(s) or the design being the responsibility of the contractor(s).

A simplified flow chart for the three main procurement routes – design and construct, traditional, and new or second-hand purchase – are set out in Figures 3.2 and 3.3, and only these routes are described in more detail in Section 3.3. For information on the other routes reference should be made to specialist publications.

The procurement route selected depends on the firmness of the functional brief for the project, the perceived need for flexibility in variations to the requirements, and the division of responsibility and risk that the purchaser wishes to retain or transfer.

> **The particular procurement route needs to be considered and decided early in the procurement process by a person with knowledge and competence in both port operational requirements and methods of procurement.**

3.1.3 The proposed roles within the project

The key roles in the procurement process are listed in Section 3.1.1 and are defined below. They have been carried out informally during the procurement of all linkspans and walkways, except for the new role of project safety auditor. Some of these roles may have different titles under some forms of contract and in some sections of the ports industry, and some of the roles may not have previously been separately defined, having been carried out as a part of a more general role.

Purchaser, employer or client

The term used to define the person or organisation procuring a linkspan or walkway, and the party to a contract for the supply, erection, installation and construction of a linkspan or walkway, depends on the form of contract adopted. Construction contracts use the term *employer* to describe this person, firm, company or other organisation, whereas consulting engineers' conditions of engagement and the CDM Regulations use the term *client*. However, throughout this section the term *purchaser* has been used to describe this person or organisation. This term is used in electrical and mechanical contracts, and its meaning is well understood by general readers.

Project adviser

The project adviser is the person who will help the purchaser to identify the options for procurement, and will assist in preparing the project brief.

The project adviser should be knowledgeable and competent about port operational requirements and in particular about the requirements for ro-ro and passenger terminals, and should have a good understanding of the procurement options for construction and equipment. The project adviser should have sufficient expertise to advise the purchaser on the best procurement route, and should be able to prepare the functional brief for the project and provide well-informed day-to-day advice, if required, throughout the procurement process. The project adviser should also need to understand the commercial and time-critical requirements for the facility.

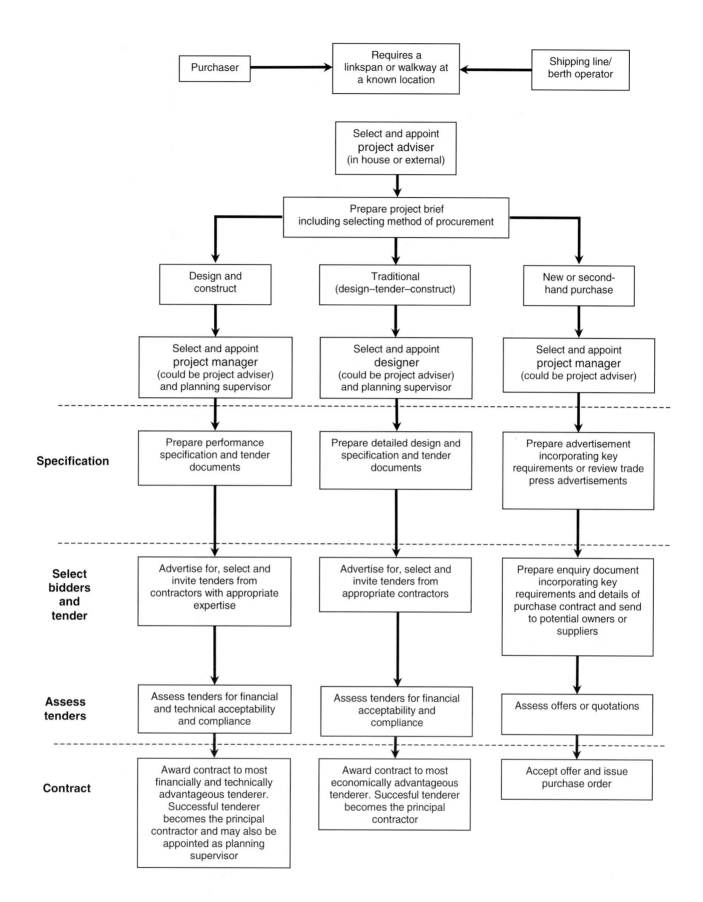

Figure 3.2 *Procurement routes for ship-to-shore linkspans and walkways: first stages*

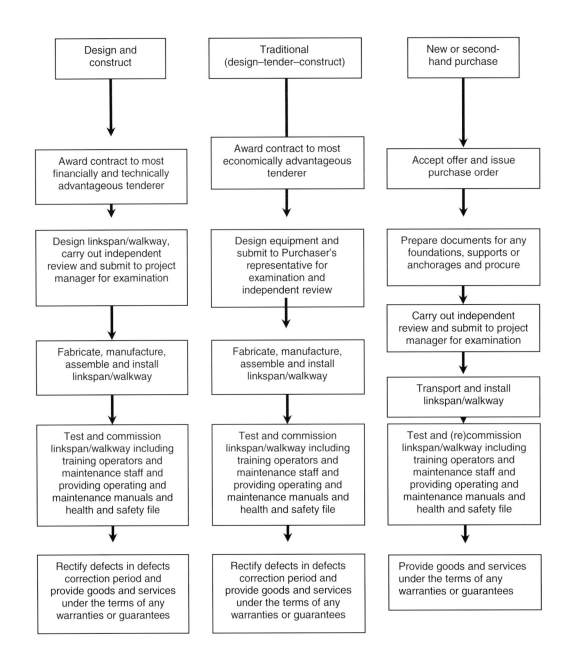

Figure 3.3   *Procurement routes for ship-to-shore linkspans and walkways: later stages*

The role of the project adviser is sometimes known as the client's representative. For many of the medium-to-large and medium-sized ports and experienced terminal operators the project adviser would usually be a member of the port or terminal operator's own organisation. However, for small ports and less experienced terminal operators it may be necessary to select and appoint an external project adviser. In either case **the purchaser should use a systematic method of selecting the project adviser that ensures that the appointee is competent and knowledgeable enough about port operational requirements and methods of procurement to be able to advise the client or purchaser properly. Note that the appointment of a project adviser would not relieve the purchaser of their regulatory responsibilities and their need to involve themselves in making decisions and controlling the project.**

The project adviser will assist the purchaser with the preparation of a functional brief for the facility and the selection of a method of procurement. The contents of the functional brief are covered in Section 3.2. Procurement routes are discussed in detail in Section 3.3.

The project adviser will then assist the purchaser to select and appoint either a project manager or a designer, depending on the procurement route selected. The project adviser may also assist the purchaser to assess the competence and resources of the planning supervisor. The project adviser could become the project manager or designer.

Project manager

The project manager could be appointed by the purchaser to co-ordinate and manage the procurement of the linkspan or walkway. The project manager's role is more effective when it is carried out independently of other roles. The project manager must be knowledgeable and competent in all aspects of the design and installation of linkspans and walkways. The project manager would draw up, or arrange for others to draw up, advertisements, selection procedures, enquiry documents, conditions of contract, technical specifications, price schedules, instructions to tenderers and the preliminary health and safety plan. Other roles include advising on the division of the procurement of the linkspan or walkway into contractual packages for appropriate elements, and assisting the purchaser to place advertisements for contractors or suppliers, carry out the selection process for contractors or suppliers, and send out tender documents to contractors with the appropriate expertise.

The project manager would assist the purchaser to assess the tenders or quotations by carrying out a systematic financial and technical evaluation, and then help to prepare the acceptance of tender and the construction contract or to issue a purchase order.

The role of project manager could be fulfilled by the project adviser, by a member of the port or terminal owner's engineering staff, by a project management company, or by a firm of consulting engineers.

Designer

The designer is selected and appointed by the purchaser, with the assistance of the project adviser, to develop the functional brief for the linkspan and walkway. The designer carries out the detailed design of the foundations, structure and machinery, and prepares conditions of contract, technical specifications, price schedules, instructions to tenderers, and the pre-tender health and safety plan.

The designer assists the purchaser in advertising for suitable contractors, and selects and shortlists tenderers. The designer would send out tender documents to the selected tenderers and assist with responding to any tender queries. The designer would carry out a systematic financial and technical evaluation of the tenders and help the purchaser to prepare the acceptance of tender and the construction contract.

The design of linkspans and walkways involves a variety of professional disciplines, and the designer may be the lead designer and manage and co-ordinate the work of other specialist designers appointed by the purchaser or subcontracted to the lead designer. Alternatively the designer may be a multidisciplinary organisation or the engineering department of a large port.

Planning supervisor

The planning supervisor's role is defined by the CDM Regulations. The planning supervisor needs to be appointed by the purchaser before decisions are made that could have health and safety implications for construction, cleaning work, maintenance and demolition. It is recommended that the planning supervisor be appointed as soon as possible after the project is confirmed. This could be either before or after the appointment of the lead designer. The planning supervisor could be either the designer or project manager or a member of a large or medium-sized port's engineering staff provided that they have sufficient competence in health and safety issues.

Engineer and engineer's representative

The engineer is an appointment defined in the particular form of contract adopted. The engineer administers the contract on behalf of the purchaser. In some forms of contract the purchaser is defined as the employer. The engineer is normally the project manager or the designer, although occasionally the purchaser's engineering manager is appointed as the engineer. **It is preferable for the engineer to be independent of the purchaser's organisation.** If the project manager or designer is part of the purchaser's own engineering staff, this separation will be more difficult.

The engineer's representative is another appointment defined in the particular form of contract. The engineer normally appoints one or more representatives to be employed at the construction site as resident engineers or to carry out inspection and examination at the factory or workshop. The engineer can delegate many of his duties under the contract to the engineer's representative.

Independent design assessor

Most structures that directly affect public safety have technical approval requirements. Examples include the Reservoirs Panel for dams and reservoirs, Building Regulations approval for new buildings, certification by the Railways Inspectorate for approval of railway works, plant and equipment, and approval by the Technical Approval Authority for complex highway bridges. Many recently installed linkspans and walkways have been subjected to an independent design assessment, and generally this role has been included within the requirements of the construction or supply contract.

> **The research has clearly shown that purchasers would wish the design verification to be under the control of the purchaser rather than the supplier.**
>
> **The purchaser would appoint the independent design assessor. The assessor would be contractually independent of the designer, supplier and installation contractor, and would report directly to the purchaser.**

The independent design assessor will review the suitability and adequacy of the technical and performance specifications and the design criteria stated in the project brief and the technical specification, including environmental, geotechnical and loading criteria. The assessor will review the provisions for inspection and maintenance, and will carry out independent analysis. The assessor will identify risks to health and safety inherent in the design assumptions and solutions. **It is most important that the assessor confirms that the capacity of the various elements and parts of the facility equal or exceed the requirements of the design criteria.**

The independent design assessor must have particular knowledge and competence in all aspects of the safety of linkspans and walkways and be experienced in the design of these facilities.

The assessor's tasks are described in more detail in Section 3.8.3.

Systems engineer

It is important that the mechanical, electrical, structural and control system elements of linkspans and walkways are fully co-ordinated and integrated to produce an ergonomically sound installation. **It is recommended that the procurement contract require the contractor or supplier of the facility to appoint a competent systems engineer to manage the day-to-day design and manufacturing activities for the machinery.** The systems engineer must be an integral member of the contractor's or supplier's project team, and would carry out the following duties:

1. Prepare or review the detailed design for mechanical, hydraulic and electrical engineering systems that have already been conceptually designed by the designer.

2. Co-ordinate detailed designs produced by the contractors for the other disciplines.

3. Contribute to the preparation of the risk analysis documentation.

4. Define any requirements for foundations or site works for the supply of the machinery not already covered by the technical specification.

5. Liaise with specialist manufacturers, suppliers and installers.

6. Witness works and site tests and commissioning, including liaising with other parties to co-ordinate attendance at tests.

7. Supervise the works on site on behalf of the contractor or supplier.

8. Prepare all necessary documentation, calculations, record drawings and information for the instruction and maintenance manuals.

9. Prepare a list of recommended spares.

10. Attend all site, technical and co-ordination meetings.

11. Demonstrate the operation of the complete installation and provide instruction and training to the purchaser's staff for operation and maintenance of the installation.

12. Demonstrate the use of any special maintenance facilities, lifting requirements, jigs and fixtures.

Procurement contracts should require the nomination of the proposed individual and the presentation of curriculum vitae at the tender stage for approval and acceptance by the purchaser. The purchaser should reserve the right to object to the employment of any individual in this position. This nomination should be made and accepted before a contractual commitment is established with the potential contractor or supplier. Practical considerations make it desirable that under specific exceptional circumstances both parties should have the freedom to require a change of the individual appointee, subject to mutual approval of the replacement.

Project safety auditor

> This role has not been formalised before, and should previously have been carried out by the purchaser. In order to provide evidence that the purchaser has taken all reasonably practical steps to ensure the safety of the facility it is strongly recommended that safety matters are properly audited, and that this role is formally identified. The project safety auditor must be knowledgeable and competent in health and safety matters related to linkspans and walkways. The auditor should preferably be independent.

The auditor will be appointed by the purchaser, and will carry out the following tasks:

1. Review the documentation produced by the supplier and contractor under the various relevant regulations, particularly the CDM Regulations, SM(S)R and other relevant regulations, such as the Pressure Systems and Transportable Gas Containers Regulations 1989 and the Pressure Regulations, which are due to come into force in 1999.

2. Carefully review the assessments of risks to health and safety.

3. Review the methods adopted to eliminate hazards, and ensure that the objectives of the essential health and safety requirements have been met.

4. Review the risks identified by the designer and independent design assessor.

5. Check that the necessary procedures required by the regulations and any quality management system have been carried out.

The auditor should produce a safety audit certificate that would systematically record any unsatisfactory findings of the audit. However, note that while the auditor is reviewing that procedures have been followed, he is *not* carrying out design checking.

It is acknowledged that the supplier of the machinery should have carried out its obligations under the regulations, and that the machinery should be safe. However, as soon as the facility is put into use the employer of the operators becomes responsible for the health and safety of employees and members of the public using the facility.

> The purchaser must take all reasonably practicable steps to ensure that the facility is in fact safe. It is recommended that this duty be supported by a formal safety audit carried out on behalf of the purchaser by the project safety auditor.

This description of the duties of a safety auditor is much wider than the duties of a planning supervisor described in the CDM Regulations. If it is decided to appoint a safety auditor, the same organisation could also be appointed as planning supervisor, provided they were competent.

3.1.4 Relationship between roles

Figures 3.4 and 3.5 have been produced in order to clarify the organisational and contractual relationships between the parties to the contract, such as the purchaser, contractor and designer, and the key roles and tasks identified in the previous section.

Figure 3.4 shows the contractual relationship and communication routes in a traditional design–tender–construct procurement method. The purchaser has direct contracts with the project adviser, designer, planning supervisor, contractor, independent design assessor and project safety auditor. In turn, the contractor has direct contracts with the machinery suppliers, materials suppliers and specialist subcontractors. Similarly these subcontractors have their own contracts with specialist materials suppliers. The communication routes for the exchange of information are shown in broken lines in the figure. These routes clearly show the strategic importance of the new project safety auditor role in receiving information from all parties and therefore in ensuring that there are no gaps in the evaluation of safety or in the provision of statutory information.

Figure 3.5 shows the contractual relationships and communication routes in a design and construct procurement method. The purchaser has similar direct contracts with the various parties, except that the project manager replaces the designer/engineer. The contractor has similar direct contracts too, but with the addition of the contractor's designer. Again, the communication routes show the strategic importance of the project safety auditor.

Note that a number of the roles could be carried out by a single organisation. For example, the purchaser might also provide the project adviser, project manager, planning supervisor or the designer/engineer. It is also possible that the construction contractor could be a specialist contractor or the machinery supplier. The independent design assessor *must* be fully independent of the other parties, and ideally the project safety auditor would also be independent of the purchaser or other parties.

3.1.5   Selection procedure

The selection of individuals and organisations to fulfil the roles outlined above should involve an assessment of competence. In order to assess the competence of an individual or organisation for any of these roles, it will be necessary for the purchaser to set down minimum criteria and some benchmark for evaluation. The criteria might include the following:

* knowledge of relevant regulations
* experience in the design, manufacture, supply and installation of linkspans and walkways as appropriate
* experience in the inspection of linkspans and walkways
* knowledge of the maintenance requirements for linkspans and walkways
* understanding of ship and floating structure motions
* experience of risk assessment and identification of hazards.

Evidence about the competence of the individual or organisation against these criteria can be best obtained through a variety of methods. Guidance is provided in CIRIA Report 172, *CDM Regulations – practical guidance for clients and clients' agents*.

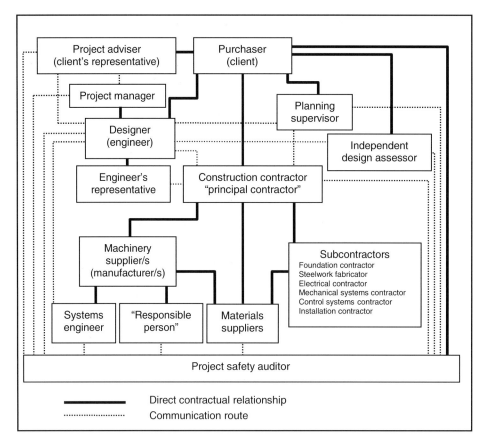

Figure 3.4 *Relationship between the participants in the procurement of linkspans and walkways: traditional approach*

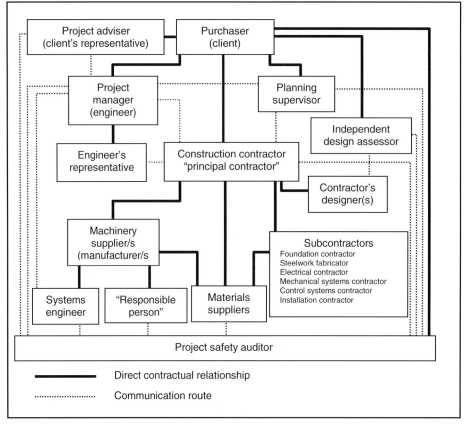

Figure 3.5 *Relationship between the participants in the procurement of linkspans and walkways: design and construct approach*

3.2 PREPARING THE BRIEF

This section assumes that, in general terms, the need for a ship-to-shore linkspan or walkway has been established and the location of the facility is known. If this is not the case, a feasibility study will be required to define the need and the location before the project can proceed further.

The need for a new linkspan or walkway has to be developed into a project brief providing a description of the project that will form the basis for the preparation of the detailed design and the specification. The project brief would be prepared by the purchaser with the assistance of the project adviser, and should include:

- the location of the facility together with a site plan

- the general scope of the work required – whether it is only the supply of a linkspan or walkway or whether there is also a need to provide infrastructure and foundations or significant shore works

- the nature of the traffic that the facility will serve, and the types of cargo

- the classes of ship and if possible the names of the ships that will use the facility, and their basic dimensions, displacements and particularly threshold heights for the linkspan or walkway interface

- the expected frequency of use

- information about the site, including sea bed levels, site surveys, tidal data, wind and wave data and tidal levels

- whether there is a possibility that a different type of traffic may be required in the future – that is, how much flexibility is needed in the design of the facility for future requirements

- the experience, skills and likely qualifications of the staff that will operate the facility

- the experience, skills and likely qualifications of the staff that will maintain the facility

- the expected mode of operation for traffic on the linkspan or walkway – how is the traffic to be controlled, will reversing be required, will turning space be required near to the ship's ramp?

- the expected mode of operation of the ships using the berth alongside the linkspan – does the linkspan/walkway system require fenders to allow the ship to berth directly bow on or stern on (whether these fenders are directly mounted on the facility or whether they are mounted on dolphins alongside the facility)

- the effect of passing ships on buoyant structures

- the level of accommodation for the operators – whether to provide an enclosed control booth and, if so, whether it should be sited so that the operator can reasonably control other operations such as traffic movements and bunkering, without leaving the booth, by means of his sight lines or communications facilities

- any general requirements, such as "it shall have the same control system as our existing linkspan", or indeed that it specifically does not include any problems that may exist on the existing linkspan

- any special requirements, such as might be required if the facility were to handle railway traffic, where particular attention to movements and deflections is required

- other duties of operators

- details of any hazardous cargoes

- information about the economic and logistical criticality of the facility

- the date by which the facility needs to be operational.

It is not intended that the project brief should give a detailed performance specification for the facility, but it is a checklist of information that the person writing the project brief will need in order to be able to properly interpret the requirements of the purchaser. For information on the specification of the facility see Section 3.6.

Where possible, and unless the purchaser strictly desires it, **the project brief should not define the means by which these aims should be achieved.** For instance, it would not be necessary to require that the facility should be lifted by any particular system, be it rope winches, hydraulic cylinders, a pontoon or other buoyant system, except where the wave climate precludes floating structures. However, if the purchaser has achieved particular satisfaction with a type of facility, then this aim should be included in the project brief. **The research has shown that organisations that had expressed greatest satisfaction with their facilities were those that had developed satisfactory systems over a long period and applied these requirements when procuring new facilities.**

3.3 METHODS OF PROCUREMENT

3.3.1 Introduction

Once the project brief has been prepared, some decisions about how to procure the facility can be made.

The three procurement routes most frequently used for linkspans and walkways are shown in the flow charts in Figures 3.2 and 3.3. These routes are described below, but other non-conventional methods, including partnering and negotiated package contracts, can be considered. These non-conventional methods are described in specialist references, but the framework of activities outlined here generally applies when these methods are used.

3.3.2 Design provided to the contractor (traditional method)

In this traditional form of procurement the purchaser enters into separate contracts for design and construction. Normally the design team leads the process. The purchaser selects a competent designer to carry out the detailed design of the facility and prepare tender documents. For larger ports the competent designer could be the engineering department of the port, but in most cases it will be an engineering consultancy company. The selection and appointment of the designer should be based on their expertise and competence in the design and procurement of linkspans and walkways.

The designer should be appointed under a suitable contract, which would normally be one of the standard conditions of engagement for designers. The purchaser may choose to appoint each of the separate disciplines of the design team – such as mechanical, electrical and structural engineers – individually, although it is more usual to appoint a lead designer, who would appoint other specialists as subconsultants. In either event the design team leader needs to be identified, and all communications should be channelled through this individual. The design team leader is responsible for co-ordinating the work of the rest of the design team, whether they are individually appointed or subconsultants.

The designer may review the site information that is provided with the project brief and decide that additional information is needed in order to produce a satisfactory and safe design. The designer may recommend further wave studies or soil investigations. These investigations are important to ensure satisfactory procurement of the facility, and sufficient time should be allowed for them. The designer will carry out the detailed design of the foundations and structure of the linkspan or walkway. However, the designer normally only produces an outline design for the machinery and then prepares a performance specification. The outline design requires careful consideration of space requirements, because the fully detailed machinery may affect the detailed design of the structural members. The designer also prepares a materials and workmanship specification, conditions of contract, instructions to tenderers and a price schedule.

The traditional approach can be carried out in a single stage, with the contractors tendering for a fully designed facility, or by a two-stage method in which selected contractors receive preliminary design information and a competitive price schedule. The most economically beneficial first-stage tenderer is appointed, and works with the designer on the development of the detailed design. This is particularly advantageous where specialist machinery that affects the detailed design of the structure is involved, or where the method of installation relies on specialist construction plant.

In another variation on the traditional method, the procurement of the facility is divided into separate contract packages. This is a form of **construction management** where the contractor acting as construction manager (which could also be a design organisation) advises on the packaging of the separate contracts and oversees the co-ordination of the separate contracts. The individual contracts for the various trade contractors and design team members are still directly with the purchaser. This method is more suitable for experienced purchasers, but it can allow an earlier start on site for long lead-time construction items such as the foundations. This method also provides for the distinctly different expertise required for marine foundation construction, structural steelwork fabrication and machinery supply.

> **The interface between the various packages needs to be properly managed, as the development of the design of each package can have an effect on the other packages. Note that the purchaser carries more risk and responsibility with multiple contracts than with a traditional single main contractor method. The contract package method is described in more detail in Section 3.3.5.**

3.3.3 Design and construct: outline performance specification only

This is the more basic version of two possible design and construct methods of procurement. There are five steps in this procedure.

1. Having decided to carry out the project, the purchaser provides an outline performance specification, which may simply involve rewriting the project brief by the project manager.

2. The purchaser must decide whether additional information should be given to the tendering contractors. For instance, wave studies or ground investigations may be required. If the purchaser or project manager judge themselves incompetent to decide on these matters, they will need to seek the assistance of engineering consultants or other specialists to complete the production of the outline performance specification and contract documentation.

3. The purchaser may wish to persuade the tendering contractors to assume all risks associated with the information described in Step 2 above. In effect, this might lead to the tendering contractors needing to obtain their own site information. Since site investigations are quite expensive, and will substantially increase the cost of tendering, it is likely that the contractor will either decline to tender or will submit a qualified tender and risk rejection. It is preferable for the purchaser to procure the site information using the procedure referred to in Step 2 above.

4. It is essential that the outline performance specification indicate the required design life of the facility or the design lives of the various items of equipment. The outline performance specification will not normally specify the quality of individual materials or workmanship. Therefore the required design life is an essential parameter in determining quality.

5. Each tendering contractor will then submit a tender based on its outline design. If selected, the contractor must then turn the outline design into a detailed design before beginning construction work.

As in Section 3.3.2, it is possible for the work to be procured as several contract packages, and the comments that were made in that section are equally valid here.

Such a procedure has the merit of requiring a comparatively low pre-contract cost. It also theoretically results in a "one point of contact" responsibility. However, this will only achieved if the tendering contractors are persuaded to assume both the risk and the responsibility of doing their own site-specific investigations. As explained above, it seems unlikely that such a project will be large enough to persuade contractors to assume these risks and responsibilities, so the responsibility for supplying some critical information will probably remain with the purchaser. If a failure or fault is caused by inaccuracy in this information, the purchaser may incur costs that cannot be recovered.

The other disadvantage is that the purchaser may not be offered what they would like, and it may be difficult to negotiate additional work to alter the contract specification to match the desired result more closely.

> **The research carried out to produce the guide indicated that the organisations expressing greatest satisfaction with their facilities were those that had the most hands-on approach and specified the work in considerably more detail.**

Although a design life may be specified, it may be difficult to demand the action that is required to achieve this design life at the start of the contract. If after construction the design life has not been achieved, it may be possible to pursue the contractor for contractual damages. However, there is no guarantee that the contractor will still be trading at such a time, and even if it is, ensuring that the contractual obligations are fulfilled may prove difficult. Note that the contractual obligations are likely to be valid for a much shorter period than the design life of the facility.

3.3.4   Design and construct: detailed performance specification

The more usual design and construct approach follows the procedure below.

1. Having decided to carry out the project, the purchaser arranges to provide an outline scope design and a detailed performance specification. If the in-house engineering department does not have a high level of capability, the purchaser will probably have to engage a consulting engineer or other specialist to provide these documents.

2. In these circumstances, the organisation carrying out the scope design and production of documents will advise whether more information – such as wave studies or ground investigation – will be required for the tendering contractors.

3. It is probable that the purchaser will offer enough information to allow the tendering contractors to make an adequate judgement and to assume the risks associated with ground conditions or wave conditions for the purposes of submitting a tender. The tenderer may then need to make allowance for obtaining more detailed information, but at least a reasonable tender can be submitted.

4. The scope design will indicate the layout expected and indicate certain restrictions concerning visual appearance and position. The purchaser must decide whether it requires the nature of the facility to be specified in detail or only the performance. For instance, if the purchaser already has some facilities, it is probably useful to ensure that the design of the equipment is specified to use the same technologies, so that the operational staff will be fully familiar with the finished product, and the same stock of spares can be used.

5. It is also usual for the specification to include much standard information on general requirements for workmanship and quality. It should therefore be possible to ensure that the specification has sufficient requirements for good practice to be followed and for there to be a low risk that the required design life and durability will not be achieved.

6. Each tendering contractor will then submit a tender based on an outline design that it produces during the preparation of the tender. If selected, it has to turn this into a detailed design before beginning the construction work.

The work required to produce the contract document for this type of approach is extensive, though not as extensive as if a full detailed design were to be provided. The advantage of this approach is that all the purchaser's experience of the linkspan or walkway can be incorporated into the specification. This should reduce dissatisfaction with what the contractor offers, while still firmly maintaining the contractor's responsibility for the design.

The provision of the scope design will give the purchaser a strong influence on the final appearance of the facility as well. This is probably more important for the provision of passenger walkways than for the provision of vehicle linkspans. Walkways are often in prominent locations such that the ferry operator will have an interest in the quality of the visual appearance, which should complement the appearance of its ships.

Although this theoretically offers a one-stop approach, it is still true that the provision of any information to the contractor on the site or the surrounding environment may lead to dispute. The contractor may be able to claim that the deficiency leading to the dispute arose from information offered by the purchaser or his advisers. The purchaser needs to consider the acceptable level of risk to be allocated between the parties to the contract.

3.3.5 Contract packages

Introduction

The descriptions given in Sections 3.3.1 to 3.3.4 assume that the facility will be considered as a single contractual entity, which would be managed under a main contract led by a civil engineering contractor. The contract would include provisions to ensure that the appropriate regulations are followed. For instance, the Construction (Design and Management) Regulations (CDM Regulations) will require that a planning supervisor and a principal contractor are appointed, and the main contractor should be able to fulfil the role of principal contractor. The Machinery Regulations will require that the manufacturer or his appointed responsible person provide the required safe machinery, and there is little difficulty in ensuring that the manufacturer is appointed by the main contractor.

However, a different approach is possible.

A project incorporating a linkspan or a walkway is usually typical of any heavy engineering project in that there are a few large and fairly easily identifiable sections to the project. For instance, a project for the development of a ro-ro berth could include the construction of dolphins, the construction of foundation blocks, the manufacture and installation of a shore ramp, and the manufacture and installation of the machinery to lift the shore ramp. There is therefore an opportunity to separate the construction operations into a number of packages, each to be implemented by different contractors.

There are reasons for considering such an approach:

1. There is an opportunity to save the administrative mark-up costs of the main contractor. These can be significant. On the other hand, one organisation must be responsible for managing the overall project, and the costs associated with this must not be underestimated (although they usually are).

2. The numbers of manufacturers with experience of linkspans and walkways, or experience of the machinery of linkspans and walkways, are small. The purchaser may therefore want to ensure that the contract is awarded to firms either with a proven track record or that are believed by the purchaser to be competent. Most civil engineering contractors will not be involved with linkspans or walkways often enough to know of such competence or track record. It is therefore not unreasonable to want to influence the shortlist of specialist contractors and engage them directly.

3. In the case of an experienced purchaser, it would allow closer control of engineering standards to suit the particular requirements of the purchaser's operating and maintenance organisation.

It is essential that both the physical and the regulatory interfaces between the packages are sensible and easily identified. To do this successfully requires considerable care and knowledge. This guidance is not concerned with the procurement of an overall project incorporating quays or dolphins, dredging or mooring facilities. It is concerned only with the elements immediately associated with linkspans or walkways. Table 3.1 indicates the main parcels of work associated with a linkspan or walkway and the physical and regulatory interfaces that exist.

Physical interfaces

Table 3.1 presents a list of the typical physical interfaces that need to be resolved in any construction packaging system with reference to the main package headings shown in Figure 3.4. There are many such interfaces to be resolved, and if it is intended to package the contract in this way then it is essential that the project manager be competent to manage them.

Table 3.1 *Typical interface issues for consideration*

Interface	Items for consideration
1 Between the machinery elements and the structural elements	
Bearings between hydraulic cylinders and the main bridge or hoist structures	Must be suitably articulated so that all the anticipated movements can be accommodated. Must be manufactured to compatible tolerances. Must be of materials suitable for the environment and duty required. It is strongly recommended that the supplier of the machinery should supply all such bearings and install them into the main structure.
Routes for cables and services, compressed air pipes	Appropriate articulation structures, such as catenary saddles for hanging cables, are required. Supporting and fixing arrangements must be provided.
Plant rooms for machinery	Must be suitably designed to provide the appropriate environment for the machines and control systems. Attention to salt water ingress, temperature control, if required, and humidity control, if possible. Must be sized to suit space limitations and ergonomic requirements.
2 Between the main structure and the foundations	
Bearings between structure and shore	Must be designed to suit the anticipated method of installation: very tight tolerances are difficult to achieve with very heavy lifting operations. Bearings of link bridges to pontoons (whether linkspans or walkways) need to allow for all anticipated movements of the pontoons during operations or under environmental loads, including pitching and rolling movements due to moving loads or waves.
Pontoon restraint devices	Must be able to allow the pontoon/linkspan to move freely over all stages of the tide. Restraint piles should be as parallel as possible, and restraint collars should either be loose or the flexibility of the piles designed so that undue binding forces are not generated by piles being out of vertical.
3 Between foundations and machinery	
Foundations for machinery	Mounting blocks for power packs and other machinery must be secure and comply with the requirements for the machinery. Pulley sheaves require adequate fixings or foundations to keep ropes in the correct positions relative to the machinery system.

Figure 3.6 shows three examples of possible solutions to the problem of physical interfaces.

1. The bearings between a hydraulic cylinder and the structure. It is recommended that the lifting machinery supplier provide the cylinders, the cylinder seatings and the pin plates.

2. The support of a dynamically controlled platform for a walkway. It is recommended that the lifting machinery supplier be responsible for the hydraulic cylinders, the fixing pin plates to the main structure and the entire lifted platform.

3. The restraint collars for a pontoon. It is recommended that the supplier of the pontoon would be responsible for the supply of the collars attached to the restraints.

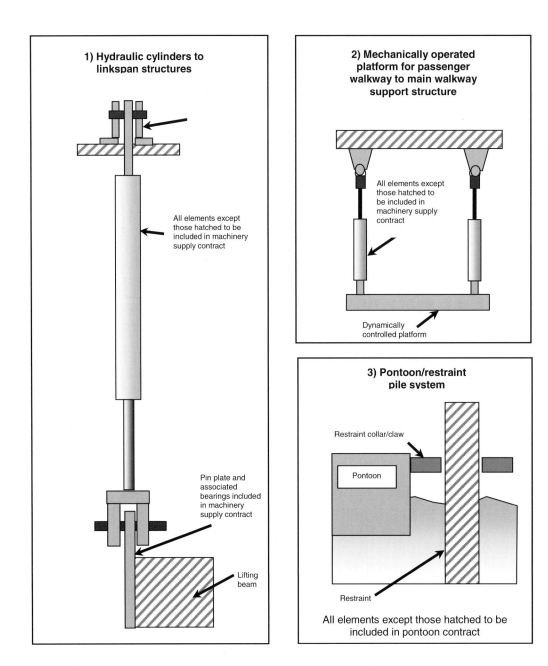

Figure 3.6 *Some examples of recommended positions where the physical interfaces between packages should be located.*

Regulatory interfaces

In addition to the physical interfaces, there are equally important regulatory interfaces to resolve. Figure 3.7 illustrates the areas where the Construction (Design and Management) Regulations and the Supply of Machinery (Safety) Regulations are particularly relevant.

In the context of a packaged project, it is important to assign the various responsibilities under the regulations correctly. A declaration of incorporation will be issued for elements of machinery that will be assembled with other machinery or incorporated into other machinery by the responsible person elected for that element of machinery. The linkspan or walkway is machinery by definition of the Supply of Machinery (Safety) Regulations, but if the elements of the machinery are separated across more than one package, the assembler of the machinery is likely to be the installation contractor that

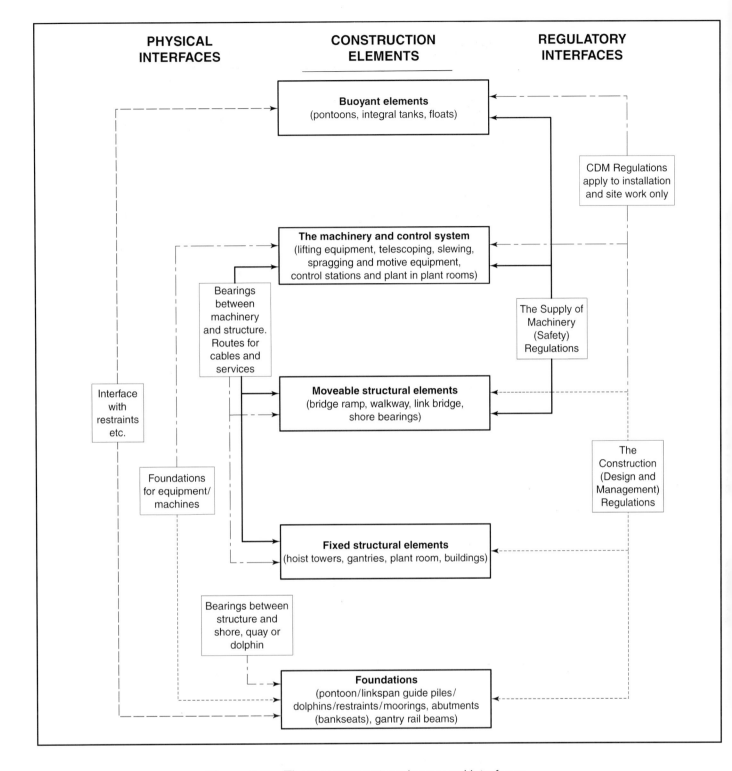

PHYSICAL INTERFACES

CONSTRUCTION ELEMENTS

REGULATORY INTERFACES

Buoyant elements
(pontoons, integral tanks, floats)

CDM Regulations apply to installation and site work only

The machinery and control system
(lifting equipment, telescoping, slewing, spragging and motive equipment, control stations and plant in plant rooms)

Bearings between machinery and structure. Routes for cables and services

The Supply of Machinery (Safety) Regulations

Interface with restraints etc.

Moveable structural elements
(bridge ramp, walkway, link bridge, shore bearings)

The Construction (Design and Management) Regulations

Foundations for equipment/machines

Fixed structural elements
(hoist towers, gantries, plant room, buildings)

Bearings between structure and shore, quay or dolphin

Foundations
(pontoon/linkspan guide piles/dolphins/restraints/moorings, abutments (bankseats), gantry rail beams)

Figure 3.7 *The procurement packages and interfaces*

will be the manufacturer putting the machinery into service under the terms of SM(S)R, and therefore will be the responsible person or must appoint the responsible person and provide the declaration of conformity.

In the case of a lifted type of shore ramp, **it is recommended that this person be within the organisation that supplied and installed the machinery rather than the organisation that fabricated or constructed the structure**. The machinery element is often of a similar monetary value to the structural elements, but the complexity of the arrangements for the machinery is usually greater than the complexity of the structures.

In addition, the construction of the facility and its foundation will be subject to the CDM Regulations, and a planning supervisor and a principal contractor will need to be appointed to carry out duties under these regulations. If the facility is being procured in packages, one of the contractors will have to be designated the principal contractor.

The application of the SM(S)R to buoyant structures is less certain. However, by definition a buoyant facility is an assembly of linked parts or components that moves, and is therefore machinery.

Using the strict definitions within the CDM Regulations, it is apparent that the machinery, the buoyant structures, the foundations, the roadway or walkway structure and the supporting structures will all be subject to the CDM Regulations. Therefore all sections of the facility except the foundations and fixed structures have to satisfy both sets of regulations. Only the foundations and fixed structures are subject solely to the CDM Regulations.

Contractual interfaces

There are many interfaces to be resolved in the internal workings of the contract to construct a ship-to-shore linkspan or walkway. Therefore the management of the interfaces becomes not only a physical and design problem but also a regulatory compliance issue.

> **It is strongly recommended that the purchaser procure all the elements of a linkspan or a walkway under a single contract.**

This will ensure that the supplying or installing contractor, or whoever is designated as the principal contractor, is responsible for resolving all these interface problems, which will greatly simplify the task of the purchaser.

However, it is also true that in most cases the purchaser or purchaser's advisers will be more knowledgeable than a potential principal contractor for assessing the suitability or competence of the possible subcontractors. It is likely that the purchaser will achieve a facility much closer to its requirements if it has some powers to ensure that subcontractors are selected from a preferred list of tenderers.

In this case, the tenderer should be required to provide the names of key suppliers and subcontractors in their tender.

> **They should also be instructed that the key suppliers and subcontractors should not be substituted during the normal course of the project. Failure to do this can lead to considerable delays in awarding subcontracts and hence time pressures, resulting in poor standards of design and workmanship.**

The purchaser should be prepared to consider procuring the specialist elements of the facility by directly setting up subcontracts from suppliers that are considered competent and reliable. These subcontractors will preferably be incorporated into the main contract by a process of novation. If time does not permit this, then it is preferable for the subcontractors to be nominated in the contract, despite the potential contractual disputes that nomination can produce.

3.3.6   Second-hand facilities

Although the research that led to this guide did not reveal any examples of second-hand linkspans or walkways, ports or ship operators do sometimes purchase second-hand facilities, and the industry is known to be keen to consider their use from time to time.

It is always difficult to assess the condition of second-hand equipment. Some knowledge of its history is required to assess whether fatigue or similar effects might have reduced its design life. The facility must comply with the regulations when it is brought back into use. This will require risk assessments on whether the facility will perform safely for its remaining design life. Detailed surveys, calculations and investigations may need to be carried out to provide assurance that it is safe to bring the equipment back into use.

The assessment of second-hand equipment is much more reliable if there are accurate drawings of the facility. If there are not, a detailed survey will be required. The extent of the survey may depend on risk assessments. The risk assessment will help to focus the investigations on the most safety-critical areas. Pre-purchase surveys and inspections of the equipment can then be targeted effectively.

The detailed survey will need to cover the following:

- a visual survey

- a survey of thicknesses of metal or concrete

- a dimension survey of the equipment if drawings do not exist

- non-destructive testing surveys, such as ultrasonic or radiographic testing, to ascertain the condition of key welds

- taking of material samples and testing to ascertain steel types

- tests of safety and functionality on electrical and control systems, and assessment of the condition of the equipment and installation

- pressure testing, inspection and verification of safety facilities associated with air/fluid pressure systems and equipment, and assessment of the condition of the equipment and installation for all lifting systems.

These surveys must be carried out by competent persons or organisations.

If drawings are available, the survey should determine whether any loss of material thickness has occurred. If drawings are not available, the dimension survey will become the basis for design work to incorporate the second-hand facility into a new scheme.

Historical information should then be assessed to decide whether there is evidence that the structure has been subjected to repeated wave or other loadings that may have caused a reduction in the fatigue life of the structure. If there is no historical information, the risks associated with the lack of knowledge of the residual fatigue life of the structure will have to be assessed. If a reduced fatigue life of certain joints or splices may result in safety-critical damage, these joints may have to be reconstructed and rewelded, or the structural configuration redesigned to alter the load paths.

The refurbishment of second-hand pontoons is a potential source of problems. Such pontoons may have been old ro-ro facilities from another port, or they may have originated as crane or transport barges. They can often be very rusty and battered. It may be found that the steel in the pontoons does not comply with modern codes of practice, particularly with respect to notch ductility tests. Such findings may not in themselves warrant a rejection of the pontoon, but a careful survey should be carried out before a purchase order is issued.

The risk assessment and calculations may show that the hull of the pontoon retains sufficient life to be able to serve for a useful period. However, often it will be necessary to reinforce the deck of the pontoon substantially to allow it to support suitable wheel loads. The arrangements for fixing restraint collars or claws to the pontoon can also require extensive localised reinforcement work to allow the loads to be spread across the structure. Such refurbishments are often more expensive than might be expected.

Passenger walkways are sometimes relocated or modified for a different purpose. However, current standards of safety are higher than when these walkways were first installed, so it is likely that these walkways will require considerable refurbishment and strengthening before they can be brought back into use.

These examples probably explain why there were no references to second-hand structures in the questionnaire survey.

When complete, the new scheme must comply with the regulations. The responsible person must be able to provide the declaration of conformity with the regulations, having satisfied himself that the conversion work has been carried out in accordance with appropriate standards and codes of practice. At the end of this process, the second-hand equipment will have to have been as carefully assessed for strength, safety and performance as a new facility.

The classification procedure available from the classification societies offers a means of providing a reliable history of the facility. A facility that has been classified and maintained in class will have been subjected to a regular inspection routine. This would enhance the second-hand value of any facility that a port owner or operator might wish to sell in the future.

3.4 FORMS OF CONTRACT

3.4.1 General

There is a range of standard forms of contract for the procurement of the supply and construction of linkspans and walkways. There are also several conditions of engagement for the appointment of designers and consultant advisers. It is outside the scope of this guide to give detailed guidance on the appropriate forms; readers should refer to one of the publications on the requirements of the various forms of contract. **Purchasers should seek advice from the project adviser on the most appropriate form of contract to use for the supply and construction of the linkspan or walkway, and for the appointment of any specialist consultants, advisers or subcontractors.**

None of the forms of contract is ideal for the supply and construction of hybrid combinations of foundations, structures and machinery. However, substantial amendments to standard forms of contract can lead to contractual arguments due to misunderstandings of the meaning of the amendments between the parties. **It is advisable to use the form of contract without amendment.**

The research showed that the most linkspans and walkways were procured using the fifth and sixth editions of the ICE Conditions of Contract. The reason for this is almost certainly because many linkspans and walkways have been procured as part of larger developments of ro-ro terminals or berths within ports.

Most forms of contract include provisions for the following:

- definitions of certain words and expressions used in the contract
- the appointment of an engineer and engineer's representative, with their duties and powers defined
- the duties and obligations of the purchaser
- the duties and obligations of the contractor
- limitations on assignment and subcontracting of the works
- requirements for a programme and details of the method of construction and installation
- procedures for approval of drawings and other documents
- methods of dealing with valuation of the works and with variations
- procedures for rectifying defective work
- details of testing and quality control
- insurances
- accidents and damage to the works
- procedure for dealing with disputes and arbitration.

Most forms of contract include the appointment of an engineer to make certain decisions under the contract and to administer the contract on behalf of the purchaser. They also envisage the appointment of an engineer's representative, who is normally based at the construction site and is delegated some of the engineer's duties.

3.4.2 Civil engineering forms

Civil engineering forms of contract include:

- ICE Sixth Edition 1991
- ICE Design and Construct 1992
- Engineering Construction Contract ICE 1995.

Civil engineering forms usually assume that the supply and construction of the linkspan and walkway will be measured against various items described using a standard method of measurement and will allow the contractor to price each item in order to obtain a tender sum. Breaking down the supply and construction into a number of items enables the engineer to evaluate any variations to the supply or construction. However, unless special arrangements are made for the payment of equipment and materials off site at the manufacturer's or fabricator's workshops, suppliers can incur cash flow problems.

The design and construct form provides for a schedule of prices, and in general does not envisage major variations to the supply and construction of the linkspan or walkway.

3.4.3 Mechanical and electrical plant forms

The 1988 edition of Form MF/1 Revision 3 is the current model form of *General Conditions of Contract for the supply of electrical, electronic or mechanical plant – with erection*. It includes clauses for inspection and testing of plant before delivery, which are considered to be essential in the procurement of any linkspan or walkway. There are also clauses about tests on completion and performance tests not covered by other forms of contract. MF/1 rev 3 provides additional special conditions for contracts involving the supply of programmable or sophisticated electronic hardware or software. These are very useful in view of the complexity of control systems on linkspans and walkways.

Form MF/1 rev 3 envisages that the machinery will be supplied against a lump sum or a relatively limited schedule of prices, and that there will be no major variations to the supply and construction of the machinery. It provides for variations that do not involve more than 15 per cent addition to, or deduction from, the contract price, unless the contractor and the purchaser have mutually consented to a larger variation. It does not make any provisions for unforeseen circumstances in foundations or weather conditions.

> **This form of contract should be used with care for single package procurement where the ground conditions are likely to affect the form of construction and the amount of construction work required.**

3.5 SELECTING SUITABLE DESIGNERS AND CONTRACTORS

3.5.1 Introduction

Most purchasers use procurement procedures that set out provisions for the selection of designers and contractors. They usually define the number that have to be invited to tender for each contract within various ranges of contract value. Developments that are wholly or partly publicly funded and are above a certain value must be advertised in the *European Journal* and receive submissions from designers or contractors.

Linkspans and walkways are hybrid facilities consisting of foundations, fixed structures, movable structures, machinery and control systems. As such they require input from a range of professional disciplines. Parties to the procurement process need to be experienced in the procurement of linkspans and walkways. Therefore it will almost certainly be necessary to go through some form of pre-qualification or pre-selection process to identify specialist designers and contractors with sufficient experience. Because of the specialist nature of linkspans and walkways it may be appropriate to follow a negotiated procurement process to ensure that the particular expertise required is available for the design and/or supply of the linkspan or walkway.

3.5.2 Selecting designers

The names of design organisations can be obtained from professional associations, including the Association of Consulting Engineers and the British Consultants Bureau. Other ports or terminal operators that have recently procured a linkspan or walkway can also provide a list of names. Alternatively the requirement can be advertised and designers requested to apply. Whichever method is adopted, **a list of evaluation criteria and thresholds should be prepared for the selection of suitable designers**. Potential designers should be asked to submit the same information about their organisation.

> **Information should be requested about the recent experience of the designer in the design of linkspans or walkways, together with the names and CVs of individual members of the designer's organisation who would actually be employed on the design of the linkspan or walkway. It is essential to ensure that each discipline is co-ordinated by a responsible and experienced designer.**

The purchaser and the project adviser should evaluate the information and come to a preliminary decision about the most appropriate design organisation. It is usual for the purchaser and the project adviser to interview the most likely potential designers before appointment. This interview can be used to explore the experience of the designer's organisation and to confirm the availability of specialist design staff for the development.

3.5.3 Selecting a planning supervisor

The appointment of the planning supervisor can be carried out in a similar way to that for the design organisation. In many cases the design organisation will provide the planning supervisor, provided that the purchaser is satisfied that the design organisation is sufficiently competent and adequately resourced to handle health and safety issues. It is important that the planning supervisor acts independently and not under the control of the designers. The planning supervisor should be able to demonstrate that they have successfully undertaken the relevant health and safety duties for the construction of other linkspans and walkways, and should be required to provide information demonstrating this experience.

The planning supervisor should also be asked to provide information about the methods they will adopt to co-ordinate the work of the designers to ensure the production of the pre-tender health and safety plan. It may be useful to request copies of previous health and safety documentation.

> **The purchaser should decide on the criteria on which the evaluation is to be made and set benchmarks that are required to be achieved by the prospective planning supervisor if they are to be considered for selection.**

3.5.4 Selecting contractors

Lists of contractors can be obtained from their trade associations or from ports or terminal operators that have recently procured linkspans or walkways. **It is important that the selected contractor has the appropriate experience of the supply and construction of linkspans or walkways.** The purchaser or their advisers should prepare a questionnaire that seeks details of the experience of the potential contractor, responses to the issues raised in the pre-tender health and safety plan, details of the site management staff who would be engaged on the development, information about proposed methods of construction, and details of the contractor's financial standing.

> **The purchaser will have to establish evaluation criteria and benchmarks that the contractors will have to achieve.**

It is unlikely that one contractor will have the range of experience and expertise required for the supply and construction of a linkspan or walkway. It may therefore be necessary for the purchaser to carry out several selection procedures for the different types of contractor required.

3.5.5 Selecting a principal contractor

> **The main contractor is normally appointed as the principal contractor under the CDM Regulations, but the purchaser has a statutory duty to ensure that the chosen contractor is competent to carry out this duty. The contractor should therefore be requested to provide details of its experience in acting as principal contractor and examples of construction health and safety files prepared for previous developments. The purchaser should also request the names and CVs of the key staff who will be involved in health and safety issues and details of their experience in carrying out the duties of the principal contractor.**

3.6 SPECIFICATION OF THE FACILITY

3.6.1 Information required by the designer from the purchaser

The designer must receive certain critical information to allow the facility to be designed successfully and reliably. The purchaser should be ready to supply the designer with the following information:

- the ships to be served

- the expected ranges and speeds of movements of the ships

- the availability of electrical power, capacity and the nature of the power source(s)

- electrical standby provisions (available and/or to be supplied)

- the degree of supervision likely to be applied to the use of the facility

- type and magnitude of loadings required

- whether the port has a preference for particular lifting systems (spragged, directly lifted or buoyant)

- any bunkering requirements

- whether there is a need for refuse or effluent disposal facilities for the ship

- tide levels at the site of the facility, including the extreme high or low tide levels for the return period appropriate to the design life of the facility

- any water levels in impounded docks, including information on extreme circumstances that can occur, such as when basin pumping equipment fails or lock gates fail to operate

- the wave climate at the berth. This should be in the form of significant wave heights for the appropriate return periods. It is also necessary to state whether the wave heights at the site arise from reflections between dock or river walls in case standing wave conditions exist. If the port operator does not possess such information, it will be advisable to carry out a wave climate assessment study

- the effect of passing ships

- the expected mode of operation of the berth (normally provided by ship operator). The decision to include fenders on a linkspan or on dolphins adjacent to linkspans will often depend on the method of berthing adopted

- the expected level of competence of the operating staff. It will usually be sensible to design control systems and their operator interface to be simpler rather than more complicated, but the means by which malfunctions are indicated to operating staff need to be discussed jointly, otherwise personnel may find themselves operating a facility which incorporates alarms and flashing lights that may confuse them

- the expected level of competence and availability of maintenance staff. If the design needs to be suitable for operation and simple maintenance by non-specialist staff in remote island locations, complex or delicate controls should be avoided altogether. There is a good case for aiming to supply the simplest adequate controls even where more sophisticated maintenance staff are available

- facilities that the operator has found by experience to be useful. For instance, one operator has had sensors installed that verify that operating staff are on actually duty during operation of a ramp. If extra features are desired, such requirements must be specified

- communications facilities at the linkspan or walkway

- any unusual characteristics of the site that might not be reasonably predictable by a designer who is not familiar with the berth location.

3.6.2　Information required by the purchaser from the designer

At various times during the procurement of a linkspan or walkway the purchaser needs information to ensure that the facility is suitable and to allow the co-ordination of associated aspects of the installation.

The purchaser must be fully conversant with the procurement of linkspans or walkways in order to ensure that the legislative requirements are satisfied.

The designer or contractor usually provides information:

- before agreement to purchase in order to demonstrate the adequacy of the proposals
- during the design and manufacturing period to ensure co-ordination with other aspects of the development
- following installation, testing and commissioning, and at handover to demonstrate the sufficiency of the installation.

Information provided before the agreement to purchase by the contractor should comprise:

- outline drawings showing proposals
- characteristics of design (load criteria etc)
- commentary outlining how the equipment will be designed, manufactured, tested, commissioned and handed over
- commentary outlining how the equipment operates
- completion of schedules outlining the type of equipment to be provided, manufacturer's names, model or reference numbers, construction materials etc
- regulations to be complied with
- name and CV of responsible person with respect to the Machinery Regulations
- Construction (Design and Management) Regulations information
- warranty proposals.

During the design, manufacturing and installation period the contractor should provide:

- general arrangement drawing(s)
- initial and intermediate risk assessments in a desk study, to demonstrate compliance with regulations
- detailed and working drawings with associated calculations, component details and logic diagrams for programmable control systems
- details of interface with existing facilities
- design verification
- method statements for manufacture and installation
- method statements and procedures for testing and commissioning
- operating and maintenance manuals in preliminary format
- staff training programme (operating and maintenance personnel)
- Construction (Design and Management) Regulations documentation.

It is particularly important that the preliminary operating and maintenance manuals are received in sufficient time for the purchaser's operational and maintenance staff to carry out their own risk assessments, to prepare their own operational procedures and instructions, and to prepare planned maintenance schedules before handover.

At handover the contractor should provide:

- materials test certificates, NDT records and protective treatment data
- works and site testing and commissioning data, test records and certificates
- load testing records
- as built/fitted drawings including logic diagrams, program listings, etc. with associated calculations
- operating and maintenance manuals in final format
- risk assessments to demonstrate compliance with regulations
- declaration of conformity for machinery, pressure systems, construction products etc
- staff training records (operating and maintenance personnel)
- certification records (as applicable)
- handover certificate
- programme for future inspection and testing of the installation
- works and site inspection data, record sheets etc
- health and safety file in compliance with the CDM Regulations
- warranties
- technical file prepared under Machinery Regulations made available by the manufacturer.

3.6.3 Specifying the facility

The type of specification depends on the procurement route adopted. For a design and construct procurement it is necessary to write a detailed performance specification that sets out the following:

- general requirements related to the particular site, port operations and health and safety matters
- requirements for testing and commissioning
- documentation and design criteria, including the geometrical movements (ranges and speeds) required for the facility
- performance requirements for the foundations, concrete structures and structural steelwork
- operating sequences
- maintenance facilities
- operational and maintenance access requirements
- details of any specific technical standards to be followed
- a description of the performance requirements for the mechanical equipment, control system and electrical equipment.

For a traditional approach, the specification will include the above requirements together with more detailed requirements for the supply of materials and standards of workmanship.

The precise contents of the specification will depend on the type of facility, and purchasers should seek the advice of the project manager or designer for the development.

3.6.4 Particular problems with automation

There are two contrary perceptions of the value of automation in installations such as linkspans and walkways. They may be represented by the following statements.

1. Provision of automatic control and operating features will lead to greater reliability, efficiency and safety, by eliminating the otherwise inevitable human operator errors and malpractice.

2. The presence of a human operator, in control of the installation, will avoid the potentially disastrous effects of equipment failure and enable corrective actions to be taken in unforeseen circumstances, with inherently superior levels of overall safety and efficiency in operation.

3.6.5 Requirements for programmable electronic systems

Potential problems related to automation are discussed in more detail in Appendix C. This appendix also includes commentary on programmable electronic systems.

3.7 ASSESSMENT OF TENDERS

3.7.1 Receipt of tenders

The instructions to tenderers in the tender documents should give precise details of the time and date for receipt and the address for return, together with the list of forms and documents that must be submitted with the tender. The instructions should also indicate the type of packaging for return; the envelope should not bear any indication of the name of the tenderer. The envelope or package should normally be marked "tender documents" and with the name of the development. It should be noted that tenders are confidential documents and should not be copied or circulated more widely than is necessary to evaluate and report on the tenders.

Tenders should be opened by responsible staff within the purchaser's organisation – normally the secretary or financial director of the company. At the appointed time, the tenders should be opened and a record kept of each tenderer's name and the tender sum, together with any other important information relating to the tender. This record of opening should be signed by the responsible member of staff and witnessed.

Most port organisations and terminal operators already have tendering procedures that cover these matters.

In a limited number of cases tenders are invited in two stages: a technical submission and a financial submission. This is more usual in tenders for advisory services than for the construction of a facility. In this event only the technical submission should be opened and evaluated. The financial submission of the selected tenderer should be opened only after the technical evaluation has been completed.

The purchaser and the project adviser (when appointed) will normally evaluate tenders for advisory services. The project manager, in consultation with the designer, will normally evaluate tenders for the supply and construction of the facility.

3.7.2 Compliance with instructions

The opened tenders should be reviewed to ensure that tenderers have complied with the instructions. A checklist should be drawn up and completed for each tender. Where tenderers have not supplied information required by the instructions to tenderers, the evaluating organisation and the purchaser will need to decide whether or not the tender should be disqualified. The circumstances under which tenders are disqualified should be clearly set out in the instructions to tenderers.

It is particularly important that late tenders are not accepted, but are returned unopened to the tenderer. Where the instructions to tenderers allow alternative designs and proposals to be submitted, the evaluation should ensure that the submission complies with the requirements set out in the instructions to tenderers. It is normal for alternative designs to be accepted only if a compliant tender, strictly in accordance with the tender documents, has also been submitted. It is also normal for the tenderer to be required to give notice before the return of the tenders that an alternative design is to be submitted. The alternative design needs to be accompanied by drawings, calculations and a price schedule in order to allow it to be properly assessed. It is essential that tenders are submitted on the same basis, and therefore qualifications should not be accepted. The instructions to tenderers should make clear how any qualifications will be dealt with during the evaluation, and should indicate whether or not the qualified tender will be rejected. However, the evaluating organisation should discuss the qualification with the purchaser before rejection.

3.7.3 Financial evaluation

All the tenders should be checked for arithmetical accuracy, and if there are errors then these should be corrected by the methods set out in the instructions to tenderers. It is normal to take the rates as being correct and to alter the extension where the corrected product of the rate and quantity give a different extension.

The rates and prices in the various tenders should be compared to identify whether mistakes have been made in pricing particular items. However, contractors use a variety of methods to price tenders, and the evaluating organisation needs to use judgement on whether differences are significant. Where there is doubt, these items should be clarified by the tenderer in writing.

3.7.4 Technical evaluation

The tenderers should provide evidence of compliance with the technical specification, including:

- method of installation
- comprehensive and detailed methods of construction
- sufficient details of the proposed machinery
- details of site construction plant
- technical data sheets for key items of machinery or structure (stating information that confirms their compliance with the technical specification).

This information should be reviewed to ensure that the contractor has identified all the hazards and put forward proposals for eliminating or mitigating the risks. Any non-compliance with the performance specifications should be identified. The financial risk associated with particular construction and installation methods should be considered, as this may affect the economic as well as the technical acceptability of the tender.

3.7.5 Method of installation

The evaluation should review the tenderer's method statement regarding supply, fabrication, installation and construction for the various elements of the facility. Where the specification puts constraints on any of these methods, the statement should be reviewed to ensure that the tenderer has complied with the specification requirements. Any inconsistencies or impracticalities in the method statement should be identified, and if necessary, clarification should be sought from the tenderer. It is particularly important that the procedures for commissioning and testing are described satisfactorily.

Where the installation and construction is likely to take place at a berth that is used by shipping during the period of construction, the method of construction and installation should describe the procedures that are to be adopted to avoid interference to shipping and to protect the works from damage.

3.7.6 Evaluation report

The evaluating organisation should write a tender evaluation report setting out the actions taken to review, check and correct the tenders, and giving conclusions and recommendations to the purchaser regarding which tender to accept. It is normal that the tender evaluation process will identify the lowest tender, and that this tender will be recommended for acceptance. However, because linkspans and walkways are complex, hybrid facilities, the lowest tenderer may not necessarily best serve the purchaser or provide the best value for money. For example, on design and construct tenders, some assessment should be made of the whole-life cost of the facility, taking into account operating and future operating and maintenance costs (see Section 5.2.4).

In addition, many linkspans and walkways have to be completed within tight schedules, and the tender evaluation report should assess the ability of the particular contractor to complete the works within the time stated.

3.8 THE IMPLEMENTATION PROCESS

3.8.1 Award of contract

The successful tenderer should be informed that the offer is to be accepted, and all the tenderers should be informed of the outcome of the tender evaluation process as soon as possible. A formal letter of acceptance should be prepared and sent by the purchaser to the successful contractor. This letter is normally prepared on behalf of the purchaser by the project manager or designer. The letter of acceptance should refer to all matters that have previously been clarified or agreed after receipt of tenders. The letter should also state where subsequent contractual correspondence should be addressed and to whom. The letter of acceptance should not be qualified in any other way.

In some cases, the formal letter of acceptance takes some time to prepare, and a letter of intent is issued. The letter of intent should state that it is intended to enter into a formal contract in the near future and, where necessary, give instructions to proceed with the ordering of materials, for example, up to a financial limit. The letter of intent should also state when the letter of acceptance is to be issued. Note that a properly formulated letter of intent is an enforceable contract.

In some forms of contract, the contract is formally implemented by the signing of a form of agreement. This process normally takes place a number of weeks after the acceptance of the tender.

3.8.2 Manufacture, supply and installation

Linkspans and walkways are combinations of foundations, structures and machinery. They often involve a number of different professional disciplines, manufacturers, suppliers and trades. It is essential to the successful completion of the facility in the time stated for completion in the contract that a detailed programme is prepared between two and four weeks of the start of the work. This programme should be a "living" document, and will need to be revised and updated as work proceeds and elements of the programme are completed either earlier or later than originally planned. For many linkspan and walkway developments a simple bar chart programme is sufficient. **However, where the time for completion *must* be achieved, then a critical path programme may be required.** This programme will make it easier to monitor the effect of any delays in the completion of elements of work. For example, if a particular part of the machinery is to be delivered late, the critical path programme would identify what effect this would have on the overall programme. This type of programme makes it possible to re-plan any changes to the programme to cause the minimum of change in the final completion date. It also enables decisions to be made about alternative sources of supply, and steps to be taken to improve supply dates.

The foundation construction is usually critical to the completion of the linkspan or walkway on time. In addition, some parts of the machinery are on long delivery, and it is essential to monitor that these items are placed on order early in the construction programme. The engineer or the engineer's representative should review these matters on behalf of the purchaser. The fabrication of the movable structure of the linkspan or walkway is normally carried out off site at a shipyard or fabrication workshop. The progress and quality of work carried out at these locations needs to be inspected from time to time by one of the engineer's representatives or a specialist inspection company. The machinery is usually supplied from a variety of manufacturers and assembled in a workshop by the lead manufacturer or the contractor. Again, these parts of machinery need to be inspected and tested at the manufacturer's factory or at the assembly workshop. Any testing of the machinery during assembly should be witnessed.

The movable structure and other items of fabricated steelwork together with the elements of machinery are normally delivered to the site close to the end of the programme. It is essential that the foundation and fixed structure works are completed in time to accept the installation of the movable structure and the machinery.

The installation process needs to be carefully and safely planned in order to ensure that it can be carried out successfully, and that parts of the construction and machinery are not damaged. Many linkspans and walkways are delivered to the site in large, pre-assembled sections so that the installation process can be relatively short. However, some linkspans and walkways are delivered in sections by road, and the restrictions imposed by road transport inevitably mean that a considerable amount of assembly has to take place on site. The site area needs to be large enough to accommodate the final assembly of the facility.

3.8.3 Verification

General

The research that was carried out to produce this guide indicated that there was considerable willingness on the part of the ports industry to arrange for and facilitate a properly structured verification process. Two main activities for this process were identified:

- verification of the design of the facility to ensure that the completed product complies with the requirements of the project brief and is both safe and in compliance with the statutory regulations

- verification that the facility has been built and installed in accordance with the specification, recognised standards and the statutory regulations.

The two activities need different approaches, but both activities need to be carried out within a systematic framework defined by the project brief. The verification activities need to encompass the overall project. For instance, it is just as important to verify that the shore foundations, pontoon restraint foundations and anchorage foundations are correctly designed and constructed as it is to ensure that the linkspan, walkway and associated tower structures are designed and installed in a manner that will produce a safe and reliable facility. The verification process can either involve classification of the facility or it can be through some form of certification. The two approaches are described below, along with a description of the steps needed to ensure that the verification activities are suitably comprehensive.

Section B4.2 in Appendix B discusses the methods by which independent verification has been carried out in the past.

The need for verification

During the consultation processes and the CIRIA workshop on 26 June 1998 it became clear that there was a strong will within the industry to apply high standards to both stages of verification, and that such verification should be carried out carefully and independently. In the United Kingdom, at least, linkspans and walkways are among the very few structures open to the public that do not have a formal verification process imposed upon them by statute or government agency regulation.

For example:

1. Buildings are subject to independent verification and approval under the Building Regulations.

2. The designs of complex highway bridges are subjected to independent verification and certification using the Category 3 check system.

3. The designs of reservoirs and dams are subject to approval by a panel of engineers, which is responsible not only for approving the design but also for carrying out regular inspections to ensure that the integrity of the dam is maintained.

4. The classification process for ships can be viewed as an independent verification of the design and construction against a specific set of rules, which have been developed and refined over 200 years. The process can be extended by periodic surveys throughout the life of the structure.

The approach to verification

The industry opinion expressed at the workshop was that verification should generally be carried out by an organisation that is independent of the supplying organisation. This organisation could communicate directly with the supplying contractor to implement the necessary technical liaison, but it would report directly to the purchaser and not to the supplying contractor. The guide is based on this approach.

The verification process should not be structured in such a way as to remove the responsibility of the supplying contractor and his own designer, or the designer appointed by the purchaser, to provide designs and installations that are both safe and functional. The guidance therefore assumes that the contractor and designer will have suitable quality control and quality assurance procedures in place. That is, the designs will be internally checked and subject to design review, and the manufacturer will carry out his own tests to ensure that the facility has been designed and constructed in accordance with appropriate standards. In these circumstances it is acceptable for the independent design assessor to carry out the assessment "with due care and diligence". In other words, the independent design assessor will have contractual liabilities only if it can be shown that he was negligent.

This approach also allows the independent design assessor to tailor the extent of the assessment to the likely safety-critical elements within the facility rather than needing to examine each element in detail. **However, the assessor should state the extent of the verification.**

Verification of the design

For the verification of the design, the following options are available:

1. If a consultant or other independent design organisation supplies the design, it could be independently assessed by another organisation appointed directly by the port or purchasing organisation (or in-house by the port concerned). The independent design assessor could be another consulting engineer, a classification society or an assessment team formed from the staff of the purchasing organisation. In such circumstances, it would be possible for the designer to become the project manager for the project, but the organisation assessing the design would be controlled directly by the purchaser and not by the project manager in such cases. This raises the possibility of contractual risks, because the performance of the independent design assessor might not adhere to pre-agreed programmes. The reasons for such failure in performance may be perfectly justifiable, but nevertheless damaging to the progress of the project.

2. If the contractor supplies the design, the independent verification could be carried out by a consulting engineer, a classification society or an in-house team reporting to the purchaser. In such circumstances, the firm carrying out the project management may have the competence to act as the independent verification organisation, but could not act as such unless it had no involvement with the development of the design concept.

It is not possible to provide a prescriptive approach to the verification of design. The amount of work required to verify one type of design will be very different from the work required to verify a different type of design.

In either case, it is recommended that the independent design assessor carries out design verification in two stages, with a report being provided for both stages:

1. **The concept design stage.** The independent design assessor will receive documents detailing the concept design, the risk assessments for the concept design, the design basis statement for the project, and a document setting out the procedures to be used by the designer to verify the design. The independent design assessor will review these documents and carry out any independent calculations necessary to satisfy himself that the concept design is acceptable. The assessor will then issue a report stating that the documents have been examined and the type examination made. The report states either that there have been no adverse findings, or it lists and describes problems that have been found. The report will also comment on whether evidence has been presented demonstrating that the designer's internal verification procedures have been followed.

2. **The detailed design stage.** The independent design assessor will receive all the detail drawings of the facility and the up-to-date design basis statement. The independent design assessor will review these documents in the light of the outline concept design, the associated risk assessments and the design criteria, and will carry out independent checks of elements considered to be important. The assessor will decide which elements of the structure or facility require calculation checks, using the risk assessment as a guide to locating safety-critical areas. The assessor will then issue a report similar to that for the concept design stage indicating what assessment has been carried out and listing the findings, if any.

> It is essential to carry out an independent verification rather than check the calculations produced by the supplier's designer or the purchaser's designer. There have been several instances where the design calculations have been incorrectly carried out but have been checked and major errors have still been missed. The independence of the proposed procedure means that the assessor is not influenced by the conceptual thinking of the original designer.

Such an independent procedure allows the structure to be assessed in an unbiased way. The assessor should focus on the important details and not spend time assessing calculations for details that are not safety critical. The independent design assessor should not be expected to carry out independent calculations for all details that require calculations for the original design work. As stated above, the assessment assumes that the original design will have been fully checked and reviewed in accordance with appropriate quality assurance procedures.

> The contract between the assessor and the purchaser needs to be carefully negotiated so that both parties understand the scope of the assessment and the related price.

The recommendation that the assessment process is carried out in two stages is useful for two reasons.

1. It is possible to programme the design work so that the concept is agreed before substantive detailed design work is started, thus reducing the likelihood of abortive work. However, time constraints may prevent this.

2. The second stage coincides with the normal services offered by the classification societies, and enables this route to be part of the overall verification process. (This is not to say that a classification society does not have a role in the concept stage, and indeed they usually welcome such involvement as being beneficial to the overall project.)

The processes described above are equivalent to the Category 3 checking procedure for the assessment of complex highway bridges in the United Kingdom.

The verification process offered by the classification societies is similar in nature and equally important, as will be described below.

Verification of workmanship

This stage of the verification process is equivalent to the supervisory tasks carried out by the engineer's representative under the construction and manufacturing phase. The verifying organisation should be able to express satisfaction that the work has been carried out in accordance with the approved designs and specifications to the purchaser.

This phase of verification requires that specialist organisations be employed to carry out specific inspections. However, the process should be controlled by an organisation that will take responsibility for the overall verification of the manufacture and workmanship on the project. Such an organisation will be competent to understand the requirements of the design and specification of the project, and to ensure that organisations selected for specialist inspection tasks are competent and correctly briefed to fulfil their roles.

If the designer of the facility was not a member of the manufacturing/supplying organisation, it is desirable that the verification of the manufacturing and workmanship should be organised by him. Otherwise, the same criteria apply to the selection of an organisation for the verification of manufacture and workmanship as apply to the verification of the design. It is reasonable to consider that these verifications are organised under the supervision of the project manager.

It is important to ensure that the contractor retains responsibility for ensuring that the work is in accordance with the specifications and regulations. Therefore it is appropriate for the independent verification of the workmanship process to be a check on the control systems of the contractor rather than a complete duplication of the contractor's own verification processes. It is necessary to set up a systematic process to ensure that the manufacture is being carried out using materials that have certificates supplied by independent testing organisations.

All the recommended procedures can be implemented by organisations such as consulting engineers, independent testing houses or the ports themselves, provided that they have suitably qualified engineers. However, it will be necessary to set up systems to ensure that every aspect of the facility has been subjected to the verification process, and to ensure that the inspection and verification teams work together in the task.

The classification process and its place in the verification process

This subsection refers to *Lloyd's Register rules and regulations for the classification of linkspans*. The rules are a set of technical standards for the design and manufacture of linkspans. The regulations define the procedures whereby the classification process using the rules is carried out, and do not have the same meaning as statutory regulations.

For the non-foundation elements of linkspan and walkway structures the classification process is available as a suitable method of verification. Classification was originally intended as a procedure to assure insurers that a ship had been built adequately and was therefore a reasonable risk. Over the years the process has developed, and classification is now an integral part of the verification process for virtually all merchant shipping. Because classification was developed to serve the shipbuilding industry, it is particularly targeted at facilities that could reasonably be produced in shipyards or associated steel fabrication works. The process has since been used for other types of steel fabrication work, and regulations have been published that define the scope of classification. Lloyd's Register of Shipping has recently produced a comprehensively revised set of rules specifically dealing with linkspans, and so the classification process is directly applicable to the majority of the elements forming such facilities.

The complete classification process for linkspans provides a unified service covering the verification of the design, construction, installation and testing of the facilities, followed by a through-life surveying regime to verify the continuing integrity of the facilities.

The classification process is well suited to the verification of the design and manufacture of steel fabrications by shipyards, which are familiar with the process.

The classification process follows the route laid out below.

1. The client decides on the need for a facility, and decides to order one.

2. The client decides on the general design parameters required and defines the environmental conditions in which the facility will operate.

3. The client engages a manufacturer/builder.

4. The manufacturer/builder usually engages the classification society. Occasionally the client may engage the classification society direct.

5. The designer usually works for the manufacturer/builder, and produces an outline design using the loadings and other criteria provided by the client with additional loading information produced in the course of the concept design.

6. When the concept design is produced, the classification society examines it using the society's rules. It produces a design appraisal document stating that the design is acceptable, and states the loadings for which the facility has been designed. This document becomes in effect a statement of the limits of use that the client can put on the facility: that is, an operating envelope.

7. The facility is built "under survey", with a representative of the classification society attending periodically at key stages to check the construction. This generally involves establishing an inspection and testing plan (ITP) and agreeing with the builder various hold-points during construction to ensure that material traceability is adequate, welding procedures are approved, welders are suitably qualified, and the construction is in accordance with the approved detail plans.

8. Steel or aluminium materials used in the construction must be produced by mills that are approved by the classification society. The society therefore has considerable power to ensure that the materials are fully traceable.

9. The facility is tested under survey before being taken into service.

10. When the facility is completed and tested a classification certificate is issued.

11. If the facility is to retain its classification certificate, it must be inspected at regular intervals throughout its life in accordance with the classification society's rules.

At the time of writing only Lloyd's Register of Shipping has rules that apply specifically to linkspans. The Lloyd's Register *Rules and regulations for the classification of linkspans* add the installation process to the items to be inspected. The classification society can also witness any towing operations required to bring the facility to the site.

The advantages of the process are as follows:

1. The classification societies have a well-established network of surveyors who can work on an international basis.

2. The procedure is well understood by shipyards, so that if the fabrication of a linkspan or walkway is carried out in a shipyard, the builder will be very conversant with the requirements of the classification society, and there may be less chance of misunderstandings

3. The classification process incorporates ongoing inspections of the facility during its operating life. This helps to ensure the facility remains safe over a long period.

4. The Lloyds Register *Rules and regulations for the classification of linkspans* include procedures for carrying out load tests on the linkspans.

There are limitations, as below.

1. The process does not deal with the stability of the linkspan's buoyant element, if applicable. This feature has arisen because ships are required to undergo stability checks under different sets of rules not controlled by the classification societies.

2. The process covers the steel fabrications and machinery, but not the foundations or restraint piles etc.

Alternatively, an additional organisation may be employed to implement the processes not covered by the classification procedure.

Part of this review can be carried out under the classification procedures set out in Lloyd's Register of Shipping *Rules and regulations for the classification of linkspans*. Those matters not covered by the rules would need to be independently reviewed by other means. These aspects include checking the stability of buoyant and semi-buoyant pontoons and linkspans, the design and construction of any foundations supporting shore bearings and restraint systems, the design and construction of hoist tower foundations for non-buoyant shore ramps, and the detailed design of electrical and control systems. If the project is being carried out on a design and construct basis, it is possible that this other organisation could be the purchaser's project manager. It is feasible to request the classification society to cover those items not covered by the classification procedure.

3.8.4 Testing and commissioning

General

The specification should set out the requirements and provide sufficient information to enable competent persons to carry out the complete inspection, testing and commissioning of the linkspan or walkway. The specification should also include a full description of how the system is intended to operate, and provide all the design and operational parameters together with all the required commissioning procedures.

The procurement contract should set out clearly and unambiguously the allocation of responsibilities for:

- detailed specification of procedures and items to be inspected, tested and commissioned
- programming and co-ordination of the activities
- provision of consumables (such as electricity supplies, diesel fuel and water) for use in testing and commissioning
- provision of test equipment (such as instruments and test loads) and any temporary installation
- recording of results and measurements
- arrangement of and payment for third-party witnessing, if required
- provision of operating personnel and all other labour
- notification to interested parties
- proposal, approval and implementation of any necessary remedial work or alterations arising from the testing and commissioning process.

Engineering testing involves some degree of hazard, and while it is the tester's duty to ensure the tester's own safety, and that of others, in the performance of the test procedures, all parties involved must take account of the effect of these activities.

Inspection and, where appropriate, testing should be carried out progressively throughout the different stages of erection and before the installation is put into service. The personnel carrying out inspection and testing of any linkspan and walkway installation must be competent. They must therefore be skilled, experienced, and have sufficient knowledge of the type of installation to be inspected, tested and commissioned to ensure that no danger occurs to any person or property.

Commissioning and testing of the engineering installation is an important task prior to the handover of a completed facility. The time required to carry out such tests can be lengthy, and sufficient time tends not to be provided in contract programmes for these activities. Even when sufficient time is allowed initially, delays in the award of subcontracts can seriously reduce the time available for commissioning.

> **Purchasers of linkspans and walkways should review contractors' programmes with a view to ensuring that the designers, contractors and testers associated with such work are given sufficient time within the contract period to carry out this work thoroughly.**

Inspection before testing and commissioning

So far as is reasonably practicable, a visual inspection should be carried out before testing and commissioning to verify that:

- all structures, equipment and materials are of the correct type and comply with the applicable requirements of the specification

- all parts of the installation are correctly selected, positioned and erected

- no part of the installation is visibly damaged or otherwise defective

- the installation is suitable for the environmental conditions

- all means of access and egress are available and safe to use

- all safety features are installed and appropriate for the conditions and intended activities.

Testing

Testing may be defined as the evaluation of the performance of an installation. It includes any checks or tests that may be required to prove the performance of the commissioned installation.

The processes of testing engineering systems are generally well established and widely described and stipulated in design codes and standards. For example, the testing of electrical installations in accordance with the IEE Regulations (BS 7671) is normal practice when new installations are completed and existing installations are modified and then routinely at appropriate intervals throughout the life of an installation. Similarly, pressure testing of fluid power systems and equipment is carried out in accordance with various regulations and standards.

Testing may be divided into manufacturer's tests at the works, and commissioning tests on site.

Just before commissioning, testing will generally involve checking and measuring the performance of individual components and subsystems while the overall machine is not capable of movement or operation. An example of this approach would be checking the operation of the braking system of a vehicle without moving the vehicle under power.

The main aim of this phase of testing is to ensure, so far as is reasonably practicable, that the whole installation is safe to operate under power for the commissioning process. Lack of attention to this phase of testing can lead to personnel and equipment being in grave danger on starting up the machinery for the first time.

Commissioning

Commissioning is the advancement of an installation from the stage of static completion to full dynamic working order in accordance with the specified requirements.

Commissioning includes the setting to work and regulating of an installation, where the term *setting to work* may be defined as the process of setting a static system into motion, and *regulation* may be defined as the process of adjusting the system to the specified tolerances. Commissioning is deemed to be complete at *the conclusion of regulation.*

The purpose of commissioning and testing procedures is to ensure that the installation as finally handed over has been properly put through all its operational procedures, with control systems functioning, and emergency and alarm facilities, safety controls, overload protection systems and the like demonstrated to operate satisfactorily.

The degree of involvement of the purchaser in the process of commissioning a linkspan and walkway should be commensurate with the available skills and experience. The commissioning period offers a valuable opportunity for personnel who will subsequently be responsible for the operation and maintenance of the facility to learn how it works and how it should perform, and to acquire confidence in handling the installation.

> **Purchasers would be advised to ensure that (as should always be the case) the contract already requires full responsibility to be taken by the supplier of the facility. The purchaser should take no action that would dilute or interfere with the supplier's responsibility.**

Load testing

Structures such as buildings and highway bridges are not generally subjected to proof load tests. Cranes and lifting equipment are subjected to proof load tests to confirm their ability to carry the working loads without undue deformation, failure or stress. Linkspans and walkways have tended to be regarded as structures with associated machinery: the structure has generally not been proof-tested, although the machinery and lifting equipment will have been tested. Various reasons have been offered to support decisions not to load test linkspans and walkways including:

- the practical difficulty of applying a suitable proof load
- there are too many possible load cases to cover them all
- it is not clearly required by the regulations and technical standards.

A linkspan or walkway installation should be subjected to appropriate load tests so far as it is practicable to do so. LOLER requires all lifting equipment to be tested to prove that it has adequate strength. The type and extent of testing would be decided by the competent person carrying out the thorough inspection of the lifting equipment.

The lifting equipment on linkspans and walkways should be subject to a proof load test carried out on the completed facility. **It is recommended that the lifting equipment is tested up to its safe working load over the full range of movement to which the lifting equipment could be subjected during the operation of the linkspan or walkway**. This test is particularly important to ensure that the lifting equipment can operate safely over the full range of movement and can be operated at the specified speeds. It should also ensure that the lifting equipment cannot come into contact with other parts of the installation during movement and that there is no risk of persons being trapped by unguarded moving parts.

The Supply of Machinery (Safety) Regulations include "Essential health and safety requirements to offset the particular hazards due to a lifting operation", which refer to working coefficients and test coefficients to be applied to the maximum working load for the particular piece of equipment. These requirements refer to a static test coefficient of 1.25 and a dynamic test coefficient of 1.1. These coefficients are considered to be rather high for the level of maximum working load likely to be specified for each item of lifting equipment on linkspans and walkways. The Type C standards, when published, should include recommendations concerning the values of these coefficients.

Dynamic load testing should be applied to relevant elements of the machinery including the slewing and telescoping equipment, mechanically operated flaps and mechanically operated hooks or pins. Dynamic tests should also be carried out on the shore bearings of linkspans and walkways and on the bearings for flaps and the like. These dynamic tests should be carried out over the full range of movement of the linkspan or walkway. In particular they should reproduce any extreme geometric movements of the linkspan or walkway that might affect the application of load to that particular bearing.

3.8.5 Training

General

Statutory instruments, such as the Management of Health and Safety at Work Regulations, place obligations upon all employers to provide the training necessary and appropriate to ensure, so far as is reasonably practicable, the safety of their employees and other persons who may be affected by their undertaking. Training of staff in the efficient and cost-effective use and maintenance of the facilities has a direct bearing on the operation and financial viability of the whole undertaking, and is an obvious requirement for a healthy business.

> **The provision of adequate and effective training for all personnel is not only a statutory obligation upon employers but also a necessary adjunct to the management of a commercially successful undertaking.**

The following extracts from British Standard Code of Practice BS5304: 1988 *Safety of machinery* give an indication of the ranges of possibly relevant aspects of the safety content of training for various typical groups of employees.

Machinery operators

Machinery operators should be trained in the following:
    (a)   *safety procedures, including emergency procedures;*
    (b)   *the correct and safe way of doing the job;*
    (c)   *knowledge and understanding of the dangers they face;*
    (d)   *understanding the purpose and function of the safeguards which protect them;*
    (e)   *reporting faults immediately,*
    (f)   *wearing and care of protective clothing and equipment;*
    (g)   *need for good housekeeping.*

Designers of machinery

Designers of machinery should be trained in the following:

    (a)   *methods of integrating safeguards into machinery at the design stage*
    (b)   *ergonomic principles*
    (c)   *factors contributing to failure to safety.*

3.9　HANDOVER REQUIREMENTS

3.9.1　Training

The supplier of a new linkspan or walkway installation has a fund of knowledge and experience arising from carrying out the design, manufacture, testing and commissioning of the installation. This should be made available to be passed on to the personnel accepting responsibility for operation and maintenance of the facility.

> **The supplier of any new facility should be required as a contractual obligation to provide high-quality input to a programme of training for all personnel who will take on responsibilities in connection with the new linkspan or walkway. This provision should be structured to suit all relevant personnel, and would probably include separate syllabuses and demonstrations for operating and maintenance personnel.**

3.9.2　Regulatory documentation

Ship-to-shore linkspans and walkways procured within the UK will be subject to the regulations implementing EU directives.

The main applicable regulations are the Supply of Machinery (Safety) Regulations, which require the manufacturer of the equipment to prepare a technical file, and the Construction (Design and Management) Regulations, which require the purchaser to ensure that a health and safety file is prepared by the principal contractor and is available for inspection.

3.9.3　Technical file

The Supply of Machinery (Safety) Regulations generally only require the manufacturer to "assemble a file containing technical information relative to the machine". The file is kept by the manufacturer, and must remain available for inspection by the national enforcement authority for 10 years.

The file should contain the following information:

- an overall drawing of the machinery together with drawings of the control circuits
- full detailed drawings, accompanied by any calculation notes, test results and such other data as may be required to check the conformity of the machinery with the essential health and safety requirements
- a list of the following documents that were used when the machinery was designed:
  - the essential health and safety requirements
  - transposed harmonised standards
  - standards
  - other technical specifications
- a description of methods adopted to eliminate hazards presented by the machinery
- any technical report or certificate obtained from a competent body or laboratory
- if the manufacture declares conformity with a transposed harmonised standard, any technical report giving the results of tests carried out at his choice either by the manufacturer or by a competent body or laboratory
- a copy of the instructions for the machinery.

The responsible person under the regulations for the elements of the machinery must also sign a declaration of incorporation for each element of machinery that is assembled with other machinery, which includes the following:

- name and address of the responsible person

- description of machinery and machinery parts

- for "relevant" machinery, the name and address of approved body issuing EC type-examination certificate and number of certificate

- for "relevant" machinery, name and address of approved body to which technical file has been sent

- transposed harmonised standards used, if any

- a statement that the element of machinery must not be put into service until a declaration of conformity has been issued for the machinery in which the element has been incorporated

- name of person signing the declaration of incorporation.

The responsible person for the manufacturer (or installer) of the complete machinery must issue an EC declaration of conformity for the linkspan or walkway, which includes the following:

- business name and full address of the responsible person and the manufacturer (where not the responsible person)

- description of the machinery, including its make, type and serial number (not particularly applicable to linkspans and walkways)

- relevant provisions with which the machinery complies

- transposed harmonised standards used, if appropriate

- national standards and technical specifications used

- name of person authorised to sign on behalf of the responsible person.

The following extract from British Standard Code of Practice BS 5304:1988 *Safety of machinery* indicates some of the detailed information that is relevant, and which should be found in handover documentation.

Clause 13.4.3   Installation, operation and maintenance instructions

The supplier should provide with each machine sufficient information, including drawings, to enable the correct installation, safe operation and maintenance of the machine with particular reference to the following:

(a)   transport;

(b)   unloading and lifting, including the weight of the machine and its attachments, with indication where it should be lifted;

(c)   commissioning and installation, i.e. the limits of travel of all moving elements should be shown;

(d)   start-up, including preparation before start-up;

(e)   operation, including description of controls and functions;

(f)   close-down;

(g)   setting/process changeover/programming;

(h)   adjustment;

(i)   cleaning;

(j)   lubrication, refuelling, recharging;

(k)   repair, including information on foreseeable failures and fault finding.

The supplier should also supply a list of recommended spare parts, and a planned maintenance schedule.

For all the phases of machine life the potential hazards should be identified, and the safeguards to protect against hazards, the safe working and operational procedures required (including emergency procedures), and the emergency equipment that may be needed should be described.

The organisation procuring an installation should ensure that documentation provided by suppliers, designers etc is integrated with the overall records, training and documentation systems of their undertaking.

> **As this information is readily available when the facility is commissioned it would be prudent to require, as a contractual obligation, that a copy or copies of the technical file be provided with the linkspan or walkway to ensure that the information contained therein is readily available to the purchaser.**

3.9.4 Health and safety file

The CDM Regulations require the client to appoint a competent planning supervisor, a competent designer, and a competent principal contractor. The client must provide information about the state and condition of the site at which the linkspan and walkway will be constructed and installed. It should include relevant information in the client's possession and information that can be ascertained by making enquiries that it is reasonable for the client to have made. Therefore, before the designer is appointed the client is likely to have to instigate investigations into soil conditions, extreme tides, ship data, environmental conditions, seabed levels and site surveys.

The client must ensure that a pre-tender health and safety plan is prepared by the planning supervisor, by the lead designer, or by the project adviser. This pre-tender plan is issued to contractors at the time of tender, so that tenderers can take it into account when planning and pricing the construction works. The pre-tender health and safety plan should include:

- brief details of the linkspan or walkway
- information about the existing site for the linkspan or walkway, and about the environmental conditions, including tidal, wind and wave data and soils conditions
- information about the design relevant to health and safety during construction of the specific facility, including hazards particularly associated with linkspans and walkways
- potential health hazards arising from particular construction materials
- potential hazards arising from shipping movements and port operations, and site procedures for dealing with these hazards
- procedures for liaison between the client and planning supervisor and the principal contractor.

On award of the contract for construction the planning supervisor must notify the HSE of the particulars of the project. The principal contractor becomes responsible for the health and safety plan, and must develop the pre-tender health and safety plan and ensure that a construction health and safety plan is issued to all those involved in the project, including the client. This plan is to be kept under review by the principal contractor and amended to suit changes to the design or to the evolution of the construction methods. These amendments must be agreed with the planning supervisor.

The construction health and safety plan must draw on information in the pre-tender health and safety plan, and should also include:

- the approach adopted for managing health and safety on the project
- procedures to ensure co-ordination of other contractors and consultation with, and training of, site personnel
- specific site rules, including the exclusion of unauthorised persons
- safe working procedures, including construction method statements, risk assessments carried out under MHSWR and other health and safety legislation (including PUWER and SM(S)R)
- emergency and welfare procedures developed in conjunction with the client's own arrangements
- procedures for monitoring compliance with health and safety legislation, such as site safety inspections and reports
- procedures for amending the plan as work proceeds.

> **The purchaser must ensure that the health and safety plan has been sufficiently developed to allow construction to start safely on site.**

> **The planning supervisor must ensure that the health and safety file is prepared, and that it is delivered to the client for safekeeping. The principal contractor, other contractors and designers must provide the information that is needed. It is particularly important that the information for the file is collected before the contractors possessing the information leave site.**

The format of the health and safety file should be discussed and agreed by the client and the planning supervisor. Once the file has been handed over to the client on completion of the works, then the client or subsequent owner is responsible for making it available for future work, and for updating the file as further work is done on the structure.

The health and safety file should contain information about the structure that will assist the planning and implementation of future construction, cleaning, refurbishment and demolition work. It should include references to schedules of as-built drawings and to operating and maintenance manuals.

Typical contents of a health and safety file for a linkspan or walkway would include:

- pre-tender health and safety plan
- design parameters affecting use of facility
- as-built fabrication drawings, including relevant schedules
- as-built construction drawings, including relevant schedules
- summarised piling records, including pile test reports
- soils investigation and interpretative reports
- materials test certificates and reports
- welding test records
- information from construction health and safety plan relevant to future cleaning, repair and demolition, including provision for temporary access
- maintenance plan for structure.

3.9.5   Operating and maintenance manuals

Considerations relating to the content, format and function of operating and maintenance manuals are discussed in Chapters 4 and 5 of this guide.

> **The supplier must provide operating and maintenance manuals at the time of commissioning, before the facility is brought into use. The technical specification should set down the matters that the manuals should address. This is to ensure that they are provided in a suitable form for the organisation operating the facility to comply with its statutory duties regarding the health and safety of its operating and maintenance personnel.**

Draft versions of the operating and maintenance manuals should be produced at an early stage for review by the purchaser and amendment and reissue, if required, before commissioning, and for use during initial training of the employer's operating and maintenance personnel.

Operating and maintenance manuals are commonly provided both as hard-copy documents and in electronic format so that the purchaser can easily update the documentation throughout the life of the installation.

3.10   RECOMMENDATIONS

The questionnaire survey and consultations showed that the industry uses a number of satisfactory procurement methods and procedures. Preceding sections have highlighted good practice and other important information. However, smaller ports and organisations purchasing linkspans or walkways may not have sufficient experience to select an appropriate procurement route, and the following recommendations are particularly aimed at such organisations.

1. The purchaser should appoint or identify within their own organisation a project adviser who is both knowledgeable and competent about operational requirements for ro-ro and passenger terminals and who has a good understanding of the procurement options for construction work and equipment supply. The purchaser should also appoint a project manager.

2. The purchaser should prepare a functional brief for the facility, with the assistance of the project adviser, including information on the ships using the facility, environmental information, and information about the operation and maintenance of the facility. It is particularly important that the limits of movement of the ship to which the facility is to be connected are defined under both operational and extreme conditions including those movements due to tidal changes, wave action, wind pressure and the effects of passing ships.

3. The purchaser should decide the procurement route with assistance from the project adviser at an early stage.

4. Once the procurement route has been decided the purchaser should select and appoint the various parties required by the particular procurement route, including the designer, the planning supervisor and the contractor. The purchaser should appoint the engineer under the terms of the particular form of contract adopted for the procurement route selected. All the parties need to have particular expertise, experience and competence in the design or supply of the linkspan and walkway.

5. The purchaser, with the assistance of the project adviser, should appoint an independent design assessor to review the suitability and adequacy of the design, to identify the particular hazards inherent in the design, and to identify to the purchaser any shortcomings in, or risk of injury from, the facility as designed. The extent of any independent checking of the design will depend on the complexity of the facility, and will be determined by the independent design assessor.

6. The supply contract for the machinery and equipment should include a requirement for the contractor to appoint a competent systems engineer. The latter should co-ordinate the checking and review of the design of engineering systems, co-ordinate integration of the design work of the other design disciplines, assist in preparing risk assessments, assist in supervision of the installation of the facility, and assist in providing the necessary documentation.

7. The purchaser should identify a person to act as project safety auditor who must be knowledgeable and competent in health and safety matters related to linkspans and walkways. The auditor will review the health and safety documentation and advise on any unsatisfactory findings.

8. Great care should be taken in ensuring that the physical interfaces between the structure and the mechanical equipment are properly resolved so that hazards are eliminated or minimised to a safe level.

9. All the elements of linkspans or walkways are subject to risk assessment under the requirements of both the Construction (Design and Management) Regulations and the Supply of Machinery (Safety) Regulations.

10. The purchaser should ensure that the contract specification includes sufficient definition of the testing and commissioning procedures required to ensure that the facility can operate safely throughout its full range of movements and under its maximum loading conditions before the facility is put into use.

11. The purchaser should ensure that the contract specification includes requirements for training of the facility's operating and maintenance staff before it is put into use.

12. The purchaser must receive a copy of the health and safety file under the CDM Regulations. The contract specification should ensure that the purchaser also receives a copy of the technical file produced under the Machinery Regulations. The purchaser should also receive copies of operating and maintenance manuals and other documentation giving instructions for the safe operation and maintenance of the facility and descriptions of the methods adopted to eliminate hazards.

4   Operation

4.1   INTRODUCTION

4.1.1   General

This chapter gives guidance on best practice for the safe and efficient operation of ship-to-shore linkspans and walkways. The guidance assumes that readers will have familiarised themselves with the requirements of legislation regarding health and safety, and that they have some knowledge of the management and record-keeping requirements for safe operation of items of port equipment with movable parts. The guide also assumes that readers will have an understanding of broader port safety considerations, and will be reasonably familiar with the operational aspects of berthing and unberthing roll-on/roll-off ships and ferries, the handling of cargoes by roll-on/roll-off methods, and the handling of ferry passengers.

4.1.2   Operational availability of facilities

Ship-to-shore linkspans and walkways are essential for ro-ro cargo handling and passenger ferry operations. Many ports do not have spare ro-ro berths so it is essential that their linkspans operate without suffering breakdowns. Good management of linkspan and walkway operations contributes significantly to the identification of potential problems at an early stage and to ensuring that safety-critical operations do not take place if the facility is not working correctly.

To ensure that the facilities perform safely and reliably operators and supervisors must monitor the operation of the facility, and have appropriate training in its operation and in the identification of defects.

4.1.3   Dangerous parts

Most port equipment is potentially dangerous, and managers and operators will be familiar with the hazards presented by moving parts. However, linkspans and walkways differ from most other port equipment in that they are used by the general public, and in many cases are subject only to intermittent movements that can catch persons unawares. Therefore, apart from the continuously rotating and moving parts of machinery within the power sources for the facilities, there are structural parts that move intermittently under the action of lifting equipment, berthing forces, tides and waves. These parts include transition and finger flaps, and traps created by one piece of structure moving relative to another. Special attention needs to be paid to these areas to ensure that they are sufficiently protected to prevent employees and members of the public from becoming trapped.

Unusually for port equipment, linkspans and walkways are connected to ships during operation, sometimes in such a way that the facility has to accommodate ship motions. They are also at risk of collision impacts from ships that can occasionally exceed the capacity of the facilities' impact-absorption systems. Some operators fail to appreciate the large amounts of energy produced by the impact of a ship on a linkspan and the extent of movements that may be so generated.

4.2   OPERATING REQUIREMENTS

4.2.1   Management

General

The continued safe and reliable operation of linkspans and walkways depends on having a clearly defined management system. Those with management responsibilities must be familiar with the requirements of health and safety legislation, which are described in Section 2. Approved codes of practice and guidance on health and safety matters of particular relevance include:

- Docks Regulations 1988 and Guidance
- *Management of health and safety at work*
- *Workplace health, safety and welfare*
- *Safe use of work equipment*
- *Safe use of lifting equipment.*

The port or terminal operator must organise a management structure that provides a clear route for communications and a clear chain for reporting problems. The management system should ensure that the facility is operated safely at all times, and that it is not misused by overloading, by operating outside its performance envelope, or by being subjected to extreme environmental loads or ship impacts beyond its capacity.

Reference should be made to *Safe working at ro-ro terminals*, Safety Panel Briefing Pamphlet No 10 published by ICHCA in association with the Through Transport Club.

Key personnel

At each port there are a number of key functions that need to be fulfilled. The titles of the personnel performing these functions and the control of them will depend on the nature of the facility and the amount of traffic it handles. The roles are defined below:

- **Terminal manager:** controls all aspects of the shore side of the terminal and is responsible for the operation of the facility. As well as having overall managerial responsibility for sub-managers in charge of traffic control within the port area, the terminal manager may be responsible for one or more berthing superintendents.

- **Berthing superintendent:** organises the mooring of the ship and oversees the operation of the linkspan or walkway. This person controls the mooring gang and manages linkspan or walkway operations.

- **Linkspan or walkway operator ("the operator"):** a person specifically trained and authorised to operate a particular linkspan or walkway.

- **Harbour master:** controls all shipping movements within the harbour. For day-to-day contact with specific berthing operations, this person delegates tasks to duty managers.

- **Port control duty manager:** issues instructions to the masters of ships using the port, including ro-ro or ferry berths, concerning berthing and unberthing procedures. Has direct contact with the person in authority at the berth.

- **Facility maintenance engineer:** the person responsible for the maintenance of the facility, and for repairing it when it malfunctions. This person will probably also act as an adviser to the person responsible for agreeing standing orders, and for composing operating instructions and risk assessments.

Although each key role has been given a name that defines the essential functions, the distribution of tasks associated with each function will depend on local circumstances. The location, degree of usage and design of the facility all affect this. For instance, a ferry berth in the Western Isles of Scotland might not include a terminal building or infrastructure, and berthing operations may be infrequent enough for them to be controlled by part-time staff. In such circumstances, one person might be able to fulfil most of the functions described above, with the remaining ones carried out by the ship's master and engineer. However, this will only be possible if the facility has been specifically designed to be simple to operate by personnel without formal engineering or port management qualifications, with a minimum of training. The geography of these sites is often such that sightlines are clear enough to enable one person to see all areas of the facility from a single location.

An alternative strategy might be to use the ship's personnel to fulfil all the functions that would otherwise require shore-based personnel, provided that the appropriate training has been given.

In certain circumstances, a specialist company employed by the operating organisation might carry out the facility maintenance engineer's role.

Risk assessments, operating instructions and emergency procedures

The operating organisation needs to turn the information provided by the supplier into safe operating instructions, standing orders, training procedures and emergency plans. These are illustrated in the flow chart in Figure 4.1. The timing of the activities in the flow chart indicates two possible scenarios, depending on the procurement route.

1. The facility is handed over, and there is a period when the supplying contractor operates the facility on behalf of the port while the port prepares its operating procedures.

2. The port prepares its operating procedures before taking possession of the facility on the basis of information provided by the supplying contractor in advance of handover.

It is strongly recommended that the latter timetable be followed.

The Management of Health and Safety at Work Regulations (MHSWR) requires that "suitable and sufficient" risk assessments are carried out to identify risks, and that the risks are evaluated and appropriate action taken to avoid them, mitigate them, or else warn personnel using the facilities of the existence of risks. It is a requirement under the Provision and Use of Work Equipment Regulations (1988) (PUWER) that the risk assessments carried out under MHSWR are used to design safe operational procedures for each task and to ensure that safe access is available to carry out the required tasks. Similar regulations exist or will soon exist for the other European Union countries.

For the operation of a linkspan or walkway, the responsibility for producing such risk assessments will lie with the terminal manager. Since the production of risk assessments demands a high degree of technical awareness, the advice of the facility maintenance engineer will be needed. The latter will have received, and been responsible for storing, the facility's operating and maintenance manual. If the guidance given in Chapter 3 has been followed, the facility maintenance engineer will also have access to the technical file (produced to comply with the SM(S)R) and the health and safety file (to comply with the CDM Regulations). The facility maintenance engineer should review these

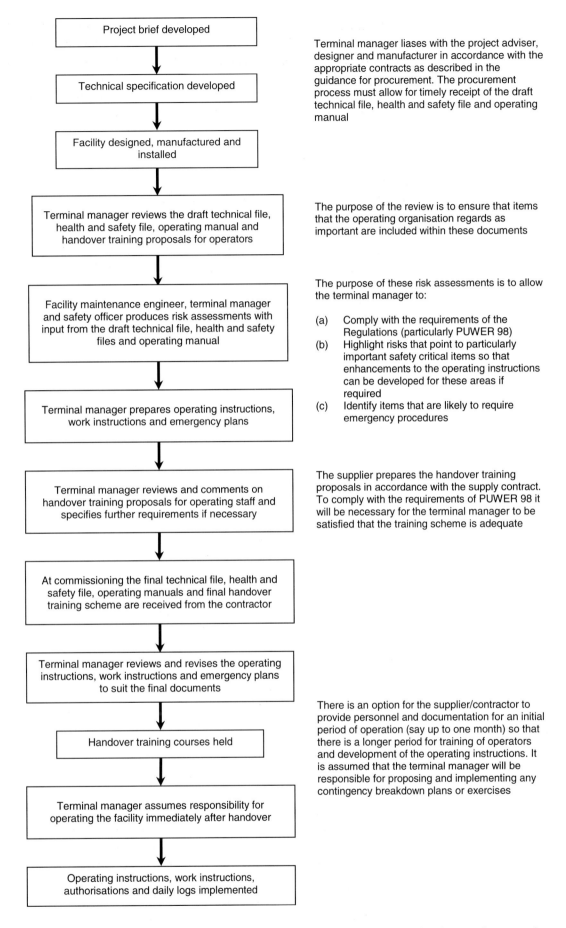

Terminal manager liases with the project adviser, designer and manufacturer in accordance with the appropriate contracts as described in the guidance for procurement. The procurement process must allow for timely receipt of the draft technical file, health and safety file and operating manual

The purpose of the review is to ensure that items that the operating organisation regards as important are included within these documents

The purpose of these risk assessments is to allow the terminal manager to:

(a) Comply with the requirements of the Regulations (particularly PUWER 98)
(b) Highlight risks that point to particularly important safety critical items so that enhancements to the operating instructions can be developed for these areas if required
(c) Identify items that are likely to require emergency procedures

The supplier prepares the handover training proposals in accordance with the supply contract. To comply with the requirements of PUWER 98 it will be necessary for the terminal manager to be satisfied that the training scheme is adequate

There is an option for the supplier/contractor to provide personnel and documentation for an initial period of operation (say up to one month) so that there is a longer period for training of operators and development of the operating instructions. It is assumed that the terminal manager will be responsible for proposing and implementing any contingency breakdown plans or exercises

Figure 4.1   *Flow chart of procedures to produce operating instructions, work instructions, training procedures and emergency plans*

documents in order to produce a well-informed risk assessment. Aided by these documents, the risk assessment will incorporate knowledge imparted by the facility's designers in addition to the facility maintenance engineer's own local knowledge.

It is important that the risk assessments should consider the unthinkable. Scenarios including risks that may arise from a major structural failure of the facility should be considered. These will be required to identify those scenarios that might be mitigated by preventive inspections or action. They will also be required to identify emergency scenarios that could usefully be turned into emergency training exercises. An emergency plan should be prepared covering failure of the facility, whether due to breakage, operational error, collision or misbehaviour, and operators should be trained to respond to such emergencies in a safe manner. The emergency plan for the facility needs to be co-ordinated with the overall emergency planning for the terminal or port.

The contingencies to be considered will depend on the type of facility, its surroundings and the location of emergency services. For linkspans they will probably include:

- ship collision
- failure of sensors on shore or on board ship
- fire on shore or on board ship
- structural failure of linkspan lifting equipment
- failure of linkspan bridge components, including bearings
- vehicle failure or collision with linkspan
- extreme weather conditions (waves, wind, snow, ice)
- sabotage, especially of vulnerable components
- operational error
- strike action
- failure of ship's equipment required for linkspan operation.

A similar assessment is required for walkways.

It will then be possible to write the operating instructions and design the training schemes for the operators.

4.2.2 Capabilities and training

Managers need to ensure that operators are able to carry out their work without risk to themselves or others. The operator's capability should be assessed in the light of the individual's level of training, knowledge and experience; if additional training is required it should be provided.

When upgrading or refurbishing the facilities and introducing new machinery or control systems a further assessment of the training needs of the operator should be undertaken. Significant changes to the facilities are likely to require additional training.

It is particularly important that operators receive regular training in emergency procedures so that they are able to respond quickly and safely. Emergencies occur only rarely, so it is important that regular simulations of emergencies are practised to enable operators to become familiar with procedures.

> **Training should provide systematic and methodical approaches to dealing with emergencies, as these occur in situations that lead to pressure on the operator and could lead to poor decision-making.**

4.2.3   Competence, training and authorisation

General

The level of competence required by operators and supervisors will vary according to the type of facility and its complexity of operation. It is essential to make an assessment of the level of competence required for operating a particular facility so that suitably capable operators can be identified, appropriate training provided and definite authorisation given.

Competence

The assessment of competence is difficult. However, it should certainly include some evaluation of the knowledge and experience of the particular operator and of the training or qualifications that they have received. One relatively simple definition is that "occupational competence is the ability to perform the activities within an occupation or function, to the standards expected in employment". It is important that supervisors and managers of operators are also competent, and the appropriate knowledge and experience should exist at all levels of an organisation.

Training

The Docks Regulations require the operator of the lifting appliance to be appropriately trained. Training should consist of a mixture of theoretical instruction and practical work. The supplier provides the majority of the operational training when the facility is installed. Operators are normally trained as part of the commissioning process, but recently purchasers have introduced a requirement for operators to be trained as part of the procurement process. In such cases the supplier provides some on-the-job training, plus limited classroom training on the contents of the operating instructions. However, many facilities are old and operators are changed over time. The operating organisation should ensure that a training system is set up so that new operators can be appropriately inducted and existing operators can have their training reinforced.

There is no national or industry-wide scheme for training operators of ship-to-shore linkspans and walkways. Training arrangements vary from one organisation to the next. In general the industry has adopted two approaches to training operators.

1. Large ports with a number of facilities have established their own effective in-house training and development for their own use. In some cases these training schemes are offered on a commercial basis to other operators.

2. A few companies offer commercial training services to operating organisations that are not large enough to support an in-house training scheme.

The operation of ship-to-shore linkspans and walkways affects the safety of large numbers of members of the public in addition to many employees, including the drivers of heavy goods vehicles. It is important that training schemes recognise the need to establish and maintain the confidence of the general public and of the relevant enforcement authorities. Operating organisations can seek further advice from:

*   British Ports Industry Training (BPIT), which offers advice on the availability of training schemes and training facilities

*   the Ports' Safety Organisation (PSO), which offers guidance on the requirements for competence, training, authorisation and health and safety advice generally.

Authorisation

The Docks Regulations require employers to keep a record of the names of employees who operate powered lifting appliances. The record should include particulars of any relevant training provided. The operator should undergo a test after completing training, and be given a certificate specifying the type of lifting appliance on which the test was carried out. In addition the operator must be authorised by his employer to operate a powered lifting appliance. Conversely, no employee should operate a powered lifting appliance unless authorised by his employer.

Any authorisation should take into account the operator's fitness in terms of general health, vision, hearing and any disabilities that might affect their ability to operate a facility safely. This will probably involve a periodic medical examination. However, operating organisations should be aware of the need to ensure that operators must not operate the facility when they are temporarily impaired by alcohol or other drugs. In the long term this may mean operators be subjected to a drug test or breathalyser test. Individual organisations currently have a wide range of policies on the use of drugs.

In other specialist sectors of industry various training systems, competence assessments and licensing have been set up, and some of these schemes have degrees of public scrutiny and control. These industry sectors include railways, where a licensing scheme has been operated for safety-critical work since 1993, and highway works, where certificates of competence are issued to street works operatives and supervisors.

> **A similar system of licensing should be considered for operators of linkspans and walkways.**

4.2.4   Operating procedures

General

The operational requirements of different types of linkspan are fairly similar. Within these types there are different methods of powering the lifting equipment, different control systems, and numerous detail differences. There are some standard types of linkspan, such as the Marine Development semi-submersible linkspan, but in general linkspans are tailor-made for a particular berth, and each one may be slightly different. Ports with several linkspans have attempted to standardise the equipment and operational systems to allow the ready interchange of spare parts, operators and maintenance staff. However, even in those ports linkspans supplied at different times will have variations in equipment and control systems. Walkways are supplied in an even greater variety of types, and these are described in Chapter 1. Each walkway tends to be tailor-made for the particular berth and ferry, and each walkway has different lifting equipment, control systems and operating procedures.

The following sections aim to give guidance on general operational matters that are common to all or most linkspans and walkways. The detailed operating requirements for a particular facility will be found in the operating manual or instructions for the machinery contained in the technical file.

Figure 4.2 is a simplified flow chart that sets out operational procedures during a complete cycle of berthing and unberthing.

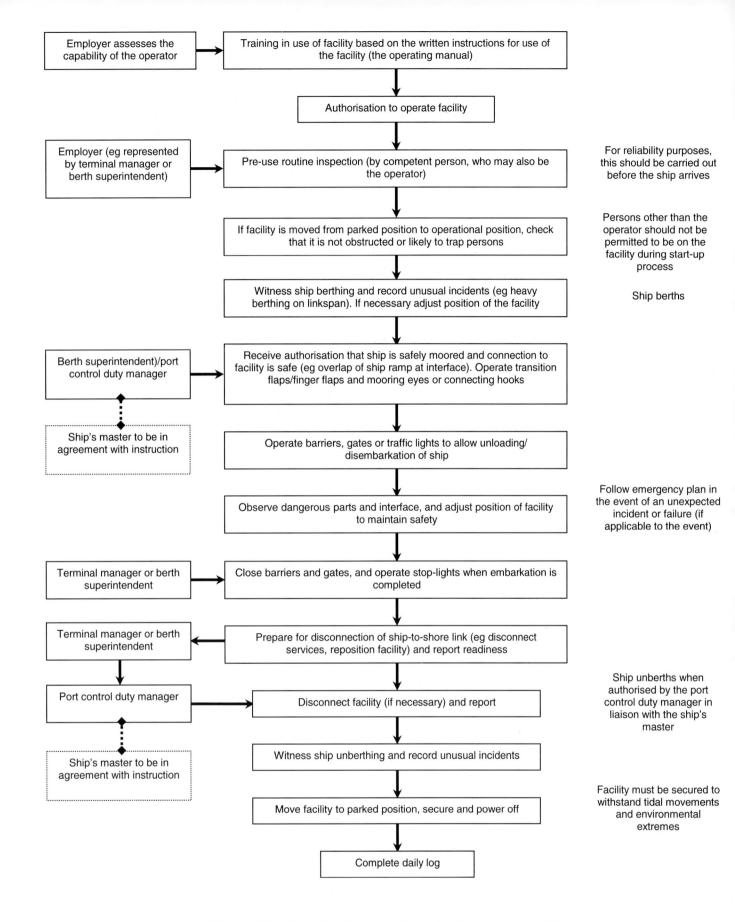

Figure 4.2 *Flow chart for operating a facility during a berthing*

Pre-arrival inspection

Before the linkspan or walkway is started up, the operator or some other competent person should carry out a routine inspection. The extent of this inspection will vary with the complexity of the linkspan or walkway and with the criticality of certain parts. For example, it might just involve the inspection of transition flaps, finger flaps and bearings, and a check that the linkspan or walkway is in its correct parked position and does not appear to have suffered any new impact damage. For a floating facility the inspection would also involve a check on the draught or freeboard of the floating part of the facility and an inspection of the restraint system. Some of the larger ports have developed quite extensive pre-use inspection check sheets that require the operator or other competent person to inspect the facility and complete the inspection sheet.

Start-up process

Once the facility has been inspected, and the operator is satisfied that it is safe to energise the machinery and move the linkspan or walkway from its parked position to an operational position, then further checks should be carried out. These should ensure that the appropriate indicators have appeared on the control panel, no alarms have been triggered, and that the linkspan or walkway can be moved safely without obstruction or persons becoming trapped. For most facilities no person other than the operator should be on the facility during the start-up process, and gates and barriers need to be provided to prevent casual access.

All the pre-arrival inspections and checks are normally carried out some time before the ship berths so that if there are problems the port control and the ship's master can be advised and alternative arrangements for berthing made or repairs put in hand.

Berthing and connection to ship

It is important that the operator checks that no damage is caused to the linkspan or walkway during ship berthing operations. The operator should be trained to recognise any unusual aspects of the berthing operation, including heavy berthing, and should be required to make a record in the log of any abnormal event and to consider immediately initiating a report to the engineering staff, through the supervisors. Many linkspans are designed to receive berthing impacts from the ship, but in extreme weather conditions, or when ships lose power, accidental heavy berthings can occur, and these can damage the linkspan. Often damage is restricted to the fendering, but occasionally it can occur to the structure and to the mechanical equipment. Following a heavy berthing the operator *must* re-inspect the safety-critical parts of the linkspan. Walkways are normally installed where there is no likelihood of damage from ships before they are deployed.

When the ship has berthed and is safely moored the final connection between the ship and the shore can be made. The operator should receive authorisation to make this final connection from the berthing superintendent or port control manager, who will have confirmed with the vessel's master that he is in agreement and that the vessel is in a condition to accept the connection safely. The position of the facility may need to be adjusted slightly to enable a safe connection to be made. In the case of linkspans one of the following operations will need to be performed.

1. The ship ramp with finger flaps is lowered on to the linkspan.
2. The ship ramp is lowered onto the linkspan and finger flaps on the linkspan are lowered onto the ship ramp.

3. The linkspan (if semi-submersible) is attached to the ship either by lowering onto the ship's transom or by the attachment of pennants before a ship ramp or other structure is positioned to complete the link. This is followed by limited ballasting to pre-load the pennants.

For walkways the final link is deployed onto the ship's coaming into the ship's passenger access door, or onto the passenger deck at a suitable opening. For all facilities the connection should be made in accordance with the requirements of the operating instructions and should be safe. Before public access to the facility is allowed the operator should receive authorisation from the berthing superintendent or port of control manager that the connection is safe.

The operator can then open barriers or gates or change traffic lights to allow unloading of vehicles onto the linkspan or disembarkation of passengers through the walkway.

Operational considerations often make it necessary to establish a shore connection with the ship and to maintain it for extended periods when no loading/unloading is in progress (for example because of early or delayed arrivals, or layovers). Such situations require careful consideration before any action is taken that would reduce the level or competence of supervision on the berth during such "quiet" periods.

Operation

While the facility is in operation the operator should check that warning lights and alarms are not triggered, and should continue to observe potentially dangerous parts and the interface between the ship and the facility, to ensure the facility remains safe to use. It may be necessary to adjust the position of the facility during operation to cater for tide variations and changes in ship draught and trim. Some linkspans incorporate sophisticated control systems linked to centres that operate the machinery and lifting equipment, adjusting the position of the facility automatically. For these linkspans the operator can carry out tasks such as routine maintenance during ship unloading and loading. Linkspans that do not have automated facilities require only infrequent adjustment, and operators on these facilities are often given other tasks such as routine maintenance.

> **It is recommended that the interface between the ship and the shore is observed at all times in case sudden movements of the ship occur. In addition, when the facility is adjusted, potentially dangerous parts should be observed.**

At some ports members of ship's crew delegated to control unloading or loading operations carry out observation. It is important that the shore-side management collaborates with the ship's master to ensure that the requirement to maintain the safety of the connection is carried out properly.

Should an exceptional occurrence, incident or facility failure occur, the emergency plan should be followed. Instructional manuals deal with a range of possible incidents, and the operator should be familiar with the routines involved in making the facility safe in the circumstances. However, unexpected incidents can happen, and the facility managers should ensure that suitable emergency plans are in place. As a minimum requirement for safety the emergency plan should be initiated by preventing further unloading or loading of vehicles, or disembarkation or embarkation of passengers.

Closing down

On completion of loading vehicles or embarking passengers the berth superintendent or terminal manager should authorise the operator to cease operations. The operator should close barriers or gates, operate stop-lights on the roadway and prepare to disconnect the ship-to-shore link, making sure that services are disconnected, and reposition the facility as required in preparation for disconnection. When the operator is satisfied that the facility is prepared for disconnection, the berth superintendent or terminal manager should be notified and permission should be obtained from the port control duty manager. The latter will have liaised with the vessel's master to ensure that he is in agreement and that the vessel's condition is such that the connection may be safely removed. The facility should then be disconnected from the ship. In the case of some linkspans this is as simple as allowing the ship ramp to be stowed. Successful disconnection should be reported through the line managers to the port control duty manager so that the ship's master can be authorised to sail.

The operator should observe the unberthing manoeuvre of the ship to check that the facility does not receive any exceptional impact. It can then be moved to its parked or stowed position, secured, and the machinery powered off. The facility should be secured so that it can withstand extreme wind loads and – in the case of floating linkspans – can cope safely with the anticipated tidal movements and wave action. In harbours where waves can impact on lifted linkspans, the linkspan should be secured at a safe level.

The operator should then complete the daily log for the facility, including recording any unusual incidents or damage that has occurred during the cycle. A sample daily log is shown in Figure 4.3.

4.3   OPERATORS' FACILITIES

4.3.1   Access

To carry out their duties, operators need adequate safe means of access to their control stations and to safety-critical parts that need to be inspected before facility start-up. The Docks Regulations, PUWER, LOLER and the Supply of Machinery (Safety) Regulations all require the provision of safe access. The approved codes of practice for the first three regulations give extensive guidance on the requirements for safe access. Safe access for operation must also be considered under the CDM Regulations. The essential health and safety requirements in the Supply of Machinery (Safety) Regulations require safe access by means of stairs, ladders, catwalks etc to all areas used for operation. Those parts of the machinery where operators or users are liable to move about must be fitted with guards or barriers to prevent falls. The regulations will be supported by a harmonised European standard in four parts for use in the design, selection and assessment of access facilities. The standard is in the final stages of development as *Safety of machinery – permanent means of access to machines and industrial plant* (prEN12437).

> **The questionnaire survey and consultation discovered that access for the purposes of operation of linkspans and walkways is relatively poor, and the design of access is an area that requires major improvement.**

Because linkspans and walkways provide facilities for the general public, it is important to prevent unauthorised and inappropriate access to moving and dangerous parts. Barriers, gates and guards will be required for many safety and security purposes on linkspans and walkways.

ANYPORT

DAILY LOG FOR LINKSPAN OR WALKWAY

Reference No ....

Date .... Time .... From .... To .... Operator ....

Ship arrives or departs during shift period:

	No of events	Satisfactory?	Time/s	Comments
Berthing	☐	☐	....	(Please note unusual ship impact, damage and excessive movements of ship while linked to the facility)
Unberthing	☐	☐	....	....

Name/s of ship/s ....

Pre-shift inspection
Manager to type in activities including pre-inspection procedures
....
....
....

Activities during shift
Operator to write in activities carried out (one task per line)
....
....
....

Performance of machinery
List the machinery in use (one piece of machinery per line)
....
....

Note: Please tick "satisfactory" box or else cross and fill in comment

Figure 4.3 *Example of a daily log form*

4.3.2 Welfare

Employees' welfare is covered by various regulations including the Docks Regulations, Management of Health and Safety at Work Regulations, and Workplace (Health, Safety and Welfare) Regulations. It is assumed that operating organisations will provide welfare amenities within the terminal, and that the reader will refer to the appropriate approved code of practice for guidance on the extent of amenities to be provided.

In the case of linkspans and walkways particular consideration needs to be given to the provision of suitable shelter for use during bad weather and to the supply of protective clothing. Most walkways offer reasonable protection against inclement weather, although to ensure adequate visibility the operator's control station is often sited near the open ship end of the walkway. Linkspans offer little shelter from poor weather, and the operator's control station is usually located inside a weatherproof cabin or kiosk.

Consideration also needs to be given to the provision of rescue, life-saving, first aid, fire fighting and similar facilities on a linkspan and walkway. The requirements depend on the relationship between the linkspan and walkway and any adjacent welfare facilities. However, it would be normal to provide life-saving equipment such as buoyancy aids in areas next to water. Similarly, fire-fighting and other safety facilities are required in plant rooms. Commonly, basic first aid facilities and an eye-wash are provided within plant rooms, particularly where substances potentially hazardous to health are involved.

The design and supply of ship-to-shore linkspans and walkways should take account of the many factors that affect operator welfare, including, but not limited to, the following:

- ergonomic factors in the arrangement of operator positions

- the provision of a safe working environment

- the provision of information to the operator, in an easily assimilable form, relating to the condition of the plant and machinery under his control

- the appropriate application of automatic features to assist the operator by reducing fatigue, stress, risk etc

- an indication of faults, remedial actions etc, to assist the operator's speed of response and its relevance

- guarding of potentially hazardous areas, and safety interlocks to prevent inadvertent entry/access to danger areas

- the reduction of noise, vibration, radiation and solid/liquid/gaseous emissions that may be hazardous.

- the avoidance of hazards such as radiation, fire and explosion

- suitable markings, instructions, notices for information and warnings to the operators, such as safe working loads and access limitations.

The questionnaire survey and consultations revealed aspects of existing installations that did not fully meet the welfare requirements for operators – see Section B2.8.

> **It is recommended that sufficient thought be given at the design stage to the welfare requirements of operators, and that operating organisations and the specifiers or designers communicate adequately with each other at an early stage in the procurement of a facility to enable the particular requirements of that facility to be implemented.**

4.4 DOCUMENTATION

4.4.1 Technical file

The Supply of Machinery (Safety) Regulations require the responsible person to draw up a technical file for the relevant machinery. The contents of the technical file, which are described in Chapter 2, will include a copy of the instructions for the machinery. The essential health and safety requirements in SM(S)R include details of what is to be included in the instructions, and the information relevant to operators is set out below.

- details of workstations likely to be occupied by operators
- instructions for safe putting into service
- instructions for safe use
- instructions for safe adjustment
- training instructions
- if necessary, instructions describing ways in which the machinery should not be used
- drawings and diagrams necessary for checking correct operation
- all useful instructions with regard to safety
- instructions on the reduction of airborne noise emissions from the machinery.

> **The wording and layout of the instructions for use should cover the essential requirements, but must take into account the level of knowledge and training that can be expected from operators of machinery.**

The Regulations only require the technical file to be drawn up by the responsible person, and it is not a requirement to provide the complete technical file to the purchaser. However the instructions for the machinery would need to be provided.

> **It is recommended that the procurement documentation requires the technical file and all other associated documentation to be provided to the purchaser with the supply of the machinery.**

4.4.2 Operating manuals

Operating manuals should be provided in accordance with BS 4884:1992 *Technical manuals*. Operating manuals should be supplied for every item of machinery and lifting equipment, and should be integrated to provide a comprehensive operating manual for the whole facility, covering its structural, mechanical, electrical and control aspects. It is recommended that operating manuals be prepared by a specialist company with experience of this type of work. Operating manuals must be in the English language for facilities in the United Kingdom.

The relationship between operating manuals and risk assessments should not be overlooked. The need to confirm the validity of risk assessments previously carried out, before the public uses the facility, must not be overshadowed by the intense activities occurring for all parties around the commissioning phase.

> **Operating manuals should cover the safe starting-up, running and close-down of all systems. They should be written specifically for the particular facility. Generalised operating manuals are not acceptable for ship-to-shore linkspans and walkways.**

The operating manual should be provided during the course of the procurement, and a draft copy should be provided for review during commissioning. This will allow the operating manual to be revised to suit matters that are found not to be successfully covered during commissioning. Operating manuals should be of high quality in both presentation and technical content.

Manuals are often supplied to purchasers in electronic format for retention purposes.

Operating instructional labels also need to be provided and displayed adjacent to the control panel and adjacent to any electrical panels in the plant room. These labels should set out operational procedures in simple terms. The labels should cover what action is to be taken when fault alarms are initiated. The operating manuals and operating instructional labels should be provided with suitable surfaces such as plastic-coated, wipe-clean sheeting to allow for the environment in which they are used.

4.4.3 Daily logs

An operating log should be kept for every facility and completed on a shift or daily basis by the operator. Where the facility is not used daily it may be appropriate to complete the log less frequently, although it should be completed at least every time the facility is used. The daily log should include details of ship arrivals and departures, and should note any unusual incidents, including ship impact, excessive movements of the ship or machinery and equipment defects.

The daily log should also record the findings of the pre-use inspection of the structure, lifting equipment and machinery, any damage found during this inspection, the adjustments to the facility carried out during the shift, including any unusual alarms or operating conditions, and a comment on whether the lifting equipment, machinery and control systems performed satisfactorily. Figure 4.3 shows a sample daily log.

The setting up of a daily log system should take account of other record-keeping functions already existing, to ensure maximum benefit and efficiency. It may not be essential in a given port to duplicate records kept in other contracts, such as Shipping Register entries of vessel movements, or meteorological records of weather conditions.

4.4.4 Other instructions

Authorisation to operate

Every operator of a linkspan or walkway should receive a written authorisation to operate the facility. The authorisation will be valid for a defined period of time, say one year. This should include the name of the operator and the description of the particular facility to which it applies, and should be signed and dated by the employer or his representative, who may well be the person responsible for the operator's specific training. The authorisation must be reviewed in accordance with a defined procedure.

Work instructions

Essential instructions covering safety-critical items on a particular linkspan or walkway should be issued in the form of work instructions. An example of a work instruction is provided in Figure 4.4; this gives typical general headings for various operational procedures. Additional work instructions may also cover particular operational procedures such as the safe connection and disconnection of the link to the ship. There may also be a specific work instruction covering procedures for closing down and making secure the facility at the end of the shift.

ANYPORT

WORK INSTRUCTION

FACILITY No: PARTICULAR LINKSPAN/WALKWAY

TITLE: **DESCRIPTION OF OPERATION INVOLVED**

TO: **NAME OF/TYPES OF PERSONNEL**

1.0   **IMPORTANT SAFETY NOTICE**
Description of particular safety problems associated with this particular operation

2.0   **BEFORE VESSEL ARRIVES**
There may be three or four groups of operational instructions for specific tasks. Should also include notes of importance. Give each task a reference number. Section to be expanded to fit appropriate numbers of tasks.

3.0   **OPERATIONAL INSTRUCTIONS FOR MOORING VESSEL**
There may be three or four groups of operational instructions for specific tasks. Should also include notes of importance. Give each task a reference number. Section to be expanded to fit appropriate numbers of tasks. Reference should be made to berthing impact on fendering to the facility and to suitability of mooring arrangements.

4.0   **OPERATIONAL INSTRUCTIONS FOR WHEN VESSEL IS ON BERTH**
There may be several groups of operational instructions for specific tasks. Should also include notes of importance. May require references to operating and instructional manual. Give each task a reference number. Section to be expanded to fit the appropriate number of tasks. Particular reference should be made to operators related to normal or extreme movements of ships.

5.0   **BEFORE SHIP DEPARTS**
There may be three or four groups of operational instructions for specific tasks. Should also include notes of importance. Give each task a reference number. Section to be expanded to fit appropriate numbers of tasks. A checklist for disconnection and communication route between shore and ship for authorisation to depart should be included.

6.0   **OPERATIONAL INSTRUCTIONS TO RELEASE MOORINGS TO VESSEL**
There may be three or four groups of operational instructions for specific tasks. Should also include notes of importance. Give each task a reference number. Section to be expanded to fit appropriate numbers of tasks.

7.0   **SHUTTING DOWN FACILITY**
There may be three or four groups of operational instructions for specific tasks. Should also include notes of importance. Give each task a reference number. Section to be expanded to fit appropriate numbers of tasks. Instructions required for securing the facility before personnel leave it overnight or at end of shift. Particular attention may need to be paid in such facilities for tidal movements or other features to ensure security.

Author	**Version Number**	**Issue**
Approved	**Port Manager**	**Date**

Figure 4.4   *Example of a pro-forma for work instruction for linkspans and walkways*

Standing orders

It is essential for safe and efficient operation, and to satisfy legal obligations, that operating organisations and shipping lines collaborate on matters related to interactions between the ship and the facility, so that the safety of the facility is maintained. Such standing orders would cover the restrictions placed on ship berthing manoeuvres adjacent to the linkspan, limiting wind or sea conditions for berthing or operation of the facility. The standing orders should also cover the constraints on berthing impacts, in terms either of speed or of angle of approach.

4.5 RECORDING AND INVESTIGATING INCIDENTS

4.5.1 Incident reports

One of the most important responsibilities of operators of ship-to-shore linkspans and walkways is the making of clear and accurate records of breakdowns, failures, damage and other unusual occurrences. This is essential if lessons are to be learnt about the behaviour of the facility. Such records can also provide information about repetitive incidents. From them, the causes of these incidents can be identified, enabling the facility to be modified so that such incidents are eliminated or reduced in number.

An immediate response to any incident is essential to the value and reliability of any eventual conclusions. Awareness of the need to preserve evidence and avoid unnecessary disturbance of the site should be part of the training of all supervisors and managers who may be in a position to influence these matters. Training in the management and investigation of incidents should be extended to all relevant personnel.

Day-to-day incidents will be recorded on the operator's daily log, but significant incidents, particularly those that affect safety-critical items, or the overall safety of the facility, should also be reported on incident records. Such incidents might include a ship collision with the linkspan beyond the capacity of the fendering. They might also include a vehicle collision causing damage to kerbs, barriers, plant rooms, control cabins, lifting equipment or machinery on a linkspan, or to the support of upper decks and overhead walkways, or damage to transition flaps and finger flaps. Incidents would also include repetitive control failures and possibly unusual occurrences or noises where the daily record does not provide sufficient space for their description.

An example of a typical incident record is given in Figure 4.5.

The survey questionnaire and consultations revealed that there was considerable under-reporting of incidents, and that even where incidents were reported, record-keeping was extremely poor. In many cases, proper records of incidents were not made at the time, and this often led to difficulties in interpreting the exact cause of the incident.

> A "no blame" management culture needs to be established so that incidents are accurately and properly recorded at the time that they occur, and witnesses or record keepers should not have to concern themselves with the attribution of blame, insurance matters, loss adjustment and possible legal proceedings. It is recommended that all operating organisations and facility owners introduce policies on the reporting of incidents, and that a much higher priority is given to the proper reporting of these incidents and to providing feedback to the ports industry.

> **Daily logs and incident records tend to refer to actual damage and failures. However, it is equally important that near misses are reported, as repeated near misses are a sign that an accident will happen in future. These near misses should be reported and acted on in the same way as an incident that causes damage or failure.**

4.5.2   Investigations

The completion of an incident record is only the first step in ensuring that the facility is still safe to operate. Where superficial damage is involved, such as the denting of a steel fender frame or damage to a vehicle barrier, detailed investigations would not be required. However, where there is a major mechanical or control failure, an unexplained occurrence or a major ship collision, then further investigations should be carried out.

Investigations should involve the thorough examination of the lifting equipment and of the machinery in order to determine whether any damage has occurred, and to confirm that it is safe to resume operations. Where structural damage is involved from ship collision or overloading then a structural survey will be required, and this would need to pay particular attention to highly stressed areas and to the bearings at the shore end, and to any lifting equipment.

In the event of a major incident these investigations need to be started as soon as possible, particularly as linkspans and walkways are critical items of port equipment. The initial investigation should establish whether the facility may be safely put back into use. Further investigations will determine what repairs and replacements are required.

> **It is important that such investigations are carried out in a systematic and thorough way despite the pressures of time due to the shipping line and operating organisations wanting to bring the facilities back into operation as soon as possible.**

The further investigations should normally result in the production of a brief report. It has been found that the availability of photographic evidence and where possible video recordings of either the actual incident or the aftermath are extremely helpful in identifying both the causes of the incident and the extent of damage.

Incidents involving injury to persons should follow statutory reporting procedures, and serious incidents will involve investigations by the appropriate enforcing authority.

It should be noted that where the facility is "in class" all damage to the structure, equipment and machinery should be reported to the classification societies' surveyors, and repairs would need to be agreed with them before being implemented and be carried out to their satisfaction. If permanent repairs are not carried out straight away the surveyors may impose a "suitable condition of class" on the facility. If the incident involves alterations to the structure or machinery then details of these alterations should be submitted to the classification society for approval before starting the alterations.

> **Lifting equipment or machinery that has been involved in an accident or dangerous occurrence must be examined before it is put back into use. It may be that the competent person will decide that a test is necessary before the lifting equipment is put back into use. The details of such a test should take account of information provided by the manufacturer of the lifting equipment.**

ANY PORT

Facility reference number ....

INCIDENT REPORT

Date and time ....

Ship involved?   **Yes** ☐   **No** ☐

Name of ship/registration no. of vehicle ....

Description of incident ....
....
....
....
....
....
....
....

Damage

To ship/vehicle ....
....
....

To facility ....
Structure ....
Fendering ....
Mechanical/electrical equipment/machinery ....
Barriers ....
Transition flaps ....

Name of ship's master: ....

Name of berth master: ....

Estimate of ship/vehicle speed: ....

Tug?   **Yes**   **No**   **Name of tug:** ....

Any witnesses?   **Yes**   **No**   **Name of witnesses:** ....
                                    (Attach contemporary statement if possible)

Environmental data at time of incident

Ship end level of facility: ....   **Est. wave height:** ....

Tide level: ....   **Visibility:** ....

Wind speed/direction: ....

Name ....   **Signed** ....   **Date** ....

Figure 4.5 *Example of an incident report pro-forma*

4.5.3 Feedback

Daily logs and incident records can be used within an operating organisation to provide information for use by the maintenance organisation in modifying its planned maintenance systems and also in identifying requirements for repairs and replacements.

> **Feedback would also be useful on an industry-wide basis, so that repetitive incidents that occur at several facilities can be made known to the industry and appropriate remedial steps taken to reduce or eliminate these incidents.**

4.6 RECOMMENDATIONS

The questionnaire survey and consultations showed that reasonably satisfactory operating instructions were provided at the majority of facilities and that the operating requirements were understood. Much of the guidance given in this section arose out of the consultation with four of the major ports and one shipping line facility operator. However, smaller ports and new operating organisations may not be fully conversant with the operating requirements for ship-to-shore linkspans and walkways, and the following recommendations are particularly aimed at such organisations.

1. Every operating organisation should be familiar with the relevant regulations

2. A chain of communication and management should be established, and every person involved in the operation of ship-to-shore linkspans and walkways should understand the routes for communication, authorisation and reporting incidents.

3. Operators of all facilities should complete daily logs recording any significant occurrences.

4. Instructions on operational limitations should be known to operators and displayed at an appropriate location on the facility. These operational limitations would include loading, environmental conditions (wind speed, wave heights, tidal extremes) and other parameters that define the performance capacity of the facility. Such information should also, wherever practicable, be made known to the vessel's master, who will necessarily be involved in the process of decision-making regarding any berthing or unberthing of his vessel.

5. Operators should be given suitable training and be authorised to operate the particular facility for which they have been trained.

6. Standing orders should be prepared in collaboration with the shipping line in order to identify constraints on ship manoeuvring adjacent to the facility.

7. Special consideration should be given to the operational requirements of remotely controlled equipment, particularly radio controls operated from the ship and automatic tide-following systems.

8. All incidents of damage, failure or misoperation should be recorded in writing and investigated.

9. An industry-wide feedback system for promulgating information about incidents involving ship-to-shore linkspans and walkways should be set up.

5 Maintenance

5.1 INTRODUCTION

5.1.1 General

A long service life may be achieved by selecting machinery suitable for the arduous working conditions expected within a marine environment, combined with judicious use of corrosion protection measures. Attention to the details of the equipment is necessary to ensure a long working life. Specialist advice may be needed at the procurement stage (see Chapter 3), to outline the alternatives available and to advise on selection.

Duty/standby equipment may, where provided, be arranged for either automatic or manual initiation of changeover in the event of failure. This may involve either the duplication of equipment or the duplication of the operating mechanism. For example:

1. The duplication of equipment may involve the provision of an additional prime mover (for example, an electric motor-driven hydraulic pump).
2. The duplication of the operating mechanism may involve manual operation of a hydraulic fluid directional control valve that is normally operated by electric solenoids.

These aspects need to be considered at the procurement stage so that satisfactory equipment availability is achieved and the appropriate level of maintenance adopted.

5.1.2 Safety

It is important that maintenance work on ship-to-shore linkspans and walkways can be carried out safely. The ability to carry out maintenance safely is largely dependent on the original design of the structure, lifting equipment and machinery and the adequate provision of access stairs, ladders and catwalks. Safety may be greatly enhanced by ensuring that maintenance items are not sited in places that are difficult to reach nor are in potentially hazardous locations (confined spaces, for example), in compliance with CDM Regulations.

The training of maintenance personnel makes a substantial contribution to safety. Initial training should be provided in the maintenance of linkspans and walkways, which should be backed up by practical experience in carrying out specific tasks and by periodic refresher training. Additional specialist training may be required for particular maintenance tasks. Only persons authorised to carry out maintenance work should be allowed to work on the structure, lifting equipment and machinery. All such work should be properly planned, with written procedures showing clearly how the tasks are to be performed efficiently and safely.

Before maintenance work is started on a linkspan or walkway it is important to advise the terminal manager and operator, who should then notify the ship operator or owner. Planned maintenance work can be scheduled to suit periods when the linkspan or walkway is not in service. However, for emergency repair work the authorised person should contact the terminal manager so that the linkspan or walkway can be safely taken out of service. Special precautions or procedures should be agreed if the ship is still on the berth and handling of vehicles or passengers has not yet been completed. Otherwise, appropriate notification should be given to the ship operator or owner. Reference should also be made to the permit-to-work systems described in Section 5.3.5.

5.1.3 Regulatory requirements

The detailed requirements of the various regulations are described in Chapter 2. There is a general requirement of the Health and Safety at Work etc Act that maintenance work is carried out safely. The Workplace (Health, Safety and Welfare) Regulations require that the workplace, equipment, devices and systems be maintained in a safe state and in good repair. These regulations also require that equipment such as linkspans and walkways should be subject to a suitable system of maintenance. A suitable system of maintenance would include regular servicing and inspections carried out periodically, the rectification of dangerous defects, the prevention of access to defective equipment, and the keeping of suitable records to ensure that regular maintenance is carried out properly.

PUWER 98 also requires that work equipment is maintained in efficient working order and good repair, and – for work equipment such as linkspans and walkways – that the necessary maintenance log is kept up to date. The extent and complexity of maintenance need to be assessed so that a maintenance management scheme can be prepared that deals appropriately with those parts that are more likely to fail or to deteriorate or may present a high hazard to safety. Risk assessment should be carried out so that the appropriate maintenance techniques can be selected to suit the types of risk involved. These are referred to in more detail in Section 5.2. PUWER 98 also requires that work equipment should be constructed or adapted so that maintenance operations can be carried out while work equipment is shut down, or maintenance operations can be carried out without exposing the maintenance personnel to risk, or appropriate measures are provided to protect the maintenance personnel from risks. The supplier should have addressed the issues of safe maintenance under the essential health and safety requirements at the design and supply stage.

Under the CDM Regulations the health and safety file must include details of significant or unexpected risks or hazards that may arise during maintenance and requirements for the structure. Manuals produced by specialist contractors and suppliers that outline operating and maintenance procedures, and schedules for plant and equipment installed as part of the structure, may be referred to in the health and safety file.

Those responsible for planning and implementing maintenance work should have knowledge of HSWA and the relevant regulations.

> **It is important that those responsible for planning and implementing maintenance work are involved in the creation of the project brief and in the technical specification of the maintenance requirements for the linkspan or walkway when it is procured.**

5.2   MAINTENANCE STRATEGIES

5.2.1   Types of maintenance

Different maintenance management approaches are required, depending on the results of the risk assessment for the various parts of the structure, lifting equipment and machinery. Reference should be made to BS 6548: Part 4: 1993 *Maintainability of equipment – guide to the planning of maintenance and maintenance support*. The approaches are set out below.

Breakdown maintenance

This involves rectification of faults or failures that require immediate remedial action because they present an immediate risk.

Planned preventive maintenance

This approach includes shutdowns for planned maintenance and major overhauls. It also includes replacing parts and making adjustments at pre-planned regular intervals so that the particular part or adjustment does not deteriorate or fail in the intervening period. The frequency of replacements and adjustments would be determined by the risk assessment and experience of breakdowns, or would be specified by the manufacturer. Under this system, faults and failures that have been reported but do not require immediate maintenance can be scheduled for inclusion in later planned preventive maintenance schemes.

Planned condition-based maintenance

This type of maintenance involves scheduling work on the basis of monitoring the condition of safety-critical parts so that wear or failure trends can be detected. The aim is to avoid hazards and carry out work before breakdowns occur. It should include long-term activities such as the repair or renewal of protective treatments.

Planned modifications

As a result of monitoring breakdowns and the frequency of planned preventive maintenance and the wear of items under condition-based planned maintenance, the structure, lifting equipment or machinery can be modified in order to improve reliability or to facilitate maintenance work. These planned modifications may also occur when it is necessary to upgrade the facility to suit different ships or to take advantage of technological improvements.

Periodic surveys

The regulations of classification societies provide for periodical surveys of facilities. Lloyd's Register of Shipping *Classification of linkspans – rules and regulations* sets out periodical survey requirements, including:

- annual surveys to maintain the linkspan "in class"

- docking or in-water surveys for buoyant linkspans carried out at least twice in a five-year period and at a maximum interval of three years

- an intermediate survey to be held two or three years after completion instead of the particular annual survey due at that time. Linkspans are also subjected to special surveys every five years in order to remain "in class". The special survey would include a complete survey of the machinery and electrical equipment. Any significant repairs to the structure, lifting equipment and machinery are to be carried out to the satisfaction of the surveyors.

Annual surveys involve checking that the linkspan is operating in the specified location, and that ships using the linkspan do not exceed the maximum displacement, berthing speed or approach angles specified in the current approval. It should be noted that Lloyd's Register of Shipping requires evidence that the specified limitations have been communicated to all the users of the installation. Details of the requirements of the various surveys are to be found in Lloyd's Register of Shipping *Classification of linkspans – rules and regulations*.

The questionnaire survey and consultation indicated that most maintenance work on ship-to-shore linkspans and walkways was carried out on a planned preventive maintenance basis.

5.2.2   Maintenance audit

In order to ensure that a planned preventive maintenance scheme can be properly prepared and that all the risks associated with the operation and maintenance of the facility can be assessed, it is important that a maintenance audit be carried out. The initial maintenance audit should be carried out during the procurement stage, and should involve the maintenance organisation. From the outset, reference should be made to BS 6548: Part 2: 1992 *Maintainability of equipment – guide to maintainability studies during the design phase*.

The initial maintenance audit at the procurement stage would usually involve a review of the port's brief and of the detailed drawings, the list of essential health and safety requirements, and the descriptions of the methods adopted to eliminate potential hazards. This will require interaction between the facility maintenance engineer and the suppliers. It will also involve a review of the draft maintenance instructional manuals. The maintenance audit would normally be carried out as part of the review by the project manager or purchaser's representative during the procurement process. However, it is important that the facility maintenance engineer has some involvement in the review because their understanding of the detailed requirements for maintenance is likely to result in the identification of improvements that can be made in the structure, lifting equipment and machinery being supplied.

A physical maintenance audit should be carried out, preferably at the commissioning stage, and subsequently if it is found that the planned preventive maintenance system or the fault reporting system involves excessive or unnecessary maintenance. An audit should also be instigated if it is found that maintenance work is difficult to carry out, so that access can be improved.

The physical maintenance audit of the facility involves a detailed inspection of the structure, lifting equipment and machinery and the provisions for maintenance. The audit also reviews the maintenance instructional manuals provided and the planned preventive maintenance system that has been set up. It highlights specific maintenance requirements, and identifies areas for improving ease of maintenance.

Figure 5.1 sets out a flow chart for the preparation of a maintenance system.

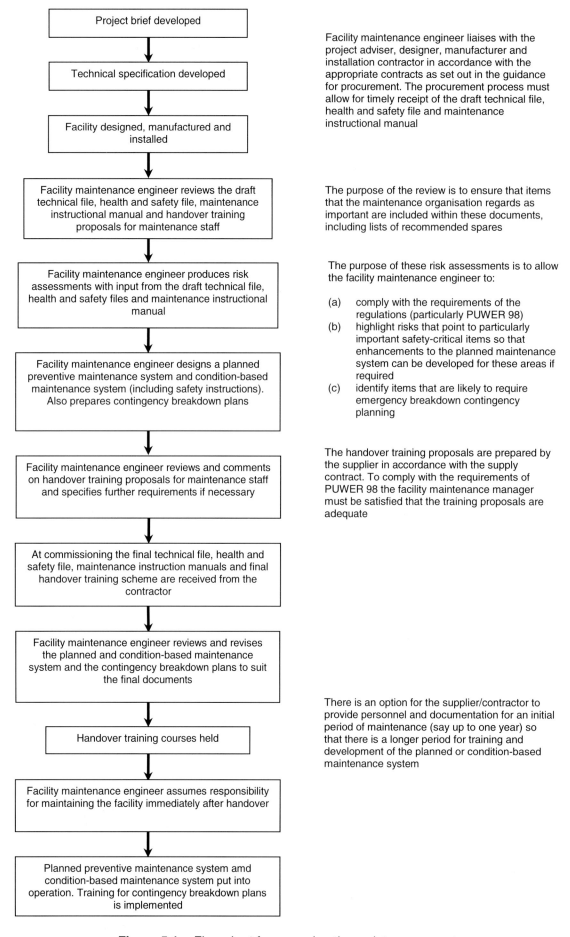

Project brief developed

Facility maintenance engineer liaises with the project adviser, designer, manufacturer and installation contractor in accordance with the appropriate contracts as set out in the guidance for procurement. The procurement process must allow for timely receipt of the draft technical file, health and safety file and maintenance instructional manual

Technical specification developed

Facility designed, manufactured and installed

Facility maintenance engineer reviews the draft technical file, health and safety file, maintenance instructional manual and handover training proposals for maintenance staff

The purpose of the review is to ensure that items that the maintenance organisation regards as important are included within these documents, including lists of recommended spares

Facility maintenance engineer produces risk assessments with input from the draft technical file, health and safety files and maintenance instructional manual

The purpose of these risk assessments is to allow the facility maintenance engineer to:

(a) comply with the requirements of the regulations (particularly PUWER 98)
(b) highlight risks that point to particularly important safety-critical items so that enhancements to the planned maintenance system can be developed for these areas if required
(c) identify items that are likely to require emergency breakdown contingency planning

Facility maintenance engineer designs a planned preventive maintenance system and condition-based maintenance system (including safety instructions). Also prepares contingency breakdown plans

Facility maintenance engineer reviews and comments on handover training proposals for maintenance staff and specifies further requirements if necessary

The handover training proposals are prepared by the supplier in accordance with the supply contract. To comply with the requirements of PUWER 98 the facility maintenance manager must be satisfied that the training proposals are adequate

At commissioning the final technical file, health and safety file, maintenance instruction manuals and final handover training scheme are received from the contractor

Facility maintenance engineer reviews and revises the planned and condition-based maintenance system and the contingency breakdown plans to suit the final documents

Handover training courses held

There is an option for the supplier/contractor to provide personnel and documentation for an initial period of maintenance (say up to one year) so that there is a longer period for training and development of the planned or condition-based maintenance system

Facility maintenance engineer assumes responsibility for maintaining the facility immediately after handover

Planned preventive maintenance system amd condition-based maintenance system put into operation. Training for contingency breakdown plans is implemented

Figure 5.1 *Flow chart for preparing the maintenance system*

The maintenance audit could be carried out either by the maintenance organisation's own staff or by another specialist organisation. The results of the maintenance audit should be used to improve the planned preventive maintenance scheme, to improve procedures for responding to breakdowns, and to monitor the performance of parts, particularly those that show rapid wear or frequent failure.

5.2.3 The ergonomic design of equipment

The questionnaire survey and consultation identified that the ease of maintenance of most facilities was unsatisfactory. Experience and observations also indicate that there is considerable room for improvement in the design of facilities to allow maintenance to be carried out safely. Minor changes at procurement and design stages can greatly improve the ease of maintenance. This can be achieved by better co-ordination between the purchaser, designer, supplier, operating organisation, maintenance organisation and the respective structural, mechanical and electrical engineers. The facility maintenance engineer should be involved in this co-ordination. The consultations with major ports and shipping lines operating several remote facilities confirmed that feedback from maintenance organisations to the supply of new facilities considerably improved the satisfaction of the maintenance organisations with the ease of maintenance.

The Supply of Machinery (Safety) Regulations and the supporting harmonised standards will lead to an improvement in the safety of maintenance work. Many new harmonised standards have been prepared, and these provide considerable guidance on the provision of maintenance access, space and hardware such as cranes and hoists.

5.2.4 Whole-life costs

Whole-life costs are concerned with the specification and design for reliability and maintainability of plant, machinery, equipment, buildings and structures; with their installation, commissioning, servicing requirements, repair, modification and replacement; and with feedback of information on design, performance and costs.

The effective management of whole-life costs depends on the ability to balance a number of procurement factors that are important for a particular facility, including the required life. It requires an understanding of management and accounting practice and a general knowledge of the engineering associated with the technological expertise appropriate to the port equipment industry.

More specifically, the application of whole-life costs brings together the whole or parts of various techniques and disciplines. These are shown in Figure 5.2.

The questionnaire survey revealed that poor communication between the purchaser and the supplier, particularly about the operational and maintenance requirements, is often responsible for subsequent operational and maintenance problems.

Only the owner, operator and maintenance organisation are able to specify the overall requirements, but the suppliers and manufacturers can and should have responsibility for much of the detail. Equipment suppliers make an important contribution to the efficiency of the equipment because they determine the reliability and fitness for purpose of the items that they supply. They have a particular responsibility to ensure that the purchaser takes delivery of equipment that meets these requirements, in terms of both technical parameters and predicted life-cycle costs.

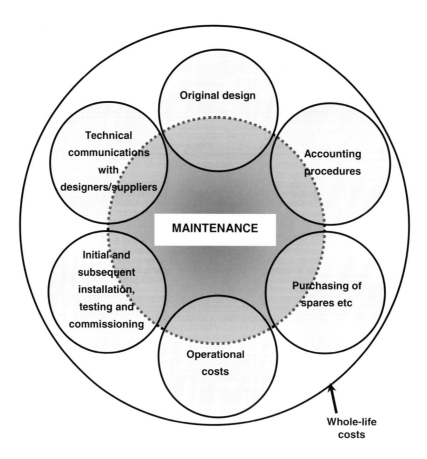

Figure 5.2 *The whole-life approach*

Closer relationships between the purchaser and the supplier are highly recommended and can result in:

- easier planning that has a better chance of success

- easier transition from specification to installation

- the programme being more readily met

- increased purchaser, operator and maintenance organisation effectiveness and greater chance of meeting market requirements.

The maintenance requirements are an important aspect of whole-life costs.

Understanding and collaboration between the various disciplines can reduce whole-life costs. An organisation can be considered a good-practice company when it consciously manages the cost of owning its linkspans and walkways. The concept of cost of ownership involves the appreciation of trade-offs between the capital, operational and maintenance costs. Specialist engineering advice may be required to implement a whole-life cost appraisal. However, only the port management can assess the commercial cost of unreliability.

The application of whole-life costs requires senior management to have a thorough understanding of each specialist's discipline and role in the project. This also means that specialists need to have a broad recognition of their own contribution and that of their colleagues in other disciplines. If senior management has to make decisions on the purchase of a new linkspan or walkway with little or no information of past performance and operating costs, this can lead to wasted resources, high costs, higher downtime and lost revenue.

The full whole-life cost cycle begins at the investment appraisal stage of procurement and ends with the demolition or disposal of linkspans and walkways, but the cycle can be entered at any point. For example, a company may decide to improve maintenance and reduce downtime on existing plant. In this case the trade-off between initial capital costs and subsequent costs cannot be taken into account, but the company's decision will still have a very real effect on the cost of ownership. The fact that whole-life costs cannot be applied from the beginning of the life-cycle of a piece of equipment should not deter a company from attempting to improve reliability, or to improve or reduce the cost of maintenance.

Whole-life checklist: before purchase

- Establish effective communication with the manufacturer or supplier.

- Carry out investment appraisal/audit – assessing trade-offs between initial costs and total life-cycle costs, with particular reference to cost of ownership.

- Use any experience from previous comparable situations in pre-purchase appraisal.

- Prepare a specification that includes reference to all matters likely to affect the cost of ownership.

- Assess the maintenance requirements: plan and ensure that appropriate maintenance resources will be available (organisation, staffing levels, skills required, supervision, management, use of specialists, in house/external sourcing of maintenance support, spares policy etc).

- Assess the facilities required for maintenance (normal or special access, tools and tackle, cranage, workshop, storage etc).

- Request adequate technical information from the manufacturer, and specify when this should be available.

- Assess the reliability of the products and the availability and cost of spares during the planned life-cycle of the equipment.

- Assess the possibility of using condition-monitoring techniques as an aid to maintenance.

- Assess the requirement for trained personnel.

Whole-life checklist: after purchase

- Assess the facilities required for maintenance (normal or special access, tools and tackle, cranage, workshop, storage etc).

- Ensure correct installation and commissioning – many problems later in the life of the facility can often be traced to poor or inadequate installation and commissioning.

- Ensure that any modifications at this stage are incorporated in the operating and maintenance manuals for the facility.

- Collect, evaluate and act upon cost and performance information.

- Ensure efficient and cost-effective maintenance.

- Collect information for feeding back to the designer and manufacturer in order to improve reliability in subsequent equipment for the same type of application.

The CIRIA publication R122, *Life cycle costing – a radical approach*, provides guidance on the implementation of a life-cycle costing scheme.

5.2.5   Equipment availability

Important aspects when considering equipment availability are:

- knowing what availability is required and taking action to achieve it
- knowing the financial costs or loss of revenue that are associated with downtime.

The questionnaire survey indicated that the availability of a ship-to-shore linkspan or walkway was critical to the port's operation and that reliable operation was essential. In a few installations a breakdown could be tolerated for up to 12 hours. Only in a port with multiple installations could a breakdown in excess of 12 hours be tolerated.

However, the only way to guarantee 100 per cent availability is to have a complete back-up plant on standby. This is not a practical approach in most ports. A balance must be struck between availability, maintenance costs and downtime costs.

Figure 5.3 demonstrates the relationship between these aspects. As the 100 per cent availability is achieved the downtime costs decrease and maintenance costs rise. Optimising equipment availability means knowing about these factors and understanding them at senior management level. The cost of maintenance will include the financing charges, or similar, associated with the value of spares and consumables held in stock. These may be notionally balanced against part of the costs attributed to loss of revenue or penalties incurred by extended downtime of the facility due to breakdown and the need to buy in or arrange delivery of spare/replacement parts.

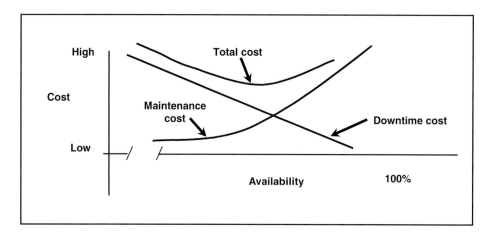

Figure 5.3   *The effect of availability on costs*

Historically, an excess stock of spares was carried to cover for any breakdown, and staff overtime was readily implemented or subcontractors were regularly used.

The survey indicated that generally the equipment was deemed to be fairly reliable, with frequency of failure being characterised as "rarely breaks down or negligible". Together with the other survey data, this indicates that the design, operation and maintenance standards being achieved are adequate, but that vigilance is required to ensure they are maintained. The breakdown faults recorded were fairly predictable, and to a certain extent are those already known within the industry. Appendix B presents the survey results and includes useful information on reliability and the extent of disruption caused by malfunctions. Table B8 indicates that electrical faults were commonest, but ship impacts appeared to cause the most disruption. Two of these faults are briefly discussed below, being examples where detailed attention is required to the design of system components to ensure a long service life.

Hydraulic hoses

Traditionally the hydraulics industry has suffered from a "dirty" image, generally prompted by the high fluid leakage rates associated with the systems. Hoses are a prime source of leakage. Leakage from some hoses could affect the structural integrity, and hence safety, of a system. Lately environmental pressures and market forces have necessitated improvements in the fluid hydraulic industry, resulting in, for example, the formation of the British Fluid Power Distributors Hose Shop Certification Scheme.

Regulations on design standards require:

- leak-free systems

- leak detection incorporated within hydraulic fluid systems

- hose assemblies selected (pressure rating/material construction) to provide a long service life

- hose assemblies cleaned and pressure-tested prior to use

- hose guarded to preclude damage to hose (and user also, should a hose burst)

- isolating valves on either side of the hose for ease of maintenance or replacement of the hose

- hose identification for maintenance records

- layout of fittings etc to predetermine formats to preclude excessive strain on hose.

The implementation of these measures should preclude hose failures.

Remote sensors/switches

Historically these have also been a source of malfunction, often caused by the arduous environment and marine atmosphere. Improvements in design, manufacturing, and application techniques have improved their working life.

Regulations and design standards may require, for a given application where safety is an important consideration, the provision of two sensors of differing technologies to satisfy the requirements, arising from the risk assessments. The provision of the sensors duplicating the sensing function can also assist with eliminating faults associated with remote sensors and switches. PLC controls can be programmed to identify the faults.

Experienced designers and operating organisations are aware of types of faults associated with hoses, remote sensors/switches and similar items, and are able to eliminate or minimise them at the procurement stage.

5.2.6   Periodic inspection and testing

The necessity for periodic inspection and testing throughout the operational life of a linkspan or walkway arises from the inevitable deterioration of any engineering system if it is not reviewed and maintained at suitable intervals. Engineering installations deteriorate because of factors such as wear, tear, corrosion, damage, excessive loading, ageing and environmental influences. Consequently there are requirements for periodic inspection and testing set out in and by:

- legislation and statutory regulations that require that various installations are periodically inspected and tested as an essential prerequisite to their being maintained in safe condition

- statutory authorities (such as the Health and Safety Executive), insurance companies and others that require periodic inspection and testing of parts of the installations.

Additionally, periodic inspection and testing is necessary:

- to verify continued compliance with design and construction standards
- on a change of use of the installation or its components
- to confirm the suitability of any alterations or additions to the original installation
- to identify and verify the acceptability of any significant change in the loading of the installation
- to identify and assess the implication of any damage that may have been caused to the installation

All installations should be regularly inspected and subjected to appropriate tests. In some cases there are statutory requirements for inspections at specified intervals (for certain items of lifting equipment, for example), but in others the designer, supplier or inspector should assess the period. Inspection periods initially recommended by designers should be continually reviewed in the light of operational and maintenance experience.

For safety, it is necessary to carry out a visual inspection of the installation before beginning any tests or interfering with equipment, removing protective covers etc. The visual inspection should verify that the safety of persons and property would not be endangered by subsequent testing activities.

It is essential to determine and plan all activities to suit the degree of operational disruption that will be acceptable before beginning inspection and testing.

The inspection should include a check on the condition of all structures, equipment and material with regard to the following:

- safety
- wear and tear
- corrosion
- damage
- excessive loading (overloading)
- age
- external influences
- suitability.

The assessment of the condition of all elements of the installation should take account of any known changes in environmental and operating conditions.

5.3 GOOD MAINTENANCE PRACTICE

5.3.1 General

This section outlines good maintenance practice based on information gleaned from the questionnaire survey and consultations. A simplified flow chart of the maintenance and repair process is set out in Figure 5.4.

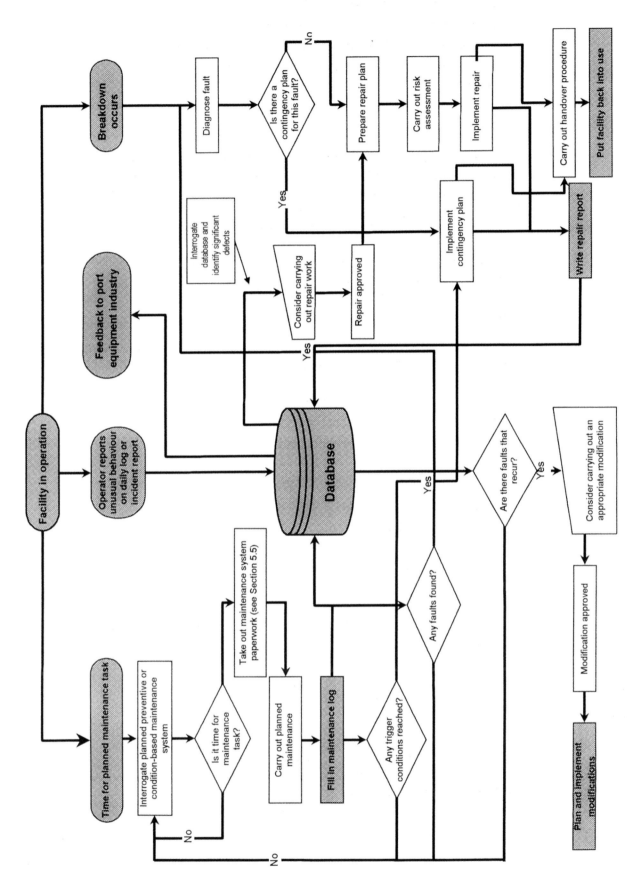

Figure 5.4 Flow chart for maintenance and repair process

5.3.2 Routine procedures

These procedures are intended to determine whether any part of the linkspan or walkway and its machinery and systems have any visible or obvious defect likely to affect the continued safe, reliable and efficient operation of the facility. The extent to which these procedures are applicable will depend on the frequency and level of planned preventive maintenance received by the facilities.

At the start of each shift or working day, the operator or other competent person should carry out routine procedures for the linkspan or walkway, which may include those below.

1. Visually examine the structure for damage or signs of distress and/or misuse.

2. Observe ropes, cylinders etc and their anchorages for obvious damage and wear.

3. Ensure, by visual inspection, that no electrical equipment is exposed to contamination by oil, grease, water or dirt.

4. Confirm that the oil level(s), coolant levels and lubrication are satisfactory.

5. Ensure that the linkspan or walkway is tidy and free from tins of grease and oil, rags, tools or materials other than those in purpose-made storage areas.

6. Drain any water from air or oil receivers.

7. Ensure that no maintenance or other personnel are on or in the immediate vicinity of linkspan or walkway or its plant rooms, access routes etc.

8. Ensure that the available operating pressures in any pneumatic and/or hydraulic system(s) are correct.

9. Operate the linkspan or walkway in all motions to confirm its satisfactory behaviour, paying particular attention to brakes and stop controls to ensure that these are working effectively.

10. Confirm, by running the linkspan or walkway to the limits of its range of travel in each motion, the operation of all limit switches or cut-outs and the dead man's handle or lever, using caution in making the checks in case of non-operation.

Should the operator or maintenance staff carrying out these procedures suspect any defect, abnormality or damage in the linkspan or walkway or in its operation they should report it immediately to their supervisor or manager or other person responsible for the safe use of the facility.

The linkspan or walkway may need to be taken out of service immediately until the faults have been corrected and the person responsible for safe operation has given clearance. Notices should be attached to the linkspan or walkway stating that it must not be used, and port control, shipping lines and operating organisations should be informed.

5.3.3 Planned maintenance

In order that linkspans and walkways may be operated safely and efficiently, it is essential that a maintenance plan is prepared so that the risk of accidents and stoppages due to breakdowns is reduced to a minimum.

> **The maintenance plan should ensure that the supplier's operating and maintenance instructional manuals are adhered to. These supplier's manuals should recommend that specific tasks are carried out at stated intervals, and these periods should in general not be exceeded.**

In addition to any statutory regulations, a record or log should be kept for all linkspans and walkways providing information on hours worked, adjustments carried out, renewal of parts, thorough examinations, maintenance work carried out and repairs made. Based on this record, the maintenance plan should be amended to provide a continuous and systematic method of ensuring efficient, reliable and safe operation. Reference should be made to BS 6548:Part 3:1992 *Maintainability of equipment. Guide to maintainability verification, and the collection, analysis and presentation of maintainability data.*

Any repairs or replacement components and consumable materials (such as lubricants) should be in accordance with the manufacturer's recommendations or specifications. To ensure that a linkspan or walkway can be maintained in an efficient and safe condition, consideration should be given to holding stocks of components and consumables.

Maintenance procedures should be carefully prepared to cover the entire facility. Many aspects of the installation are often "out of sight and out of mind", and are forgotten because they do not cause problems in the short term. The safe and efficient operation of structural bearings, restraints and similar relatively simple items requires adequate routine inspection and servicing (lubrication, wear adjustment etc) throughout their lifetime if failure is to be avoided.

5.3.4 Breakdown maintenance

Provision must be made for dealing with unexpected failures of equipment and the results of damage to the linkspan or walkway. The best and most thoroughly planned preventive maintenance regime cannot guarantee against breakdown. If the breakdown could be predicted, dealing with it would fall within the scope of planned maintenance. Breakdown maintenance deals with events that either were not foreseen or whose timing and nature were not predicted. Personnel involved are therefore dealing with the unexpected, often in circumstances far from ideal and at times that are not of their choosing. One purpose of risk analysis is to minimise the number of unexpected events.

There will often be considerable pressure to return a failed linkspan or walkway to service as soon as possible, and it is essential for the safety and overall efficiency of operation that the personnel involved are adequately prepared and supported to act properly in these circumstances.

Personnel who will be involved in dealing with breakdown maintenance must have:

- suitable experience and personal attributes to cope with the pressures and stresses that they will encounter

- adequate knowledge through education and training of principles and of the particular facility to enable them to diagnose causes of failures and to understand the implications of any proposed remedial actions

- adequate supervision and management

- adequate resources (labour, tools, equipment, parts, materials etc) to enable them to carry out effective and safe repairs

- co-operation from all other parties whose actions and attitudes might otherwise generate dangerous and unproductive levels of stress

- access to all relevant and useful information, particularly any diagnostic procedures recommended by the supplier of the linkspan or walkway in addition to all drawings, technical manuals and records

- immediate availability of all appropriate personal protective equipment, safe means of access and egress and safe places of work at all points to which access may be necessary.

The degree and scope of skills required to deal with breakdown maintenance are very different from the requirements for handling routine preventive maintenance. The specific training and background knowledge required for these two functions are quite distinct, and training and selection programmes for maintenance personnel must take this into account. Individuals may be employed to cover the needs of an organisation for either or both of these functions, but they should be recognised as separate areas of work and responsibility, in order to ensure adequate preparation for either function.

5.3.5 Safe systems of work

Before any repairs, adjustments or examinations are planned or effected on a linkspan or walkway, a safe system of work must be established and documented. Its primary purpose is to prevent the linkspan or walkway machinery from being moved or activated in such a manner as to prejudice the safety of the personnel carrying out the task and of other personnel who might be at risk.

Compliance with the employer's arrangements for safe working by all employees is a statutory obligation, and any breach should be treated as a serious disciplinary matter in all organisations.

Verbal instructions alone cannot ensure a safe system of work. A formal documented system must be devised and put into practice to ensure effective communication between all parties concerned, including operators, maintenance staff, vehicle drivers, ships' crews and contractors.

A widely applicable technique is the use of a documented permit-to-work system, which can be an effective way of achieving a safe system of working. A nominated person first isolates and locks off the electrical supply or other power sources, the means of access to unsafe areas, water, gas or pressurised fluid supplies etc. This person then issues a permit to work to the individual who is to undertake or supervise the work on that installation or in that area. On completion, this permit-to-work-holder signs that they have removed all personnel and tools etc, reinstated all systems, warned any person who is under their charge that it is no longer safe to work on that installation in that area, and successfully completed any relevant tests. On receipt of this declaration, the nominated person can restore the linkspan or walkway to service.

Permit-to-work systems should require recorded acknowledgement by operating personnel and management when installations are handed over to maintenance personnel or when work is to be carried out when the installation is in operation.

Essential components of a permit-to-work system require:

- that isolation is adequate for the work being undertaken
- that isolation remains secure while the permit to work is in force
- that the area of work and the work to be carried out are clearly printed on the permit
- that no work other than that specified is carried out
- that the safe working area is clearly defined
- that any special precautions necessary for the safe carrying out of the work, including access and clearing away on completion, are stated
- that the system should be monitored and integrated with all associated management systems
- that the schedule of shipping services is known to the maintenance team.

It is established practice to employ permit-to-work systems in connection with electrical work, work in confined spaces and other applications. It is vitally important that all permit-to-work systems operating in any given location be cross-referenced and interrelated, to avoid failures of communication that could prove to be dangerous.

5.3.6 Linkspans and walkways in remote locations

The arrangements for maintenance outlined in the preceding subsections are based on an assumption that the linkspan or walkway is located within a port that has an on-site management organisation to carry out the functions described. However, some linkspans and walkways serve small islands or are in remote locations and have no on-site management organisation. Facilities provided at such places need to be designed with simplicity of maintenance in mind. A planned condition-based approach should be adopted, and daily logs and maintenance reports should be forwarded to the appropriate management organisation or to a maintenance organisation. A competent engineer in the maintenance organisation should review the comments, notes and information on the daily logs and maintenance reports. If necessary, maintenance or repair tasks should be identified and included in periodic planned preventive maintenance visits to the remote location or, if urgent, included in emergency repair schemes.

At such locations availability of spare parts and consumable materials should be considered carefully. There will be a need to transport spare parts to the facility for every maintenance operation unless adequate local stocks of the necessary items are provided. Any such local stocks of replaceable parts etc should be checked and inspected as part of the routine maintenance procedures. Such items may include fuses, hydraulic hoses, lamps, filters and drive belts as appropriate.

5.3.7 Safe means of access

There are statutory requirements requiring that safe means of access be provided to enable inspections and maintenance work to be carried out.

It is essential that provision be made for means of escape in an emergency from any place at which any person will be working, no matter how infrequently or how briefly.

No person should be permitted to go onto a linkspan or walkway without the operator's knowledge and permission. Where the point of access is out of sight of the operator, special precautions need to be taken. Confined space procedures need to be followed where appropriate.

Personnel should be instructed to use only the proper means of access provided, and any breach should be regarded as a serious disciplinary matter. Persons who may be involved in rescue operations are often at greater peril than the victims of incidents.

Work descriptions for routine tasks should include descriptions of safe access and egress arrangements, which should be determined before any new facility is handed over, and be reviewed periodically thereafter. Unusual or infrequent activities should be subject to individual risk assessments, which will necessarily consider safe access and egress.

5.3.8 Feedback to the design process

Advances in efficiency and safety in the construction and operation of linkspans and walkways may be generated as a result of the designer's ability or by practical lessons learnt from experience of previous designs.

> **The value of designers' risk assessments is greatly enhanced, and their contribution to safe and efficient operation improved, by consideration of past incidents affecting other facilities that were not foreseen at the design stage.**

Excellent theoretical solutions are often rendered inappropriate by practical conditions. Simulation tests of the performance of materials and systems may be undertaken with great diligence but may still fail to reflect accurately the real environment.

It is of great value to the industry when operators and users of these facilities are prepared to disseminate information arising from their experiences. Positive feedback is useful. It is reassuring to designers and procurers of facilities to receive evidence of actually realised good performance. Information relating to failures or problems encountered, if made available and used in the right spirit, can make major contributions to raising levels of efficiency and safety. Appendix B should be studied by all those concerned with the design or operation of port facilities and equipment.

5.3.9   Procurement of maintenance staff

Guidance on the selection of designers and contractors is included in Section 3.5. The procurement of maintenance staff and contractors involves similar principles. Most organisations have their own recruitment procedures, which cover the engagement of in-house maintenance staff. These procedures should ensure that applicants pass a threshold of experience in the maintenance of appropriate lifting equipment and machinery, have appropriate technical training in the maintenance of similar facilities, can provide documentary evidence of this training, and are considered to be capable of undergoing any necessary additional specialist training to be able to maintain linkspans and walkways safely.

Some purchasers, owners, operating organisations and maintenance organisations may not be large enough to provide in-house maintenance support. Therefore they would need to consider the procurement of external maintenance contractors. Organisations would have to take advice on the preparation of a suitable specification covering the maintenance requirements for the linkspan or walkway, including details of any planned maintenance systems, a policy on spares, and reporting routes for the maintenance contractor. The specification should also define the extent of on-site presence required. For some facilities it may be necessary to have a full-time presence of staff from the maintenance contractor, whereas for others it may be sufficient to specify the frequency of periodic maintenance visits together with some arrangements for emergency call-out.

The organisation should ensure that the contractors submit details of their experience, their proposed maintenance personnel and managers, and details of the planned maintenance systems and emergency breakdown systems that they would adopt. The information requested should demonstrate the potential maintenance contractor's experience and competence. The procuring organisation should establish evaluation criteria and benchmarks for the selection of potential maintenance contractors.

Maintenance contractors are normally commissioned on a term contract basis. In order to provide sufficient incentive for the contractor to take a long-term interest in the proper maintenance of the facility it is recommended that the term contract run for a sufficient period – say three years – with an equitable mechanism for assessing the performance of the maintenance contractor and for extending or terminating the term contract.

5.4 TRAINING

5.4.1 General

Training for personnel with responsibility for the maintenance of linkspan and walkway facilities needs to address aspects and subjects including and beyond the scope of training necessary for operating personnel.

Commercial pressures have led to a reduction in the availability of in-house permanently staffed maintenance departments populated by traditional craftsmen, each specialising in one established branch of engineering skill. Training requirements for a safe and efficient maintenance operation must take account of the special demands of:

- the employment of long-term or short-term contract or agency personnel, whose level of skill and extent of particularly relevant experience may be widely variable

- the requirement for first-line maintenance personnel to be multi-skilled, with a broader range of trade skills and understanding than was required traditionally

- the safety-related aspects of much maintenance work, including adjustment and periodic examination, modification of control systems (short-term or long-term), repair and correct installation of spare parts.

The guidance given in Sections 4.2.2 and 4.2.3 regarding the capabilities, competence, training and authorisation of management, supervisory and operating personnel applies generally to maintenance staff. However, the considerations above relating to the breadth of responsibilities and technical knowledge and competence required lead to the conclusion that specifically prepared education programmes, training courses and capability assessments are vital for maintenance personnel.

Experience is a valuable attribute in maintenance personnel at all levels. Only the consistent employment of the same personnel over extended periods of time can develop a base of experience in a maintenance organisation. This valuable asset is lost immediately when staff depart, and it cannot be readily or quickly passed on.

> **This leads to a recommendation that, so far as is practicable, maintenance personnel should be retained on a long-term basis.**

5.4.2 Relevant experience

Education and general engineering training and appreciation of the application of sound principles are essential, but cannot replace the need for maintenance personnel to have experience and knowledge specific to the particular demands of linkspans and walkways. Within the team of personnel, supervisors and managers there needs to be sufficient shared knowledge of the characteristics of each installation and its usage to ensure that all maintenance work, particularly of breakdown outages or limited-duration planned outages where personnel are under pressure, is carried out efficiently and safely.

Maintenance personnel must have the experience, support and personal characteristics to enable them to resist and manage the considerable pressures that they have from operational management and others, particularly in the case of breakdowns.

Particularly careful assessment of the level of competence is necessary for contract or agency personnel who may be employed to maintain or repair linkspans or walkways. The owner or maintenance organisation must be aware of the limit of responsibility that it is appropriate to delegate to such personnel or to contract maintenance organisations.

5.4.3 Legislation

The legal obligations of persons involved with linkspans and walkways are discussed extensively in Chapter 2. Regulations such as the Docks Regulations and PUWER 98 place responsibilities on employers to ensure the safe maintenance of these facilities, and the appropriate approved codes of practice should be read and their requirements and recommendations implemented.

5.4.4 Particular needs of craftsmen

It is recommended that a suitable, authoritative, established and widely recognised system (for example the Engineering Industrial Training Board system) **of training be adopted for persons being trained for the maintenance of linkspans and walkways.** It must be recognised that skills embracing structural, mechanical, hydraulic, electrical and electronic engineering might be needed. Educational and practical training schemes based on a variable modular structure, such as the National Vocational Qualification (NVQ) schemes, would seem to lend themselves ideally to these needs. These would need to be augmented by appropriate classroom and on-the-job training in the needs of particular specialist skills.

5.4.5 Inspectors and engineer surveyors

A formal training and education programme for engineering inspectors and engineer surveyors is essential. **It is recommended that they be trained as a minimum to the academic standard for technician engineers.** The accredited Business and Technician Education Council (BTEC) and Scottish Vocational Educational Council (SCOTVEC) Higher National Certificate or any other qualifications judged to be of equivalent standard may be suitable. Inspectors and surveyors will also need to have knowledge of current ship-to-shore linkspan and walkway technology. Notwithstanding the above recommendations, it is acknowledged that there are many established engineers who are well trained and experienced in ship-to-shore linkspans and walkways technology but who do not hold formal qualifications. Classification societies and other organisations use the terms *inspector* and *surveyor* with a more precise application than in general parlance; an inspector would be expected to be qualified to the level of at least a technician engineer, and a surveyor would be a chartered engineer or equivalent.

It is recommended that the training should take the form of a quality assured modular programme covering all skills and knowledge of a competent engineer surveyor or inspector. The programmes may be varied and dependent upon the previous background and experience of the trainee.

5.4.6 Supervisory and management personnel

Chapter 4 discusses the general requirements of supervisors and management personnel.

Specific maintenance and engineering responsibilities will require consideration beyond that necessary for operational, commercial and other management staff.

It is recommended that every linkspan and walkway should be within the responsibility of an engineer with the appropriate level of engineering education, technical appreciation and experience relating to port equipment and operations with particular reference to linkspan and walkway facilities.

5.4.7   Assistance with provision of training

Some organisations are able to meet their overall training needs using in-house resources, others can meet them in part and numerous organisations cannot support any substantial permanent training function. Additionally, there are commercial agencies that offer various levels and types of training.

When using outside agencies to train personnel for work with specific installations it should be ensured that the training given is not limited to generalities. Background knowledge and understanding are necessary, but it is vital for personnel to be trained and be able to demonstrate their competence on the actual installations they work with.

5.5   DOCUMENTATION

5.5.1   General

The supplier of the machinery is required to provide instructions covering the following:

- safe assembly and dismantling
- safe adjustment
- safe maintenance, including servicing and repair
- details of any specialist tools that may be required to maintain the machinery
- emergency procedures
- diagnostic aids including, for example, diagrams showing condition of control system input/output status indicators for each operating and fault condition
- details of periodic inspection requirements
- any instructions required by the Supply of Machinery (Safety) Regulations.

The instructions are likely to be required to include drawings and diagrams showing the parts of the machinery and details of any maintenance, inspection or repair procedures for the particular parts of the machinery. The maintenance instructional manuals need to be written in language that covers the essential health and safety requirements but takes into account the general education and knowledge of the maintenance personnel.

Figure 5.5 illustrates a possible set of documents for this purpose.

5.5.2   Maintenance manuals

The maintenance manuals should include information from the health and safety file prepared under the CDM Regulations. These detail the maintenance facilities and equipment, maintenance procedures and requirements for the structure, and manuals produced by specialist contractors and suppliers giving maintenance procedures and schedules for plant and equipment that are installed as part of the structure. There will be considerable overlap between the manuals provided with the health and safety file and the instructions for the machinery provided with the technical file.

Maintenance manuals should be prepared by a specialist company experienced in their preparation. The company should liaise with the systems engineer as defined in Chapter 3 and with the relevant subcontractors, suppliers and commissioning personnel.

Maintenance manuals are to be provided in accordance with BS 4884 *Technical manuals*. BS 4884 is designed for the authors of manuals, and covers basic principles. The project brief should refer to the content, quality and presentation required.

BS 4884 is published in three parts as follows:

Part 1   *Specification for presentation of essential health and safety requirements*

Part 2   *Guide to content*

Part 3   *Guide to presentation.*

BS 4899 *User's requirements for technical manuals* also provides some additional information, and is published in two parts:

Part 1   *Content*

Part 2   *Presentation.*

Maintenance manuals should be provided for every item of lifting equipment and machinery. For facilities in the UK the manuals should be in the English language.

The questionnaire survey indicated that all facilities were provided with operating and maintenance manuals. However, the quality of the contents and presentation of these manuals varied considerably. The survey and experience generally show that the contents and presentation of both operating and maintenance manuals for ship-to-shore linkspans and walkways require improvement.

> **Procurement procedures should provide for a price to be stated for providing this documentation. This will provide some measure of the quality envisaged by the contractor. It is essential that manuals are of a high quality with properly co-ordinated typed pages and identified extracts from other technical documents such as catalogues.**

The maintenance manual for a facility should be prepared specifically for that facility. Maintenance manuals should be produced using word processing or desktop publishing software and be provided in electronic as well as printed format. Preparation of the maintenance manual should start at the outset of the supply of the lifting equipment and machinery in order to enable the documents to take account of the development of the design and so that they are completed by the time that commissioning takes place.

> **A draft copy of the manual should be provided to the project manager and facility maintenance engineer or purchaser's representative in order that it can be reviewed.**

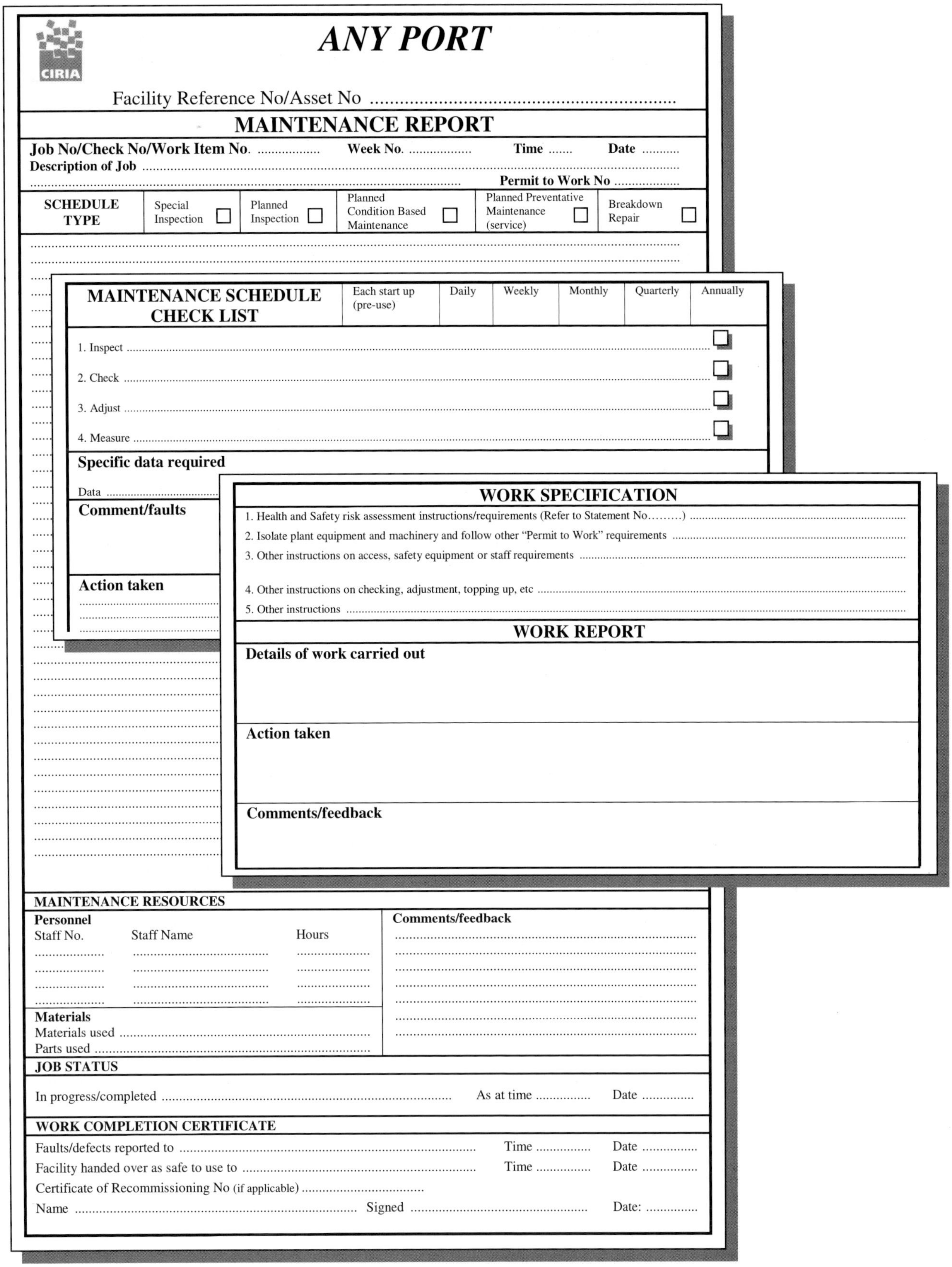

ANY PORT

Facility Reference No/Asset No ....

MAINTENANCE REPORT

Job No/Check No/Work Item No. .... **Week No**. .... **Time** .... **Date** ....
Description of Job ....
.... **Permit to Work No** ....

SCHEDULE TYPE	Special Inspection ☐	Planned Inspection ☐	Planned Condition Based Maintenance ☐	Planned Preventative Maintenance (service) ☐	Breakdown Repair ☐

....

MAINTENANCE SCHEDULE CHECK LIST

	Each start up (pre-use)	Daily	Weekly	Monthly	Quarterly	Annually
1. Inspect						☐
2. Check						☐
3. Adjust						☐
4. Measure						☐

Specific data required

Data ....

Comment/faults

Action taken

WORK SPECIFICATION

1. Health and Safety risk assessment instructions/requirements (Refer to Statement No.........) ....
2. Isolate plant equipment and machinery and follow other "Permit to Work" requirements ....
3. Other instructions on access, safety equipment or staff requirements ....
4. Other instructions on checking, adjustment, topping up, etc ....
5. Other instructions ....

WORK REPORT

Details of work carried out

Action taken

Comments/feedback

MAINTENANCE RESOURCES

Personnel

Staff No.	Staff Name	Hours
....	....	....
....	....	....
....	....	....

Comments/feedback
....
....
....
....
....
....

Materials
Materials used ....
Parts used ....

JOB STATUS

In progress/completed .... As at time .... Date ....

WORK COMPLETION CERTIFICATE

Faults/defects reported to .... Time .... Date ....
Facility handed over as safe to use to .... Time .... Date ....
Certificate of Recommissioning No (if applicable) ....
Name .... Signed .... Date: ....

Figure 5.5 *Maintenance documentation*

Maintenance manuals should incorporate the following:

- index
- general introduction
- safety aspects
- design parameters
- description of each new item of equipment or machinery
- description of controls
- description of operation of hydraulic systems, PLC LED indicating lamps etc
- mechanical maintenance requirements
- hydraulic maintenance requirements
- electrical maintenance requirements
- structural maintenance requirements
- replacement and repair procedures particularly for lifting cylinder, hydraulic pump and motor removal or replacement
- for every component, an ordering specification so that spare parts can be obtained either from the original supplier or from alternative suppliers. The original manufacturer's reference number (invoice number or purchase number) should be provided to assist in future ordering
- drawing list
- list of key parts with types and reference numbers
- list of recommended spares.

5.5.3 Maintenance schedules

The planned preventive maintenance system should involve the preparation of individual maintenance schedules for each facility at specified time intervals. The maintenance schedules may well be produced to cover daily, weekly, monthly, quarterly and annual schedules of maintenance activities. These maintenance schedules should consist of a checklist of items to be attended to, together with a maintenance work specification for each of the items.

A maintenance report should be included either as part of the maintenance schedule or as an attachment to the schedule. The maintenance report would cover the requirements for risk assessment and a statement of the measures taken to minimise or eliminate risks. The report would also provide for details of the work carried out and any materials or parts that are used or replaced. There would also be space on the report for comments to be made about the items on the checklist. For example, the comment could require an intermediate inspection of an item that did not require immediate maintenance but was showing signs of requiring future maintenance.

The maintenance report and schedule would be used to form the maintenance log for the individual facility. Ship-to-shore linkspans and walkways are complex items of machinery, and the maintenance log should preferably be entered onto a database so that the maintenance history of individual items can be analysed and their costs monitored. Historical records are extremely useful in updating the planned preventive maintenance system and in identifying items of lifting equipment and machinery that may require upgrading or replacement.

Figure 5.5 illustrates a possible set of documents for this purpose.

5.5.4 Work permits and recommissioning certificates

In order to carry out maintenance work the facility will have to be taken out of service. It is important that the maintenance management system provides for liaison between the maintenance organisation and the operating organisation so that a formal procedure is in place for ensuring that the operating organisation does not attempt to use the facility while it is under repair. This formal procedure should preferably be supported by permits to work, as described in Section 5.3.5.

Where repairs, replacements or modifications to the lifting equipment and machinery are required, or where the facility may need to be retested and recommissioned before the facility is handed back to the operating organisation for use, a certificate of recommissioning should be issued. A procedure should be developed so that the facility can be formally handed back to the operating organisation in a safe-to-use condition.

5.5.5 Notices to mariners

The maintenance organisation should liaise with the harbour master when it envisages making any major modifications that are likely to affect the availability of the facility. In situations where maintenance work, repair or modification require the facility to be taken out of commission for some time it may be necessary to issue a Notice to Mariners so that ships using the berth are aware of any restrictions on approaching the facility. This is particularly important where the facility previously provided energy-absorbing fendering for the berthing of the ship. In these circumstances the berthing and unberthing of ships may require tug assistance, particularly in windy conditions. Notices to Mariners are normally prepared by the harbour master.

5.6 TESTING AND RECOMMISSIONING

Any maintenance or repair activity has the potential to alter the linkspan or walkway in such a way that it no longer behaves as it did when originally tested, commissioned and put into service. Such changes to the characteristics of the installation may be deliberately arranged or may be the unintended result of damage, errors or lack of appreciation in the maintenance or repair work carried out.

Hence it is essential for the maintenance of efficient and safe operation that appropriate testing and recommissioning procedures are carried out following any interference or disruption to the walkway or linkspan or any of its components, associated machinery or lifting equipment.

The extent of testing and recommissioning required to be carried out after routine maintenance or minor repair tasks should be decided within the maintenance management regime. The requirements should be incorporated in the specific work instruction issued to personnel who will carry out the work.

Competent and experienced engineering managers and supervisors should determine the extent and type of tests that are reasonably practicable in each case. Care must be taken to identify any consequential effects of the tests on other sections of the facility beyond those obviously involved in the work.

It is important to retest to discover any latent faults or secondary defects existing, but not seen, before carrying out the work, or that were caused by carrying out the work. For example, if a controlling programmable logic controller relied upon an internal battery to maintain its program memory while the control system was isolated from the mains for replacement of a faulty component, and that battery had severely deteriorated, problems could arise on re-energising the system. The controlling program may have been lost or badly corrupted, or corrupted in a subtle and limited manner. Each of these possibilities contains its own dangers and problems if not identified, and each would be identifiable by sufficiently rigorous testing before returning the facility to service.

Overloading of the linkspan, walkway or its lifting equipment due to accident or misuse might damage several component parts, though obvious failure might be limited to just one part. Rectification of the obviously damaged part must be followed by thorough examination, testing and recommissioning of the whole to unearth any problems.

Consideration must be given to repeat testing carried out periodically during installation of the facility to ensure its continued efficiency and safety in use regardless of whether any damage, repair or alteration is known to have occurred. Such testing would seek to discover whether any latent defect or gradual and hidden deterioration processes were taking effect without signs being evident.

Engineering plant and installations generally will deteriorate if they are out of use for any significant length of time. Extensive mothballing procedures may be implemented, but these will not entirely negate the ravages of time and environment. Any linkspan or walkway that is not in regular use, or which is taken out of service for a long period, must be assessed by competent engineering personnel to identify any remedial work necessary before it is put back into service. Appropriate testing and recommissioning procedures must be specified and carried out. The results of all tests and trials should be recorded together with details of the nature of the testing procedures employed.

Personnel and techniques employed in testing and commissioning at any stage in the life of a linkspan or walkway need to be chosen with great care. The purpose and nature of these activities is such that dangers are greater than in the normal operation of the facility. It should be anticipated that something could go wrong during testing and commissioning, and all possible precautions should be taken to minimise danger. This has implications for:

- choice of personnel – abilities, training, competence
- provision of supervision – level and competence
- provision of safety facilities – additional personnel, rescue facilities, equipment etc
- control of environment – limiting access, working conditions etc
- provision of safe specialist test equipment
- quality of risk assessment and task arrangement.

5.7   RECOMMENDATIONS

The questionnaire survey and consultations show that the majority of facilities for which responses were received have satisfactory maintenance schemes that are consistent with the following recommendations.

1. Every maintenance organisation should be familiar with the relevant regulations.

2. A routine maintenance inspection system should be set up to ensure that the safety-critical items on the facility are periodically checked. The routine maintenance inspection could consist of a daily inspection by the operator and completion of the daily log together with a weekly (or other appropriate interval) routine maintenance inspection by maintenance personnel.

3. A planned maintenance system should be set up that identifies planned preventive maintenance items, planned condition-based maintenance items, and procedures for dealing with emergency breakdowns. The planned maintenance system should include maintenance schedules covering each item and each interval of maintenance inspection, work specifications for the maintenance of the various items, and a maintenance report.

4. In order to ensure the safety of operators, maintenance personnel and the general public, and the safe reinstatement into use of the facility, a permit-to-work system should be introduced.

5. Maintenance organisations should introduce a training system for maintenance personnel, supervisors and managers. The training system should ensure that adequate training is provided in the various specialist areas required, and that training records are kept such that each individual's competence can be readily assessed so that the individual can be authorised to carry out maintenance work for which the person is properly trained.

6. Provision for safe access and egress to all areas of the facility requiring maintenance should be provided.

7. Following major damage, repair, replacement, modification or lack of use, the lifting equipment and machinery should be thoroughly examined, appropriately tested and subjected to a recommissioning procedure determined by a competent person.

8. Information concerning repetitive faults, defects or failures of structures, lifting equipment and machinery should be recorded by the maintenance organisation and used to determine whether improvements or replacements are required. Significant problems should be reported on an industry-wide basis to other maintenance organisations, designers and suppliers.

9. The extent of testing and recommissioning required to be carried out after routine maintenance or minor repair tasks should be decided within the maintenance management regime.

A   The research process

A1   INTRODUCTION

The objectives of the research were:

*   to obtain information on incidents and experiences related to the procurement, operation and maintenance of ship-to-shore linkspans and walkways

*   to interpret the information for use in the production of the guidance.

The CIRIA project steering group specifically wanted to ensure that the research took into account the opinions of as many practitioners in the industry as possible. Information was therefore sought by means of a questionnaire.

The research project was carried out in six stages.

1. An extensive list of potential consultees was drawn up.

2. An initial questionnaire was issued to establish interest in the project and in the ability of the consultee to provide useful data.

3. Detailed questionnaires were then issued.

4. A series of interviews was held with four UK-based port operators and one ferry operator to present the information that had been gathered (subject to confidentiality) and to obtain opinions about the preliminary conclusions in the report.

5. Certain individuals were consulted in order to verify particular information presented in the questionnaire survey.

6. The conclusions of the research were presented at a workshop, arranged by CIRIA in London, which was attended by invited specialists.

A2   SELECTION OF CONSULTEES

The specification of the research contract demanded that consultations be carried out with all willing ports and with organisations in the ports industry including the relevant designers, manufacturers, insurers and statutory bodies with responsibility for regulating this sector of industry. Although UK interests funded the project, the steering group also wished other European ports to be consulted. It was known that some of those ports had experienced accidents or incidents, and it was believed that information about these accidents and incidents would increase the quality of the research.

A list of 281 consultees was produced using contacts in the industry and standard reference directories. Northwest European ferry routes were identified so that suitable Continental or Irish ports could be selected for inclusion in the survey. Consultees were classified according to Table A1.

The total exceeds the total number of 281 consultees already quoted, because some organisations belong to more than one category.

Table A1 *Numbers of consultees*

Type of consultee	Number of consultees
UK port owners	72
Non-UK port owners	32
Facility operators	5
Facility owners	2
Ship owners	21
Designers	32
Manufacturers	53
Insurers	24
Classification societies/inspection organisations	5
Contractors/installers	12
Trade associations	28
Statutory authorities	12
Others	6

A3 THE INITIAL QUESTIONNAIRE

The information gathered by the initial questionnaire was:

- the name and address of the organisation

- the type of organisation (whether a port owner, manufacturer etc)

- the name of a suitable contact person for the consultation process

- the name of each port and of each facility of which the consultee had knowledge

- the type of knowledge that the consultee could offer.

The consultees were asked to return the questionnaires in January 1998. Of the 281 initial questionnaires issued, 130 (46 per cent) were returned completed, which identified 293 linkspans and 99 walkways. The geographical distribution of the facilities identified is shown in Figures A1 and A2. The information provided was entered into a database. This database enabled recipients of the detailed questionnaires to be identified.

A4 THE DETAILED QUESTIONNAIRE

The first two sections of the questionnaire asked questions about the organisation being consulted, and the remaining sections asked questions about the facilities themselves.

The first group of sections was as follows:

G1 General

G2 Maintenance records

The following sections concerned each linkspan and walkway.

1. General data on individual linkspans

2. Procurement

3. Design and technical information

4. Electrical engineering and control system design

5. Operational matters and mechanical problems

6. Maintenance

7. Regulations and standards

8. Reports on accidents/incidents.

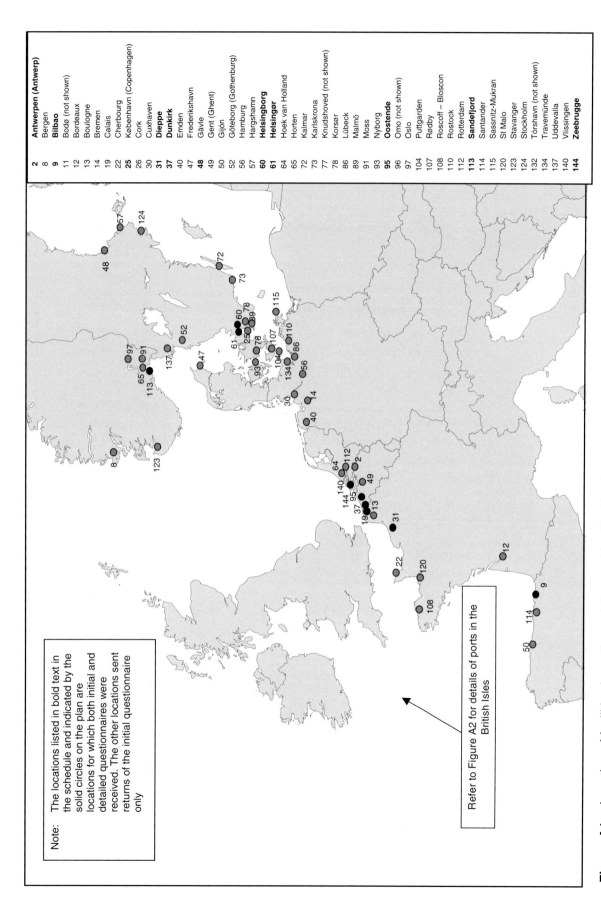

2	**Antwerpen (Antwerp)**
8	Bergen
9	**Bilbao**
11	Bodø (not shown)
12	Bordeaux
13	Boulogne
14	Bremen
19	Calais
22	Cherbourg
25	København (Copenhagen)
26	Cork
30	Cuxhaven
31	**Dieppe**
37	**Dunkirk**
40	Emden
47	Frederikshavn
48	**Gävle**
49	Gent (Ghent)
50	Gijón
52	Göteborg (Gothenburg)
56	Hamburg
57	Hargshamn
60	**Helsingborg**
61	**Helsingør**
64	Hoek van Holland
65	Horten
72	Kalmar
73	Karlskrona
77	Knudshoved (not shown)
78	Korsør
86	Lübeck
89	Malmö
91	Moss
93	Nyborg
95	**Oostende**
96	Omo (not shown)
97	Oslo
104	Puttgarden
107	Rødby
108	Roscoff – Bloscon
110	Rostock
112	Rotterdam
113	**Sandefjord**
114	Santander
115	Sassnitz-Mukran
120	St Malo
123	Stavanger
124	Stockholm
132	Tórshavn (not shown)
134	Travemünde
137	Uddevalla
140	Vlissingen
144	**Zeebrugge**

Note: The locations listed in bold text in the schedule and indicated by the solid circles on the plan are locations for which both initial and detailed questionnaires were received. The other locations sent returns of the initial questionnaire only

Refer to Figure A2 for details of ports in the British Isles

Figure A1 *Location of facilities in north-west Europe identified by the questionnaires*

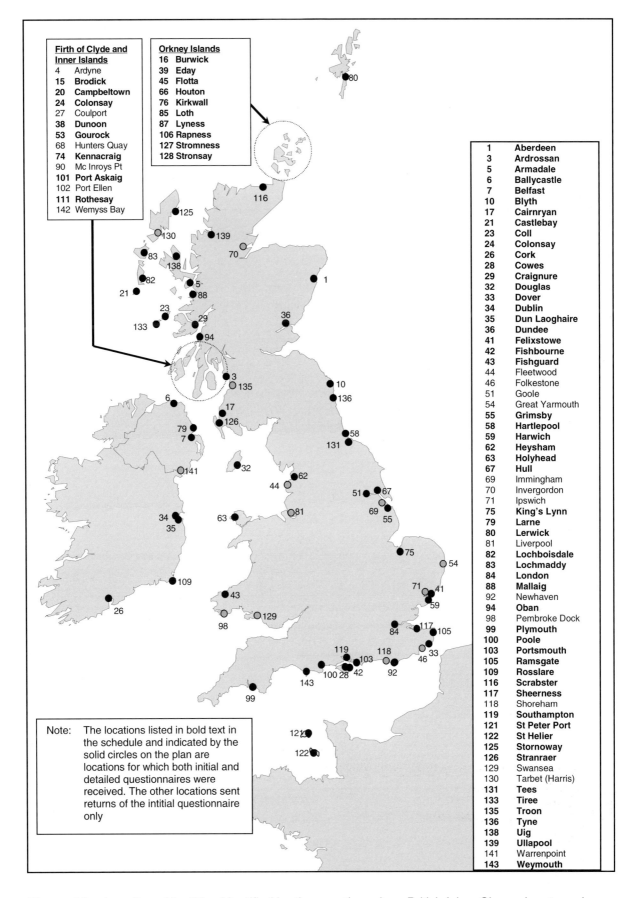

Firth of Clyde and Inner Islands
4   Ardyne
15   Brodick
20   Campbeltown
24   Colonsay
27   Coulport
38   Dunoon
53   Gourock
68   Hunters Quay
74   Kennacraig
90   Mc Inroys Pt
101   Port Askaig
102   Port Ellen
111   Rothesay
142   Wemyss Bay

Orkney Islands
16   Burwick
39   Eday
45   Flotta
66   Houton
76   Kirkwall
85   Loth
87   Lyness
106   Rapness
127   Stromness
128   Stronsay

1	Aberdeen
3	Ardrossan
5	Armadale
6	Ballycastle
7	Belfast
10	Blyth
17	Cairnryan
21	Castlebay
23	Coll
24	Colonsay
26	Cork
28	Cowes
29	Craignure
32	Douglas
33	Dover
34	Dublin
35	Dun Laoghaire
36	Dundee
41	Felixstowe
42	Fishbourne
43	Fishguard
44	Fleetwood
46	Folkestone
51	Goole
54	Great Yarmouth
55	Grimsby
58	Hartlepool
59	Harwich
62	Heysham
63	Holyhead
67	Hull
69	Immingham
70	Invergordon
71	Ipswich
75	King's Lynn
79	Larne
80	Lerwick
81	Liverpool
82	Lochboisdale
83	Lochmaddy
84	London
88	Mallaig
92	Newhaven
94	Oban
98	Pembroke Dock
99	Plymouth
100	Poole
103	Portsmouth
105	Ramsgate
109	Rosslare
116	Scrabster
117	Sheerness
118	Shoreham
119	Southampton
121	St Peter Port
122	St Helier
125	Stornoway
126	Stranraer
129	Swansea
130	Tarbet (Harris)
131	Tees
133	Tiree
135	Troon
136	Tyne
138	Uig
139	Ullapool
141	Warrenpoint
143	Weymouth

Note: The locations listed in bold text in the schedule and indicated by the solid circles on the plan are locations for which both initial and detailed questionnaires were received. The other locations sent returns of the intitial questionnaire only

Figure A2   *Location of facilities identified by the questionnaires: British Isles, Channel ports and Ireland*

It was recognised that the consultees might find it difficult to release information about accidents, incidents and certain internal management procedures because of the sensitive issues involved. Furthermore, many items of information required by the survey might be of commercial interest to competitors.

The research team therefore gave a confidentiality undertaking that was additional to the research contract condition on confidentiality. Each form had a tick box asking the consultee to state whether the information included in the relevant section of the questionnaire was confidential. The detailed responses to the questionnaire cannot be published or made available to other parties. However, it was thought right to allow an independent check on the work of the research team. Therefore the confidentiality undertaking stated that the details of the database would be shown, if required, to the chairman of the CIRIA project steering group for this research project, Professor J C Chapman, who is a well-respected independent consulting engineer and academic.

Consultees were sent those questionnaires that corresponded to the areas of knowledge that recipients of the initial questionnaire had identified. Some 2800 questionnaire sections were issued to the consultees during February 1998. The distribution system for the questionnaires is shown in Figure A3.

Of the 293 linkspans and 99 walkways for which detailed questionnaires were issued, information was returned for 142 linkspans and 40 walkways, a return of 48 per cent and 40 per cent respectively. The geographical distribution of the facilities for which information was returned is shown in Figures A1 and A2.

A5   THE ANALYSIS OF THE DATA

Lists of all the tick-box answers and a series of database reports of the written text included in the responses were produced.

The database was then interrogated to produce the information in Chapter 1 and Appendix B.

For certain of the database queries there was a difference between the answers given by different consultees. In most cases the responses submitted by port owners were given precedence over those received from other consultees.

A6   INTERVIEWS

A6.1   With port and ferry operators

Interviews were held with the owners of four major ro-ro ports in the UK and with a major operator of ferries to many small ports in Scotland.

Dover	major port with many ro-ro ramps that are rope lifted
Portsmouth	major port with several floating linkspans
Larne	major port with several hydraulically lifted facilities, one of which uses tandem cylinders
Felixstowe	major port specialising in freight-only movements and operating ramps with single hydraulic cylinder supports
Caledonian MacBrayne	ship owner operating many small ferry ports in remote locations with no on-site workshop facilities.

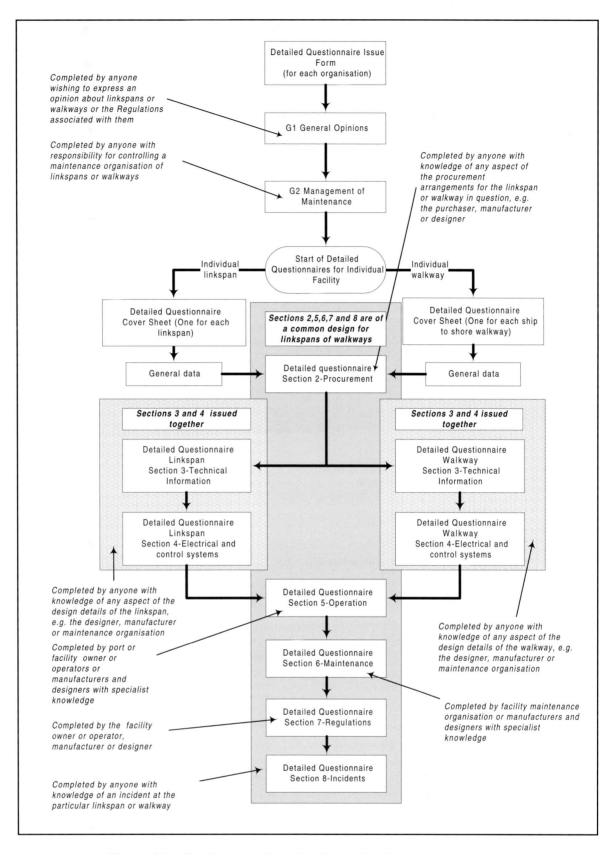

Figure A3   *Detailed questionnaire distribution diagram*

The interviewees were sent early drafts of sections of the report and several graphs and charts indicating output from the database. They were asked to provide samples of operating and maintenance records and incident report sheets.

Two of the ports were asked to consider the reasons why they more than others appeared to have achieved a relatively high level of satisfaction with their facilities.

These consultation processes included the following:

- a face-to-face discussion on the preliminary conclusions of the research contractor
- a more detailed explanation of certain incidents that were known to the consultees
- a discussion in detail of the consultee's own operation and maintenance procedures
- a discussion of the procurement process proposed in the guide.

The interviews enabled differing views to be expressed, and made possible a full discussion of the results of the survey.

All interviewees had efficient procedures and documentation for operation, maintenance and the reporting of incidents. They all had well-structured training schemes.

The experience of Caledonian MacBrayne showed the benefits of simple design, operation and maintenance of the equipment in circumstances where they needed to operate their facilities using local personnel. Such personnel had limited previous engineering experience, and were enabled to carry out their duties by means of a simple induction training process.

A6.2   With others

Face-to-face interviews and telephone consultations have taken place with the following organisations:

- Health and Safety Executive
- Ports' Safety Organisation
- Lloyd's Register of Shipping.

Consultations with the first two were to ensure that there was a consensus between the Health and Safety Executive and the ports industry on interpretation of the regulations with reference to linkspans and walkways.

It is important that the Health and Safety Executive agree with and endorse the guidance given in this document. The consultations were concerned with Chapters 2 and 3, but some issues in connection with Chapters 4 and 5 were also dealt with.

The consultation with Lloyd's Register of Shipping was to ensure that the option of carrying out verification through the route of classification was correctly described. It was also important to highlight the existence of the new *Rules for the classification of linkspans* and how they should be used in the overall process of design and verification. As a specialist organisation with extensive experience of the verification process for linkspans and walkways, it was also able to give much general information.

A7 WORKSHOP

A workshop was held in London on 26 June 1998, attended by about 50 invited specialists and members of the industry. The workshop consisted of three presentations of the research findings and conclusions, and syndicate meetings to discuss and answer a number of questions concerning:

- preparing the brief and specification
- selecting the team and assessment of competence
- ensuring supply, installation, operation and maintenance to specification
- systems, competence and training to ensure safe and efficient operation
- maintenance planning, record-keeping, training and feedback
- contingency planning, post-incident inspections and reporting.

The syndicate meetings were followed by plenary sessions to report and review the conclusions of the syndicates. The workshop confirmed a clear consensus within the industry on some important and potentially contentious issues.

B   Questionnaire survey results

B1   GENERAL

The purpose of this appendix is to present some of the detailed information found in the questionnaire survey. It amplifies the information given in Chapter 1 of the Guide.

This appendix is laid out in the same sequence as Chapter 1. Figures in parenthesis in headings cross-refer to the sections of the report for which the information is relevant.

B2   SHIP-TO-SHORE LINKSPANS

B2.1   Types of structure (1.2.1)

Table B1 and Figures B1 and B2 indicate the numbers of each type of structure that were identified.

Table B1   *Types of linkspan from the questionnaire survey*

Type of linkspan and shore ramp	Number of examples	Percentage of sample
Floating types		
Pontoon	27	20
Integral tank	5	4
Semi-submersible	16	12
Lifted types		
Rope-winch	28	21
Hydraulic cylinders	57	43
Rack and pinion	1	1
Scissor-lift	0	0
Supported by another structure (typically the upper deck of double deck)	15	11
Supported by a ship (usually additional support)	18	13

Note that lifted structures may be supported by another structure, and that floating types may be supported by a ship, hence the total of the percentages is more than 100.

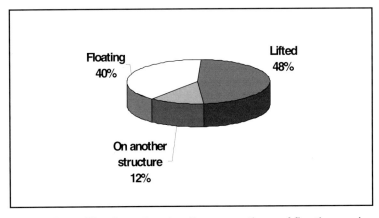

Figure B1   *Pie chart showing the proportions of floating and non-floating linkspans (from the questionnaire survey)*

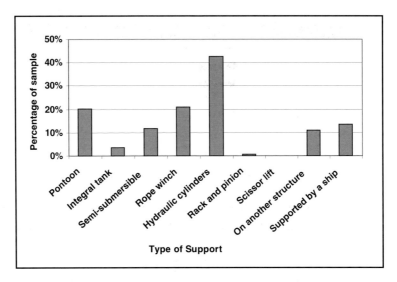

Figure B2 *Histogram showing the percentage frequency of each type of linkspan*

Table B2 shows the proportions of the different types of bridge structure that have been revealed by the survey.

Table B2 *Types of bridge structure*

Type of bridge	Numbers counted	Percentage of sample
Bridge structure type		
Box girder	26	19
Plate girder	93	68
Truss	14	10
Other	4	3
Bridge deck type		
Steel deck	125	91
Concrete deck	10	7
Other	23	2

B2.2   Causes of incidents (1.2.2 and 1.2.3)

Sections 1.2.2 and 1.2.3 show the total numbers of incidents that have occurred to linkspans and the percentages of causes. The causes are discussed in more detail below.

Mechanical failure

One of the most frequent causes of incidents is failure of the electrical or mechanical systems. This accounted for 29 per cent of the incidents. The systems in question were usually mechanical lifting equipment, such as hydraulic cylinders or rope winches. The typical incident is a malfunction of the control systems, leading to one side of the ramp being lifted farther than the other, often by more than 1 m. Such incidents usually cause significant structural damage. Perhaps surprisingly, this damage is not usually difficult to repair, and the facility is often not closed for long following such incidents.

Ship impact or movements

The other major cause of incidents is ship impact, also at 29 per cent. In theory, this type can be mitigated by fendering, but in practice the value of fendering is limited, particularly if the ship usually berths bow-on. In circumstances where a ship loses control, it is rarely possible to avoid significant damage.

Waves

Waves cause 12 per cent of incidents; at least two of the incidents occurred at facilities that were mechanically lifted. The others were associated with partial or complete failure of restraint systems to floating facilities. This latter type underlines the need to pay careful attention to the survivability of floating facilities in waves.

As an example, when there is a swell wave at the same time as a high tide, a fully enclosed box girder type of bridge deck (see Figure 1.13 in Section 1.2.3) can receive both very high wave impact (slam) forces and buoyant uplift forces. This is of critical importance to the design of the shore bearings and the compression capacity and bearings of the lifting equipment.

Failure to appreciate the effects of buoyancy is an important factor in causing incidents. Buoyancy can occur in quite unexpected places. For instance, one incident was caused when a bridge deck became submerged because of a failure of the control system and trapped an air pocket, causing buoyant uplift leading to major structural damage.

Others

Semi-submersible linkspans need to be supported at the seaward end during operation to carry the live load. This support is often provided by pennant ropes attached to eyes on the ship. Of the incidents reported, 10 per cent resulted from these ropes breaking or becoming damaged due to overloading or to the ship breaking its moorings. This might appear to be potentially highly dangerous, because it might be expected that rope failure would be accompanied by a large release of energy, leading to whiplash. Subsequent collapse of the linkspan might also be expected to cause injuries. In fact, because the ropes support only the live load, the forces in the ropes can be relatively small and the energy is released by unravelling of the rope. Also, following failure of the rope, the linkspan descends quite slowly until it floats on the surface of the water. Reports indicate that the failures have occurred as a result of unravelling of eye splices rather than a breakage of the main body of the rope. The conclusion is that hard eyes should always be provided.

Although it appears that the incidents of failure that have been reported have not been as dangerous as might have been expected, nevertheless great caution is required. For instance, a brittle type of rope fibre might well fail with a much higher release of whiplash energy.

Minor repetitive faults

The detailed questionnaire also asked for information on repeated operating malfunctions. These are discussed in Section B2.5.

Design faults

The survey has revealed that the respondents have attributed 16 per cent of incidents to design faults. The questionnaires do not make clear the basis for this attribution. However, this appears to be too high for satisfaction, and indicates that the accuracy of design with respect to linkspans and shore ramps needs to be improved.

B2.3   Prevalence of major incidents for different types of linkspan (1.2.4)

A relationship has been derived between the numbers of major incidents and the types of linkspan. The numbers of major incidents for each type of linkspan are given in Table B3. The table shows both the total numbers of each type of linkspan that have been entered into the database (the same numbers as given in Table B1) and the numbers of those linkspans for which information on incidents was received. From this, it is possible to produce Figure B3, where the bars for "% of total numbers" show percentage of numbers of incidents relative to the total numbers of the linkspans in the survey. The bars for "% of sample" show the percentage of numbers of incidents expressed as a percentage of the sample including both the linkspan type and an incident record.

The shapes of the two histograms are similar, with the semi-submersible bar being the only one to show a significant difference in distribution as a result of the different comparisons. This might be because several of the records for semi-submersible linkspans were obtained from organisations that did not have any responsibility for operating the linkspans after installation, and therefore may not have had information about incidents that occurred after installation.

Table B3   *Numbers of major incidents relative to linkspan types*

Type of linkspan	Total number of facilities in database	Numbers of facilities for which incident records were provided	Number of incidents recorded	Percentage based on total numbers in survey	Percentage based on numbers for which incident records were provided
Pontoon	27	16	2	26	44
Integral tank	5	5	9	60	60
Semi-submersible	16	10	10	50	80
Rope-lifted	28	22	4	39	50
Hydraulic cylinder	57	28	6	21	43
Rack and pinion	1	1	0	0	0

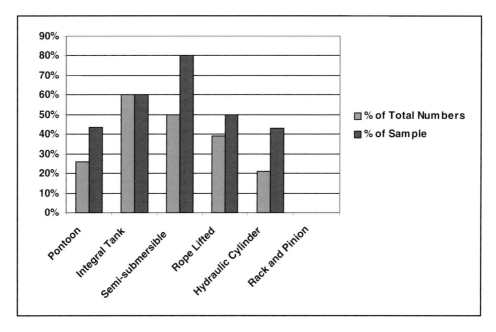

Figure B3 *Histogram of numbers of major incidents for each type of linkspan as a percentage of the total number of each type*

Whichever comparison is used, it would appear that lifted linkspans and pontoon/link bridge-type facilities are generally less troublesome than the semi-submersible or integral tank type of linkspan. However, because of the comparatively small size of the sample it is not possible to defend such a conclusion statistically.

The statistics for repeated malfunctions (see Section B2.5) clearly indicate that electrical sensors, control circuits and hose failures regularly cause problems for linkspans that contain such features. From those records for which it is possible to make a comparison between types of linkspan and the numbers of repeated malfunctions, there are 29 records of mechanically lifted linkspans that also experienced repeated malfunctions due to problems with remote sensors and switches, and only three for floating linkspans. This is not entirely unexpected, since floating systems do not rely so frequently on control systems to maintain their level.

It would appear that mechanically lifted linkspans provide a high level of general reliability with few major incidents, but suffer a greater number of minor problems than do floating facilities. Conversely, floating linkspans have a smaller regular maintenance commitment, but have a higher risk of significant incidents. The increased risk of incidents to semi-submersible linkspans may be due to their reliance on the ship providing support and the possibility of failure of this support or of the ship's moorings.

B2.4   Consequences of incidents (1.2.4)

The questionnaire survey shows that the majority of incidents that occur are relatively disruptive. For instance, 29 per cent of the incidents closed the facility for more than a month, and more than 60 per cent of the incidents closed it for more than a day (see Figure B4). Furthermore, the damage caused is usually quite severe, with 45 per cent of incidents leading to major structural damage and 35 per cent to moderate structural damage. Major mechanical damage was caused by 20 per cent of the incidents (see Figure B5).

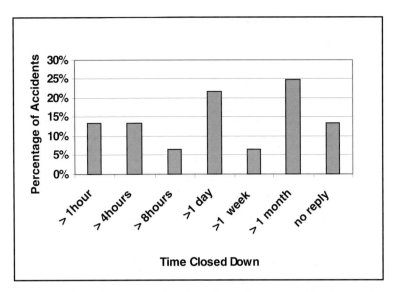

Figure B4   *Histogram showing disruption caused by incidents*

Table B4   *Definitions from questionnaire for Figure B5*

Abbreviations	Definitions
Major	Major structural damage resulting in the closure of the facility, or major mechanical damage resulting in failure of machinery
Moderate	Moderate structural damage resulting in significant loss of function, or moderate mechanical damage resulting in significant loss of performance
Minor	Minor structural damage with no loss of function, or minor mechanical damage with no loss of performance

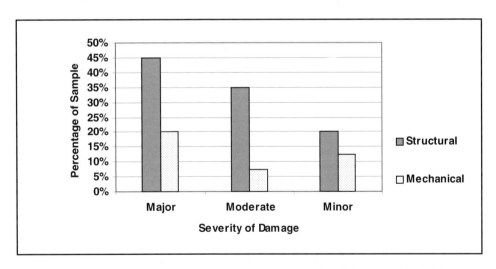

Figure B5   *Histogram showing the damage caused to linkspans by incidents (refer to Table B4 for key)*

The majority of respondents to the survey considered the operational availability of the linkspan to be essential and minimisation of downtime to be of great importance. It was only in ports where either a number of linkspans existed or where berth occupancy was low that a delay could be accepted, and this was generally only for short periods. Figure B6 indicates the importance with which the port operators regarded their linkspans.

Figure B6 *Histogram showing criticality of linkspans to operating organisations*

The numerical rating is defined in Table B5.

Table B5 *Scale of criticality used in the detailed questionnaire*

Numerical rating	Description
1	Not critical: other facilities available in port
2	Not critical: other facilities available in neighbouring port
3	Operation desirable: delay accepted for short period up to 3 months
4	Operation desirable: delay accepted for short period up to 1 months
5	Operation desirable: delay accepted for short period up to 1 week
6	Operation desirable: delay accepted for short period up to 1 day
7	Operation desirable: delay accepted for short period up to 12 hours
8	Critical: operation essential

Operating organisations have therefore taken measures to achieve the greatest possible reliability, as discussed below.

The criticality of a linkspan to the operation of a port can most easily be compared to that of a dockside crane or similar item of port equipment. If a linkspan fails, the berth is unavailable to handle ro-ro cargo. It may be possible to move a ship to another berth, but in effect the economic advantage of being able to use the length of quayside adjacent to the linkspan is lost for some time. However, in most ports there is more than one dockside crane on a berth, so if one crane fails the berth can still be used, but with a lower level of productivity.

Fortunately, the results of the research show that linkspans are generally reliable. Therefore the operating and maintenance personnel will seldom experience an emergency, and there is a danger that the operating staff will forget how to deal with the problem. Chapters 4 and 5 cover the training procedures that should be adopted to ensure familiarity with emergency procedures.

The research shows that many ports follow well-planned good practice in training staff.

1. In general the terminal staff operate the linkspan, although the shipping line provides the staff in a limited number of cases.

2. Operations are carried out in accordance with the operating manual and a predetermined training plan. Generally the training covers normal operating conditions. In a few cases abnormal or emergency operating conditions are included in training programmes.

3. Refresher courses are implemented for the operators but only for a limited number of installations.

B2.5   Reliability (1.2.4)

The detailed questionnaire included a section designed to find out how reliably the facilities included in the survey had performed. The respondents were requested to provide a numerical rating of reliability of their equipment using the scales listed in Tables B6 and B7. The results are shown in the histograms in Figures B7 and B8

Table B6   *Classification of reliability of lifting or other equipment*

Numerical rating	Description
1	Equipment breaks down frequently (weekly)
2	Equipment requires constant attention by maintenance staff to preclude breakdown
3	Equipment breaks down fairly often (monthly)
4	Equipment occasionally breaks down (quarterly)
5	Equipment rarely breaks down (six monthly)
6	Equipment breakdown is negligible
7	Equipment never fails

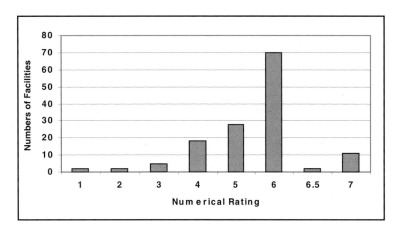

Figure B7   *Histogram showing the reported reliability of linkspans*

Table B7 *Classification of reliability of flotation restraint systems*

Numerical rating	Description
1	Restraints/moorings require weekly attention by maintenance staff to preclude breakdown
2	Restraints/moorings require monthly attention
3	Restraints/moorings require six-monthly attention
4	Restraints/moorings require annual attention
5	Restraints/moorings require no maintenance

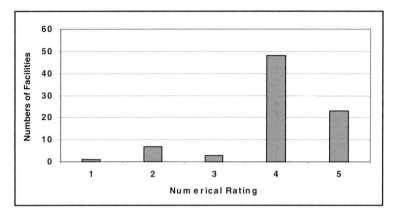

Figure B8 *Histogram showing the reported reliability of flotation restraint systems*

The numerical ratings indicate that both the mechanical equipment and the flotation restraint systems being used are considered to be fairly reliable.

The detailed questionnaire also asked for information about the areas of the facilities that were subject to repeated malfunctions of various types. The responses are listed in Table B8.

The sample size is not sufficient to have statistical significance. However, there are some clear trends that arise from these results:

1. The most important causes of regular malfunctions are electrical sensors, switches and control system.

2. Problems with ships are the second most significant cause of regular malfunctions.

3. Structural fatigue was reported as the third most significant cause of regular malfunctions.

In attempting to improve the reliability of linkspans, the factors listed above should be targeted when considering the procurement of future facilities.

Table B8 *Causes of repeated malfunctions for linkspans*

Description	No of facilities reported	Description	No of facilities reported
Structural causes		**Mechanical causes**	
Pontoon restraints	0	Electric motors	2
Vehicle impact/overload	0	Hydraulic motors	0
Structural fatigue	9	Hydraulic power unit	0
Flooring	2	Dirty hydraulic fluid	1
Cladding	5	Hydraulic control valves	2
Bearings at lifting point	1	Damaged winch wire	2
Bearings at shore end	1	Broken winch wire	0
Vandalism	0	Hose failure	3
Other	8	Sheave/bearing seizure	1
		Screw thread/nut seizure	0
		Guide wheel failure/seizure	0
		Air compressor failure	0
		Bearing failure	2
		Air dryer failure	0
		Pneumatic control failure	0
		Vandalism	0
		Other	10
Marine causes		**Electrical causes**	
Ship impact	21	Power supply	6
Fenders	11	Main operating controls	2
Bollards/mooring points	0	Remote sensors/switches	33
Capstan	0	Subsidiary operating controls	0
Navigation aids	2	Control circuits	16
Vandalism	0	Bus systems	2
Other	4	Vandalism	0
		Other	

B2.6 Electrical and control systems (1.2.4)

The current practices and trends in the provision of various aspects of motion and control systems associated with existing linkspans reflected in the survey questionnaire returns are summarised below. Not all consultees responded to all questions, so the populations appropriate to each set of answers are different.

Powered motions for following ship movements

The following percentage responses were received to questions about the availability of powered motions to follow tide or other movements:

- 22 per cent have powered tide-following provision
- 10 per cent have powered motion to follow almost all ship movement.

Faults

The questionnaire also included a question on how many disturbances in operation were experienced as a result of faults in the power or control systems. The question invited the consultee to state how often each type of event disturbed their facility each year. A simple way of displaying this data is to sum all the events from all facilities for each type of event, and the following list gives data for a total number of 199 facilities for which information was supplied.

1. There were 76 events where there was a loss of "normal" power supply.

2. There was one event due to simultaneous loss of normal and standby power.

3. There were 174 events due to power or control system component failure.

4. There were 64 events due to damage to power or control system components.

5. There were 45 events where there was a control system failure or maloperation caused by "operator error".

6. There were six events caused by incorrect reinstatement etc following maintenance or disassembly.

This indicates that control systems have a particularly large influence on the reliability of equipment.

Control system features and facilities

Of the 199 linkspan facilities for which information was supplied, 101 were provided with a height adjustment or setting control system that was usable by the operators and 27 were provided with a system to allow the ramp to automatically move to pre-set positions following initiation by the operator. Among the remainder the provision of chalk or paint marks was substantially more common than the provision of indicating dials or displays. In short, simpler systems are more common than might be thought.

Of those facilities that had such features, nearly all were considered reliable and useful.

The degree of sophistication and extent of automation incorporated in existing control systems is generally represented in the responses received as follows:

1. 67 linkspans have basic manual up/down control with few other basic features.

2. 7 linkspans have additional facilities (eg preset position) with basic control gear.

3. 16 linkspans have some automation and enhanced operator facilities via relay control.

4. 21 linkspans have similar control using programmable or electronic control gear.

5. 16 linkspans have more sophisticated controls using programmable or electronic control gear.

The survey included questions that aimed to establish the extent to which safety engineering or the adoption of specific reliability-enhancing techniques have been employed in the systems associated with existing linkspans. Some 66 per cent of the responses indicated that if one control sensor or limit switch failed, the motion would cease only when the cylinder or winch rope reached the end of its range of movement. Only 23 per cent would have been stopped by the operation of a back-up or alternative control sensor.

Questions were also asked about specific reliability and safety features of the control systems, and the questionnaires revealed that, of the responses received, the following percentages of features were provided:

- duplicated sensors   23%
- main and back-up sensors   38%
- certified "safety relays"   10%
- duplicated controllers with error checking between outputs   7%
- monitoring system separate from control system checking critical functions   3%
- programmable controllers etc with hardware or software designed or   20%
  certified for enhanced safety.

Within a total of 120 linkspans for which the question was answered, 90 per cent were still operating with their original control system, although some of these had been modified. The age profile of the existing control systems reported was as follows:

- less than 1 year old   3%
- 1–5 years old   25%
- 5–10 years old   28%
- 10–15 years old   15%
- 15–20 years old   18%
- 20–30 years old   7%
- greater than 30 years old   5%

66 control systems had been subjected to some form of modification throughout their life. Of these, modifications had been carried out for the purposes listed below:

- to provide additional operational or control facilities   30
- to remove redundant operational or control facilities   5
- to provide additional safety features   14
- to accommodate alterations to the linkspan structure   6
- to accommodate alterations to the lifting machinery   9

Power supply provision

At a significant number of installations the only supplement to a single adequately rated power supply ultimately derived from the public supply system was an independent standby power supply (such as a private generator) adequate to run the full operation. Responses to the relevant question covered 190 installations; of these, 62 installations were reported to be provided with such a standby facility.

A range of other features (including compressed-air connection, petrol-engined hydraulic pump, and limited-capacity standby supply) were reported from a relatively small number of installations.

B2.7 Operations (1.2.4 and Chapter 4)

Several questions about operational procedures and the convenience of operation were included in the detailed questionnaire. The responses were supplemented by interviews with linkspan operators. The operation of linkspans is discussed in Chapter 4, but it is worth recording here the responses of the consultees to a question about the ease and convenience of operation of the control system.

The questionnaire requested respondents to provide a numerical rating with respect to the ease of operation of the control facility. They were invited to classify the facility against a numerical rating as given in Table B9 and to give a rating between 1 and 10 as appropriate. Figure B9 shows the results, and indicates that improvements could be made with the presentation of some controls.

Table B9 *Numerical rating classification of convenience of use for operation of facility*

Numerical rating	Description
1	Represents poorly set-out controls, operating facility and fault identification
5	Represents average design, layout and some minor aspects not ideal with limited operation and fault identification
10	Represents excellent design, layout, incorporating a man–machine interface or similar facility

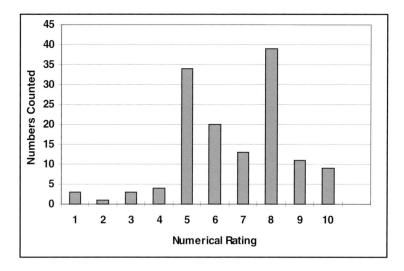

Figure B9 *Histogram showing the opinions about convenience of operation against the classification system in Table B9*

When asked which aspects of the operational features were unsatisfactory, respondents offered the following list:

- identification and labelling of controls

- location of panel (with respect to the visual appraisal of the ship/linkspan interface)

- programming of electronic control system

- freeboard control (that is, a means of ensuring that the ramp is at the correct level relative to the water line)

- grouping of operational controls associated with the linkspan, and controls associated with other aspects, including traffic lights, barriers and lighting

- implementation of emergency or standby operation

- location of emergency use control equipment with respect to the visual appraisal of the ship/linkspan interface

- layout of control panel

- complexity of control panel

- access for the purposes of operation of the facility, which is often poor.

B2.8　　　　Maintenance (1.2.4 and Chapter 5)

The maintenance problems revealed by the survey are discussed in Chapter 5. However, the responses to a question about the convenience of the facility for maintenance are set out below. Respondents were asked to provide a numerical rating to describe their opinions about the convenience of their facilities with respect to ergonomic design and ease of maintenance. The numerical rating system is given in Table B10.

Table B10　*Numerical rating classification of convenience of use and ergonomic design for maintenance of the facility*

Numerical rating	Description
1	Represents poor design/layout. Limited access around/to equipment, difficult access to equipment for personnel, tools and spares. Inadequate domestic services (power, lighting etc). Poorly thought out and executed.
5	Represents average design/layout. Some aspects/areas have limited access (perhaps infrequent access required), acceptable access route for personnel. difficult access for tools and spares. Average domestic services
10	Represents excellent design/layout. Ease of access around equipment, ease of access to equipment for personnel, tools and spares, good domestic services (lighting, communications, fire and safety etc). All well thought out and planned.

Consultees were invited to give a rating between 1 and 10, to describe their opinions about their facilities. The histogram in Figure B10 shows the responses.

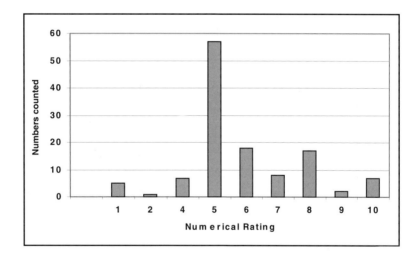

Figure B10　*Histogram showing the opinion of the consultees about the ergonomic design and ease of maintenance of their facilities*

The questionnaire also enabled the respondents to indicate which aspects of the design were not satisfactory for the purpose of maintenance. These comments have been rationalised as follows:

- lack of fixed maintenance platforms for access to external machinery (winch, cylinder, pipework, electrical controls etc)
- access to shore abutment bearings difficult
- access to underside of bridge and lifting beam difficult
- inadequate shelter for operator and equipment
- access to internal chambers of pontoons difficult
- spragging arrangements for the linkspan inadequate

- difficult to remove hydraulic cylinder clevis pins or shafts

- components that are removed easily able to fall into water: some form of retention device required, together with better-designed working platforms

- layout of hydraulic power unit components (pump, motor and manifolds) not conducive to ease of maintenance

- poor layout of plant room

- unsatisfactory visual access from control station or plant room to ship ramp/linkspan and ship doorway/gangway interfaces

- roadway not strong enough for mobile crane access and operation.

There appears to be considerable scope for improvement in the general facilities that are provided for the convenience of maintenance of linkspans. In particular, it appears that there are some facilities that do not adequately comply with the Management and Health and Safety at Work Regulations and the Provision and Use of Work Equipment Regulations. This is surprising, because the requirement to provide safe access to equipment has been enshrined in various regulations since 1974.

B3 SHIP-TO-SHORE WALKWAYS

B3.1 Consequences of incidents (1.3.4)

Figure B11 indicates the importance with which the walkway operating organisations regarded their facilities.

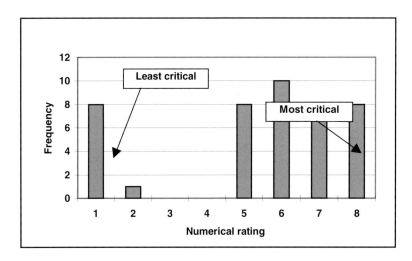

Figure B11 *Histogram showing the perceived criticality of the facility to the operating organisation*

Table B11 gives the description of the scale of criticality.

Table B11 *Scale of criticality used in the detailed questionnaire*

Numerical rating	Description
1	Not critical: other facilities available in port
2	Not critical: other facilities available in neighbouring port
3	Operation desirable: delay accepted for short period up to 3 months
4	Operation desirable: delay accepted for short period up to 1 months
5	Operation desirable: delay accepted for short period up to 1 week
6	Operation desirable: delay accepted for short period up to 1 day
7	Operation desirable: delay accepted for short period up to 12 hours
8	Critical: operation essential

It is apparent that the operators regard the passenger walkway facilities as less critical than their linkspans (see Figure B6). If the walkway is out of use, it is usually possible to find another way to unload and load passengers. If a linkspan is unavailable, there is usually no alternative means of getting the vehicles off the ship.

The consequences of a walkway being taken out of service are thus rather less than for a linkspan. However, the range of possible movements of a walkway system can mean that the control systems are more complex and require a higher degree of skill in fault-diagnosis. Personnel responsible for the operation and maintenance of walkways need a level of competence and training similar to those in charge of linkspans.

B3.2   Reliability (1.3.4)

The detailed questionnaire included a section to find out how reliably the facilities included in the survey had performed. The respondents were requested to provide a numerical rating of the reliability of the equipment. Since no floating types were included in the database, the questions about the reliability of restraint systems remain unanswered. The results of the survey of reliability are set out in Figure B12. The ratings are defined in Table B12.

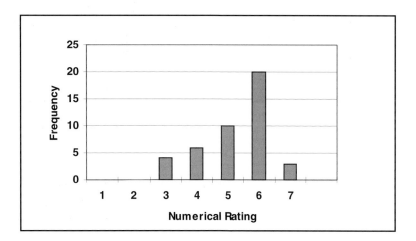

Figure B12 *Histogram showing the reported reliability of walkways*

Table B12 *Classification of reliability of equipment*

Numerical rating	Description
1	Equipment breaks down frequently (weekly)
2	Equipment requires constant attention by maintenance staff to preclude breakdown
3	Equipment breaks down fairly often (monthly)
4	Equipment occasionally breaks down (quarterly)
5	Equipment rarely breaks down (six monthly)
6	Equipment breakdown is negligible
7	Equipment never fails"

The ratings indicate that the types of equipment being used are considered to be fairly reliable. It is important that facilities that are used by the general public have a high level of reliability and safety.

The detailed questionnaire also asked for information about the areas of the facilities that were subject to repeated malfunctions of various types. The responses are listed in Table B13 below.

Table B13 *Causes of repeated malfunctions for walkways*

Description	No. of facilities reported	Description	No. of facilities reported
Structural causes		**Mechanical causes**	
Pontoon restraints	1	Electric motors	1
Vehicle impact/overload	0	Hydraulic motors	0
Structural fatigue	2	Hydraulic power unit	0
Flooring	0	Dirty hydraulic fluid	0
Cladding	1	Hydraulic control valves	0
Bearings at lifting point	0	Damaged winch wire	0
Bearings at shore end	0	Broken winch wire	0
Vandalism	0	Hose failure	0
Other	3	Sheave/ bearing seizure	0
		Screw thread/nut seizure	0
		Guide wheel failure/seizure	0
		Air compressor failure	1
		Bearing failure	0
		Air dryer failure	0
		Pneumatic control failure	0
		Vandalism	0
		Other	5
Marine causes		**Electrical causes**	
Ship impact	3	Power supply	2
Fenders	0	Main operating controls	1
Bollards/mooring points	0	Remote sensors/switches	10
Capstan	0	Subsidiary operating controls	0
Navigation aids	0	Control circuits	2
Vandalism	0	Bus systems	0
Other	1	Vandalism	0
		Other	0

The sample size here is even smaller than for the sample of linkspans, and therefore the statistical significance is doubtful. However, there are still some clear trends arising from these results.

1. As for linkspans, the most important causes of regular malfunctions are electrical sensors and switches. Control systems do not seem to have been as significant a cause of problems as for linkspans.

2. Problems with ships are the second most significant cause of regular malfunctions.

3. Structural fatigue was reported as the third most significant cause of regular malfunctions.

4. There are very few mechanical causes of regular problems. This may be a function of the very much lower loadings that passenger walkways have to withstand.

B3.3   Electrical control systems (1.3.4)

The current practices and trends in the provision of various aspects of motion and control systems associated with existing walkways reflected in the survey questionnaire returns are briefly summarised below. The total size of the sample of responses received was only 56. Certain questions were clearly answered by fewer respondents, in which case the size of the smaller sample is indicated.

Powered motions for following ship movements

The following responses were received to the question concerning provision of powered motion following deployment of the walkway:

1. 53 per cent have no powered ship-following motion.

2. 25 per cent have slow vertical powered motion (capable of following the tide).

3. 22 per cent have fast vertical powered motion (capable of following almost all ship movements).

4. 9 per cent have slow powered motion along the berth.

5. 2 per cent have fast powered motion along the berth.

6. 13 per cent have slow powered motion perpendicular to the berth.

7. 7 per cent have fast powered motion perpendicular to the berth.

Faults

The questionnaire responses indicated that if all the incidents that had occurred to all the facilities in the survey are summed, the total numbers of disturbances due to the events listed below are as follows:

- power/control system component failure   15 per year
- damage to power/control system components   6 per year
- control system failure/maloperation caused by operator error   6 per year
- loss of normal power supply   5 per year
- simultaneous loss of normal and standby power   0 per year
- incorrect reinstatement etc following maintenance/disassembly   0 per year

Control system features and facilities

In the following section, the numbers of consultees that responded to individual questions varied from question to question. Therefore there is no consistency in the total numbers of facilities for which answers were received.

Of the 56 facilities for which information was supplied, 21 were provided with some form of operator-controlled height adjustment or height settings control device. Seven were provided with a facility for the ramp to move automatically to preset positions after initiation by the operator.

Of those that had such facilities, more than 80 per cent reported that they were useful, functional and reliable.

The degree of sophistication and extent of automation incorporated in existing control systems is generally represented in the responses received as follows:

1. 15 walkways have basic manual up/down control with few other basic features.

2. 5 walkways have additional facilities (eg preset position) with basic control gear.

3. 4 walkways have some automation and enhanced operator facilities via relay control.

4. 12 walkways have similar control using programmable or electronic control gear.

5. 2 walkways have more sophisticated control systems using programmable or electronic control gear.

The survey included questions that attempted to establish the extent to which safety engineering or specific reliability-enhancing techniques have been employed in the systems associated with existing walkways. No less than 21 (37 per cent) indicated that should a single control sensor, limit switch etc fail at the end of travel of walkway motion, the motion would be caused to stop by cylinders, winch ropes etc reaching the end of their range of movement. Only 8 (14 per cent) would be stopped by operation of back-up or alternative control sensors.

Of 37 walkways for which responses were provided, 27 were provided with end-of-travel sensors etc, which stop the walkway's movement should the operator fail to do so. Eight were stopped by cylinders or winch ropes reaching the end of their range.

Twenty walkways were covered by responses to a question about specific reliability and safety features of the control systems. Responses indicated that the following features were provided.

• duplicated sensors	23%
• main and back-up sensors	37%
• certified safety relays	10%
• duplicated controllers with error checking between outputs	7%
• monitoring system separate from control system checking critical functions	3%
• programmable controllers etc with hardware or software designed or certified for enhanced safety.	20%

Thirty-two walkways (57 per cent) were still operating with their original control system, although some of these had been modified. The list below indicates the age profile of the existing control systems reported on. (Note that the sum of the ages listed below does not equate to the 32 walkways that still possess their original system.)

- less than 1 year old   0
- 1–5 years old   16
- 5–10 years old   9
- 10–15 years old   7
- 15–20 years old   3
- more than 20 years old   0

The following numbers of installations had been modified for the purposes indicated:

- to provide additional operational or control facilities   5
- to remove redundant operational or control facilities   0
- to provide additional safety features   6
- to accommodate alterations to the walkway structure   4
- to accommodate alterations to the lifting equipment   2

Six walkways had automatic adjustment for tide following, three for ship trim/draft variation and 13 to follow both tide and ship variations. The majority view was that these features were reliable and generally were used by the operators.

Power supply provision

The responses to the questionnaire indicated that the great majority of walkways are provided with a single adequately rated power supply derived from the public system. Few installations are provided with standby power. Some isolated installations do not have mains electric power supply and are provided with other facilities, such as engine-driven hydraulic pumps.

Respondents indicated that some installations were provided with sensors monitoring the extent of movement of the walkway final connection with the ship. Very few installations were provided with facilities for monitoring excessive ship movements. The number of installations concerned were:

- sensing of extreme walkway element movement – vertical   11
- sensing of extreme walkway element movement – along berth   7
- sensing of extreme walkway element movement – perpendicular
  to berth   8
- sensing of extreme ship movement – vertically   5
- sensing of extreme ship movement – parallel to the berth   6
- sensing of extreme ship movement – perpendicular to berth   7

Of the installations reported, 8 used the above sensors to generate alarms and/or operator indications; 9 used them to initiate automatic response/adjustments of the walkway. Various technologies form the basis of sensors used, as follows:

- mechanical limit switches   6
- proximity limit switches   12
- inclinometers   7
- other types of measuring device (eg radar or infra-red beam) 4

B3.4   Operation and maintenance (1.3.4, Chapters 4 and 5)

This subject has been discussed at length in Sections B2.7 and B2.8, and the survey of walkways does not add to the information reported.

B4   GENERAL ISSUES, ATTITUDES AND OPINIONS ARISING FROM THE SURVEY

B4.1   Factors considered important by purchasers

In the survey, the consultees were asked to state which factors they regarded as important in the purchase of a ship-to-shore linkspan or walkway. The question was:

- When selecting a contractor or supplier for a linkspan or walkway, would you have checked the following list of factors or questions when taking account of the tender price and submission?

The responses are listed in Table B14.

Table B14   *Responses from question about factors considered important by potential purchasers*

	Number of organisations agreeing that the factors would have been considered	
	Now	**5 years ago**
The price	45	42
Had they taken account of the wave conditions?	39	35
Did they know the wave conditions?	37	32
Had they taken account of wind conditions?	40	35
Did they know the wind conditions?	37	32
Had they taken account of the vessel approach manoeuvres?	46	41
Had they taken account of the capability of the port maintenance personnel and organisation?	37	28
Had they allowed for fail-safe devices within the operation system or structural support system	43	33
Had they allowed for the range of temperature conditions?	32	26
Did they know the range of temperature conditions?	33	27
Did they have a quality management system?	39	14
Total size of sample	54	

These responses may well not reflect true opinion, since the question prompts the respondent to consider factors that they may not have previously considered. However, the point of the question was to highlight certain features that purchasers should consider when they purchase a linkspan or walkway. It is significant that lower numbers of consultees suggested that it was important that wave, wind and temperature should be considered in assessing potential suppliers. It is necessary to ensure that the designers or contractors are competent to deal with these parameters.

It is interesting, and probably accurate, that the awareness of these factors is stated as being better now than it was five years ago.

B4.2   Past practice in purchasing ship-to-shore linkspans and walkways

The detailed questionnaires asked about the methods of purchase of linkspans and walkways and the methods of providing an independent assessment of the facilities. The methods of procurement were designated in the questionnaire as follows:

- design and construct: contractor supplied with performance requirements
- design and construct: contractor supplied with outline scope design and detailed performance specifications
- design provided to the contractor with limited design and construct elements
- turnkey contract
- second-hand purchase.

The term *turnkey contract* is not always consistently defined. In this case it was intended to apply to a situation where the purchaser wishes to have a facility procured on the basis of a general description only. An agreement is then reached with a contractor to provide all the design, construction and commissioning of the facility; the purchaser relies on the same contractor to assess all problems associated with providing a safe facility without any further amendment by the purchaser.

Out of a sample of 173 linkspans and 41 walkways, the pie charts in Figure B13 were produced, which indicate the means by which existing linkspans and walkways were purchased.

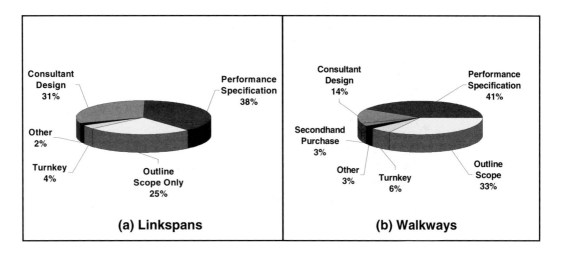

Figure B13   *Pie charts showing procurement routes for linkspans and walkways*

The labels in Figure B13 are abbreviations of the questions in Section 2 of the detailed questionnaire, and the meanings are listed in Table B15.

Table B15 *Terms used in Figure B13*

Term in Figure 1.35	Complete description given in the detailed questionnaires
Consultant design	Design provided to the contractor with limited design and construct elements
Performance specification	Design and construct: contractor supplied with performance requirements
Outline scope	Design and construct: contractor supplies with outline scope design and detailed performance specifications
Turnkey	Turnkey contract (the consultee was then invited to define this term)
Other	Other types of procurement (BOOT, management contracting etc)
Second-hand purchase	Second-hand purchase

Only one example of a second-hand purchase of linkspans or walkways was found in the survey, but it is known that several such purchases were not revealed.

The database has been interrogated to determine whether there was any relationship between the procurement route and the reliability of the finished facility. None was found that could be defended statistically.

The procurement of the majority of linkspans and walkways included an independent checking process or a process similar to ship classification.

The pie charts in Figures B14 and B15 show the distribution of checking and review methods between independent checking by consulting engineers, independent checking by in-house staff and classification, and whether the facility has been put into class and whether it is still in class.

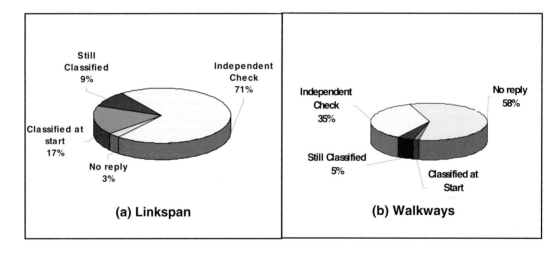

(a) Linkspan   **(b) Walkways**

Figure B14 *Pie charts showing the facilities for which independent checking or classification was carried out*

Information on the classification process is given in Section 3.8.3.

Although few facilities have been classified, the majority of independent checking procedures for linkspans have been carried out by a classification society even though not many were in kept in class. On the other hand, very few purchasers have turned to classification societies to carry out an independent check of the design of passenger walkways. The pie charts in Figure B15 indicate this clearly.

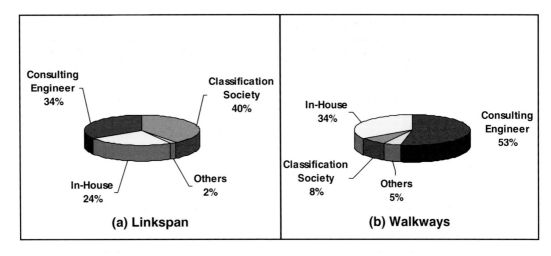

Figure B15   *Pie charts showing the types of independent checking*

It is concluded that most purchasers ensure that independent checking is an integral part of most procurement processes.

B4.3   Understanding of the existing regulations

There has been a considerable volume of new legislation in recent years relevant to the safety of linkspans and walkways. However, the survey has generally revealed a good understanding of the requirements of this legislation. The framework for the legislation and regulations is described in Chapter 2.

The opinions of the consultees with respect to the regulatory issues were sought during the survey. The questions asked and the answers given are listed in Table B16.

Table B16   *Responses to questions on regulations*

Full text of question in detailed questionnaire	Yes	No	No reply
Are you satisfied that existing regulations are satisfactory?	14	25	15
Should there be a specific standard for the design of ship-to-shore linkspans and walkways?	40	7	7
Should linkspans and walkways be subjected to a statutory independent assessment and inspection system such as under the Building Regulations?	30	15	9
Should there be a panel of expert professional engineers who approve the design and periodic inspection of linkspans and walkways as part of a regulatory framework (such as the Reservoir Panel for dams)?	17	26	11
Are there too many regulations?	13	25	16
Do you think that changing the regulatory framework will lead to fewer accidents?	28	14	12
Are you familiar with the Construction (Design and Management) Regulations?	38	6	10
Do you consider that the Docks Regulations 1988 provide sufficient regulatory framework?	15	29	10
Do you agree that shore ramps and walkways are by definition lifting appliances, machines or machinery and are therefore subject to the requirements of :			
(a) The Supply of Machinery (Safety) Regulations 1992	23	11	20
(b) The Provision and Use of Work Equipment Regulations	26	9	19
(c) The Lifting Operations and Lifting Equipment Regulations 1997	33	5	16

C Automation and programmable electronic systems

C1 PROBLEMS WITH AUTOMATION

C1.1 General

Wide experience through many industries and applications of engineering installations confirms that neither human operators nor automatic control systems are absolutely reliable. In any application they may both be subject to many diverse influences, which may, for example, cause:

- overloading, leading to failure to respond correctly or not at all
- corruption of logical decision-making process, leading to inappropriate actions
- misinterpretation of genuine signals and indications
- failure to recognise false or contradictory signals and indications
- loss of physical or mental ability to act or respond appropriately.

Machines, in particular electrical and electronic systems (computers, electromechanical relay assemblies etc), are often seen as capable of almost infinite performance in many respects. For example:

1. They never forget.
2. They never make the wrong decision.
3. They will always respond in a predictable and reliable manner.

C1.2 Reliability of control systems

It would be easy to become over-confident in the infallibility of automatic systems. However, they should never be regarded as completely reliable. In statistical terms, all components, and hence systems composed of them, have their own finite probabilities of failure within a given period of time. The statistician's or reliability engineer's concept of the *mean time between failures* for a system is based upon the fact that any system will fail, and will do so more than once.

The engineering community has long recognised this situation. Over several decades, many standards, codes of practice and regulations have been promulgated. Recently, advances in some branches of technology have proceeded at a pace previously unimaginable, and some entirely new technologies have emerged. Among the recent technologies to find wide acceptance have been electronic control systems generally, and programmable electronic systems in particular.

In 1995 the UK Health and Safety Executive published the booklet *Out of control – why control systems go wrong, and how to prevent failure*, chiefly to raise awareness of the technical causes of control system failure. Its contents are of interest and relevance to managers, engineers and technicians who hold responsibility at various phases in the life-cycle of a control system. The following extracts from the booklet's introduction indicate the wide fields of responsibility to which these considerations relate.

1. *This publication is aimed particularly at all those concerned with the technical aspects of the specification, design, fabrication, commissioning, and maintenance of control systems. The book may also help those responsible for purchasing such systems, or reviewing the safety of existing equipment.*

2. *However, it must be stressed that the achievement of safety, human and management factors are also very important. Therefore this guidance not only applies to technical managers in the control and instrumentation field, but also to those at senior levels in companies which supply and purchase control equipment. These managers carry the responsibility for ensuring that the equipment is competitively priced, and that its safety integrity is adequate in operation. The systematic approach advocated in this document will help to ensure that optimum solutions will emerge in terms of cost and safety. A general study made by HSE into the cost of accidents showed that the costs of error rectification far exceeded those which would have been incurred if a systematic approach had been employed from the outset*

10. *Section 5 highlights the importance of managerial responsibilities, since it is acknowledged that failures in control systems are not due to technical aspects alone; human and managerial factors are extremely important. Issues such as conflicting managerial priorities and incentives, lack of safety engineering training, absence of a "safety culture" and poor contract procedures etc, may contribute significantly to an eventual failure which has a technical cause.*

This booklet should be examined by all involved in the procurement, operation and maintenance of control systems for linkspans and walkways.

C1.3   Comments on EU legislation

The legislative framework within which linkspans and walkways are procured, operated and maintained is described elsewhere in this guide, but it is appropriate to draw the reader's attention to the following document:

Community legislation on machinery: Comments on Directive 89/392/EEC and Directive 91/368/EEC, Edition 1993, by Pierre Massimi and Jean-Pierre Van Ghelure. Luxembourg: Office for Official Publications of the European Communities.

The following extract from the foreword of the document, indicates its scope and applicability.

The following study sets out and comments on the text of Directive 89/392/EEC, as amended.

These comments are made by officials who are all trained engineers, and who have followed the whole legislative process (preparatory work, discussions at the Council, scrutiny by European Parliament committees and the Economic and Social committee); they are intended to answer the kind of questions which users of the Directive (manufacturers, their representatives and machinery users) are likely to ask.

Many sections of the document relate directly or indirectly to considerations affecting control systems or specific requirements thereof, and **the whole document should be considered by all having responsibilities for machinery.**

C2   PROGRAMMABLE ELECTRONIC SYSTEMS

C2.1   Safety aspects of programmable electronic systems

The Health and Safety Executive has for many years been disseminating information on good practice concerning the application of programmable electronic control systems, particularly their safety aspects. Its two-volume publication *Programmable electronic systems in safety related applications* (1987), is regularly quoted and referred to in the latest papers, discussions and standards in this field. The following extract from HSE's 1981 publication *Microprocessors in industry* relates to the demands for suitable personnel, training etc to promote safety operations involving plant and machinery controlled by computers or their equivalent.

The design, installation, maintenance and operation of a programmed electronic system may require new levels or combinations of skills, and careful consideration should therefore be given to the training or retraining of staff. The training required will obviously vary widely in relation both to the complexity of the process and the control systems, and the needs of the person being trained. It is essential however even in the simplest of circumstances (e.g. an operator or attendant responsible for a simple machine tool controlled by a programmable electronic system), that the person should be as fully aware of the operation of the Programmed Electronic System as he is of the machine itself, and in particular, be aware of the consequences of failure of the control system. Where the operator or attendant is expected, in the case of computer failure, to maintain safety by manual or other non-computerised means, adequate operating instructions and/or back-up instrumentation should always be provided.

A guiding principle when considering the application of computer-based or programmable-electronics-based automatic control to an installation or process (which previously would have been provided with manual or simple relay-based control systems) is that the new computerised system should be at least as safe as the system it actually or notionally replaces.

A thorough knowledge and understanding of the hardware and software elements of the control systems is essential to enable one to make any proper assessment of the safety and reliability thereof. This must be applied together with an in-depth knowledge and appreciation of the interfaces between the control system, the equipment under control, the human operators and the operating environment. The nature and performance capabilities of plant sensors (limit switches, operator's pushbuttons, measuring instruments etc) and control/indication devices (valves, actuatory, lamps, gauges etc) must be understood, and their compatibility with the control systems must be ensured.

Without suitable precautions being incorporated in the control systems and associated arrangements, there exist significant risks that undesirable and potentially lethal maloperation of the plant could result from seemingly trivial factors. For example:

- a single erroneous key stroke on a programming device keyboard
- a single slightly dirty switch contact
- a single minor spike/disturbance on the power supply waveform
- a single loose, broken or short-circuited connection in the plant wiring.

The possible list of such factors can be quite lengthy for even relatively small installations of limited complexity. However, if only one of the relevant factors is not adequately considered and appropriate action taken, an incident or series of incidents with potentially fatal consequences may result.

C2.2   Technical standards for functional safety

An excellent introduction for the non-specialist to the requirements for the safe design, installation and use of computerised equipment or programmable electronic systems, is provided by another of the Health and Safety Executive's publications in this field: *Programmable electronic systems in safety related applications. Part 1, An introductory guide.* This same publication provides in its considerably more extensive *Part 2, General technical guidelines* advice to those who manufacture, design, supply, select, apply, program and use programmable electronic systems that affect safety. Readers are recommended to refer to these volumes as relevant to their individual responsibilities and interests.

An international standard that will form a major reference for practitioners in this field has been under development within the scope of the International Electrotechnical Commission (IEC) procedures in recent years. Publication is taking place in sections over 1998 and 1999. Industry organisations worldwide have been working on the development of systems, products and standards in support of this exercise for some years. The present situation was reported in Issue 37 of *Safety and EMC* (published by ERA Technology, Cleave Road, Leatherhead, Surrey) on the basis of information supplied by the chairman of the responsible working group (IEC/SC66/NG10). The following is extracted from that report:

The proposed changes to the Parts 1–7 of draft standard IEC 61508 Functional safety of electrical, electronic and programmable electronic (E/E/PE) safety-related systems *(formerly IEC 1580) remain under development. Parts 1, 3, 4 and 5 are now expected to be issued as Final Draft International Standards (FDIS) in March 1998, with final publication in 1998. Parts 2, 6 and 7 are expected to be issued as Committee Drafts for Vote (CDV) in March 1998; acceptance would ensure FDIS status with final publication in 1999.*

IEC Basic Safety Publication status has been proposed for Parts 1, 2, 3 and 4, which means that IEC Technical Committees have to use these Parts when they are developing sector standards covering the functional safety of E/E/PE safety systems (the exception being "low complexity" E/E/PE safety related systems – see below). It should also be noted that IEC 61508 is intended to be used as a stand-alone standard where, for example, no sector implementation exists.

The ideas behind these considerations relating to automatic and computerised control also apply to matters of wider application. They also have impacts on the procurement and use of linkspans and walkways, as below.

1.   The safety of the installations depends upon the provision of appropriate personnel, experience, training and competence.

2.   Many other aspects (eg structural bearings) of these installations may be described as safety-related systems or components, and need to be treated as such.

D   Standards

D1   ISO STANDARDS

BRITISH STANDARDS INSTITUTION
Specification for roll on/roll off ship to shore connection: interface between terminals and ships with straight stern/bow ramps
ISO 6812:1983 (BS MA 97:1984)

BRITISH STANDARDS INSTITUTION
Specification for aluminium shore gangways
ISO 7061:1993 (BS MA 78:1978)

D2   BS EN STANDARDS

BRITISH STANDARDS INSTITUTION
Safety rules for the construction and installation of escalators and passenger conveyors
BS EN 115:1995

BRITISH STANDARDS INSTITUTION
Safety of machinery. Basic concepts, general principles for design
Part 1: Basic terminology, methodology
BS EN 292-1:1991

BRITISH STANDARDS INSTITUTION
Safety of machinery. Basic concepts, general principles for design
Part 2: Technical principles and specifications
BS EN 292-2:1991

BRITISH STANDARDS INSTITUTION
Safety of machinery. Emergency stop equipment. Functional aspects. Principles for design
BS EN 418:1992

BRITISH STANDARDS INSTITUTION
Safety of machinery. Auditory danger signals. General requirements, design and testing
BS EN 457:1992

BRITISH STANDARDS INSTITUTION
Safety of machinery. Human body measurements. Principles for determining the dimensions required for openings for whole body access into machinery
BS EN 547-1:1997

BRITISH STANDARDS INSTITUTION
Safety of machinery. Human body measurements. Principles for determining the dimensions required for access openings
BS EN 547-2:1997

BRITISH STANDARDS INSTITUTION
Safety of machinery. Two-hand control devices. Functional aspects. Principles for
design
BS EN 574:1997

BRITISH STANDARDS INSTITUTION
Safety of machinery. Ergonomic design principles
Part 1. Terminology and general principles
BS EN 614-1:1995

BRITISH STANDARDS INSTITUTION
Specifications for data logging and monitoring of lifts, escalators and passenger
conveyors
BS EN 627:1996

BRITISH STANDARDS INSTITUTION
Safety of machinery. Visual danger signals. General requirements, design and testing
BS EN 842:1996

BRITISH STANDARDS INSTITUTION
Safety of machinery. Ergonomics requirements for the design of displays and control
actuators
Part 1. General principles for human interactions with displays and control actuators
BS EN 894-1:1997

BRITISH STANDARDS INSTITUTION
Safety of machinery. Ergonomics requirements for the design of displays and control
actuators.
Part 2. Displays
BS EN 894-2:1997

BRITISH STANDARDS INSTITUTION
Safety of machinery. Guards. General requirements for the design and construction of
fixed and movable guards
BS EN 953:1998

BRITISH STANDARDS INSTITUTION
Safety of machinery. Safety related parts of control systems
Part 1. General principles for design
BS EN 954-1:1997

BRITISH STANDARDS INSTITUITION
Safety of machinery. System of auditory and visual danger and information signals
BS EN 981:1997

BRITISH STANDARDS INSTITUTION
Safety of machinery. Safety requirements for fluid power systems and their components.
Hydraulics
BS EN 982:1996

BRITISH STANDARDS INSTITUTION
Safety of machinery. Safety requirements for fluid power systems and their components.
Pneumatic
BS EN 983:1996

BRITISH STANDARDS INSTITUTION
Safety of machinery. Prevention of unexpected start-up
BS EN 1037:1996

BRITISH STANDARDS INSTITUTION
Safety of machinery. Principles for risk assessment
BS EN 1050:1997

BRITISH STANDARDS INSTITUTION
Safety of machinery. Interlocking devices associated with guards. Principles for design and selection
BS EN 1088:1996

BRITISH STANDARDS INSTITUTION
Safety of machinery. Electrical equipment of machines
Part 1. Specification for general requirements
BS EN 60204-1:1998

D3   DRAFT EUROPEAN STANDARDS

BRITISH STANDARDS INSTITUTION
Aircraft ground support equipment – specific requirements
Part 4: Passenger boarding bridges
pr EN 12312-4:1997

BRITISH STANDARDS INSTITUTION
Safety of machinery – permanent means of access to machines and industrial plant
Part 1. Choice of a fixed means of access between two levels
pr EN 12437-1:1996

BRITISH STANDARDS INSTITUTION
Safety of machinery – permanent means of access to machines and industrial plant
Part 2. Working platforms and gangways
pr EN 12437-2:1996

BRITISH STANDARDS INSTITUTION
Safety of machinery – permanent means of access to machines and industrial plan
Part 3. Stairways, stepladders and guardrails
pr EN 12437-3:1996

BRITISH STANDARDS INSTITUTION
Safety of machinery – permanent means of access to machines and industrial plan
Part 4. Fixed ladders
pr EN 12437-4:1996

BRITISH STANDARDS INSTITUTION
Safety of machinery. Technical principles and specification for mobility and for lifting
pr EN 12937:1997

BRITISH STANDARDS INSTITUTION
Specification for lifts, escalators, passenger conveyors and paternosters
Part 1. General requirements for electric, hydraulic and hand powered lifts
BS 2655: Part 1:1970

BRITISH STANDARDS INSTITUTION
Technical manuals
Part 1. Specification for presentation of essential information
BS 4884: Part 1:1992

BRITISH STANDARDS INSTITUTION
Technical manuals
Part 2. Guide to content
BS 4884: Part 2:1993

BRITISH STANDARDS INSTITUTION
Technical manuals
Part 3. Guide to presentation
BS 4884: Part 3:1993

BRITISH STANDARDS INSTITUTION
Guide to user's requirements for technical manuals
Part 1. Content
BS 4899: Part 1:1991

BRITISH STANDARDS INSTITUTION
Guide to user's requirements for technical manuals
Part 2. Presentation
BS 4899: Part 2:1992

BRITISH STANDARDS INSTITUTION
Code of practice for safety of machinery
BS 5304:1988

BRITISH STANDARDS INSTITUTION
Code of practice for scissor lifts
BS 5323:1980

BRITISH STANDARDS INSTITUTION
Stairs, ladders and walkways
Part 3. Code of practice for the design of industrial type stairs, permanent ladders and walkways
BS 5395: Part 3:1985

BRITISH STANDARDS INSTITUTION
Steel, concrete and composite bridges
Part 2. Specification for loads
BS 5400: Part 2:1978

BRITISH STANDARDS INSTITUTION
Lifts and service lifts
Part 1. Safety rules for the construction and installation of electric lifts
BS 5655: Part 1:1986 (EN 81: Part 1:1985)

BRITISH STANDARDS INSTITUTION
Lifts and service lifts
Part 2. Safety rules for the construction and installation of hydraulic lifts
BS 5655: Part 2:1988 (EN 81: Part 2:1987)

BRITISH STANDARDS INSTITUTION
Lifts and service lifts
Part 6. Code of practice for selection and installation
BS5655: Part 6:1990

BRITISH STANDARDS INSTITUTION
Maritime structures
Part 1. General criteria
BS 6349: Part 1:1984

BRITISH STANDARDS INSTITUTION
Maritime structures
Part 2. Design of quay walls, jetties and dolphins
BS 6349: Part 2:1988

BRITISH STANDARDS INSTITUTION
Maritime structures
Part 4. Design of fendering and mooring systems
BS 6349: Part 4:1994

BRITISH STANDARDS INSTITUTION
Maritime structures
Part 6. Design of inshore moorings and floating structures
BS 6349: Part 6:1989

BRITISH STANDARDS INSTITUTION
Maintainability of equipment
Part 1. Guide to specifying and contracting for maintainability
BS 6548: Part 1:1984 (IEC 706-1:1982)

BRITISH STANDARDS INSTITUTION
Maintainability of equipment
Part 2. Guide to maintainability studies during the design phase
BS6548: Part 2:1992 (IEC 706-2:1990)

BRITISH STANDARDS INSTITUTION
Maintainability of equipment
Part 3. Guide to maintainability verification, and the collection, analysis and presentation of maintainability data
BS 6548: Part 3:1991 (IEC 706-3:1987)

BRITISH STANDARDS INSTITUTION
Maintainability of equipment
Part 4. Guide to the planning of maintenance and maintenance support
BS 6548: Part 4:1993

BRITISH STANDARDS INSTITUTION
Guide to the preparation of specifications
BS 7373:1998

BRITISH STANDARDS INSTITUTION
Requirements for electrical installations
IEE Wiring Regulations. Sixteenth Edition
BS 7671:1992

BRITISH STANDARDS INSTITUTION
Code of practice for foundations
BS 8004:1986

BRITISH STANDARDS INSTITUTION
Structural use of concrete
Part 1. Code of practice for design and construction
BS 8110: Part 1:1997

BRITISH STANDARDS INSTITUTION
Structural use of concrete
Part 2. Code of practice for special circumstances
BS 8110: Part 2:1985

BRITISH STANDARDS INSTITUTION
Structural use of concrete
Part 3. Design charts for singly reinforced beams, doubly reinforced beams and rectangular columns
BS 8110: Part 3:1985

BRITISH STANDARDS INSTITUTION
Guide to occupational health and safety management systems
BS 8800:1996

References

GENERAL

BRITISH FLUID POWER ASSOCIATION
A guide to the use of the CE Mark. BFPA/P61
BFPA, 1994

BRITISH FLUID POWER ASSOCIATION
Guidelines for the flushing of hydraulic systems. BFPA/P9
BFPA, 1992

BRITISH FLUID POWER ASSOCIATION
Guidelines for the safe application of hydraulic and pneumatic fluid power equipment. BFPA/P3
BFPA, 1995

BRITISH FLUID POWER ASSOCIATION
Guidelines to electrohydraulic control systems. BFPA/P49
BFPA, 1995

BRITISH FLUID POWER ASSOCIATION
Machinery Directive – Manufacturers. BFPA/P68
BFPA, 1995

CHAPMAN, J C (1998)
"Collapse of the Ramsgate walkway"
The Structural Engineer, 76:1, pp 1–10

CONSTRUCTION INDUSTRY BOARD
Briefing the team
Thomas Telford Publishing, 1997, ISBN 0 7277 2541 6

CONSTRUCTION INDUSTRY BOARD
Code of practice for the selection of main contractors
Thomas Telford Publishing, 1997, ISBN 0 7277 2618 8

CONSTRUCTION INDUSTRY BOARD
Code of practice for the selection of subcontractors
Thomas Telford Publishing, 1997, ISBN 0 7277 2543 2

CONSTRUCTION INDUSTRY RESEARCH AND INFORMATION ASSOCIATION
Value by competition. A guide to the competitive procurement of consultancy services for construction. Special Publication 117
CIRIA, 1994, ISBN 0 86017 414 X

CONSTRUCTION INDUSTRY RESEARCH AND INFORMATION
Specialist trade contracting – a review. Special Publication 138
CIRIA, 1997, ISBN 0 86017 465 4

CONSTRUCTION INDUSTRY RESEARCH AND INFORMATION ASSOCIATION
CDM Regulations – practical guidance for planning supervisors. Report 173
CIRIA, 1998, ISBN 0 86017 487 5

CONSTRUCTION INDUSTRY RESEARCH AND INFORMATION ASSOCIATION
Life cycle costing – a radical approach. Report 122
CIRIA, 1991, ISBN 0 86017 322 4

CONSTRUCTION INDUSTRY RESEARCH AND INFORMATION ASSOCIATION
Managing the design process in civil engineering design and build – a guide for clients, designers and contractors. Funders Report CP59
CIRIA, 1998

CONSTRUCTION INDUSTRY RESEARCH AND INFORMATION ASSOCIATION
Planning to build? A practical introduction to the construction process. Special Publication 113
CIRIA, 1995, ISBN 0 86017 433 6

CONSTRUCTION INDUSTRY RESEARCH AND INFORMATION
Control of risk. A guide to the systematic management of risk from construction. Special Publication 125
CIRIA, 1996, ISBN 0 86017 441 7

HEALTH AND SAFETY EXECUTIVE
Micro processors for industry
HSE, 1981

HEALTH AND SAFETY EXECUTIVE
Out of control – why control systems go wrong, and how to prevent failure
HSE, 1995

HEALTH AND SAFETY EXECUTIVE
Programmable electronic systems in safety related applications
Part 1. An introductory guide
Part 2. General technical guidelines
HSE, 1987

HER MAJESTY'S STATIONERY OFFICE
Admiralty manual of seamanship
HMSO, 1972

ICE CONDITIONS OF CONTRACT STANDING JOINT COMMITTEE
Guidance on the preparation, submission and consideration of tenders for civil engineering contracts recommended for use in the United Kingdom
ICE, ACE and FCEC, ISBN 0 7277 0517 2

INTERNATIONAL CARGO HANDLING CO-ORDINATION ASSOCIATION
SAFETY PANEL
Safe working at ro ro terminals
ICHCA, Pamphlet No 10

INTERNATIONAL CARGO HANDLING CO-ORDINATION ASSOCIATION
Developments in handling of ro ro cargo
ICHCA, 1991

INTERNATIONAL CARGO HANDLING CO-ORDINATION ASSOCIATION
Multilingual glossary of cargo handling terms
ICHCA, Third Edition, 1987

INTERNATIONAL CARGO HANDLING CO-ORDINATION ASSOCIATION
Ro/ro shore and ship ramp characteristics
ICHCA, 1978

PERMANENT INTERNATIONAL ASSOCIATION OF NAVIGATION CONGRESSES
Ferry developments and their consequences for ports. Recommendations for the design and operation of port facilities (Port facilities for ferries. Practical guide)
PIANC, 1995

PERMANENT INTERNATIONAL ASSOCIATION OF NAVIGATION CONGRESSES
Report of the International Study Commission on the Standardisation of Roll-on/Roll-off ships and Berths
PIANC, 1978

STANDING COMMITTEE ON STRUCTURAL SAFETY
Structural safety 1994–96. Review and recommendations
Eleventh Report of SCOSS
SETO Ltd, January 1997, ISBN 1 874266 31 X

SULLIVAN, ERIC
The marine encyclopaedic dictionary
Lloyd's of London Press Ltd, 1992

LEGISLATION

HER MAJESTY'S STATIONERY OFFICE
Health and Safety at Work etc Act 1974
HMSO, 1974

HER MAJESTY'S STATIONERY OFFICE
Docks Regulations
HMSO, 1988

HER MAJESTY'S STATIONERY OFFICE
The Merchant Shipping (Means of Access) Regulations 1988
HMSO, 1988, SI No 1637

HER MAJESTY'S STATIONERY OFFICE
The Pressure Systems and Transportable Gas Containers Regulations 1989
HMSO, 1989, SI No 2169

HER MAJESTY'S STATIONERY OFFICE
The Electricity at Work Regulations 1989
HMSO, 1989, SI No 635, ISBN 0 11 096635X

HER MAJESTY'S STATIONERY OFFICE
The Construction Products Regulations 1991
HMSO, 1991, SI No 1620, ISBN 0 11 014620 4

HER MAJESTY'S STATIONERY OFFICE
Management of Health and Safety at Work Regulations 1992
HMSO, 1992

HER MAJESTY'S STATIONERY OFFICE
Workplace (Health, Safety and Welfare) Regulations 1992
HMSO, 1992, SI No 3004

HEALTH AND SAFETY EXECUTIVE
Provision and Use of Work Equipment Regulations
HSE, 1992

HER MAJESTY'S STATIONERY OFFICE
The Supply of Machinery (Safety) Regulations
HMSO, 1992, SI No 3073

HER MAJESTY'S STATIONERY OFFICE
The Supply of Machinery (Safety) (Amendment) Regulations 1994
HMSO, 1994, SI No 2063

HEALTH AND SAFETY COMMISSION
The Construction (Design and Management) Regulations 1994
HMSO, 1994, SI No 3140, ISBN 0 11 043845 0

HER MAJESTY'S STATIONERY OFFICE
The Construction Products (Amendment) Regulations 1994
HMSO, 1994, SI No 3051, ISBN 0 11 043291 6

HEALTH AND SAFETY EXECUTIVE
The Provision and Use of Work Equipment Regulations 1998
HMSO, 1998, SI No 2306, ISBN 0 11 079599 7

HEALTH AND SAFETY COMMISSION
The Lifting Operations and Lifting Equipment Regulations 1998
HMSO, 1998, SI No 2307, ISBN 0 11 079598 9

GUIDANCE ON LEGISLATION

CONSTRUCTION INDUSTRY AND RESEARCH INFORMATION ASSOCIATION
CDM Regulations – practical guidance for clients and client's agents. Report 172
CIRIA, 1998, ISBN 0 86017 486 7

CONSTRUCTION INDUSTRY RESEARCH AND INFORMATION ASSOCIATION
CDM Regulations – work sector guidance for designers. Report 166
CIRIA, 1997, ISBN 0 86017 464 6

DEPARTMENT OF TRADE AND INDUSTRY
Product standards machinery – guidance notes on UK regulations. URN 95/650
DTI, May 1995

EUROPEAN COMMISSION DGIII – INDUSTRY
Machinery. Useful facts in relation to Directive 89/392/EEC
Office for Official Publications of the European Communities, 1997
ISBN 92 827 9200 5

EUROPEAN COMMISSION/PIERRE MASSAMI AND JEAN-PIERRE VAN
GHELURE
*Community legislation on machinery. Comments on Directive 89/392/EEC and
Directive 91/368/EEC*
Office for Official Publications of the European Communities, 1993

HEALTH AND SAFETY COMMISSION
A guide to managing health and safety in construction
HSE, 1995, ISBN 0 7176 0755 0

HEALTH AND SAFETY COMMISSION
Health and Safety at Work etc Act – advice to employers. HSC3
HSE, 1995

HEALTH AND SAFETY COMMISSION
Management of health and safety at work. Approved Code of Practice L21
HSE, 1992, ISBN 0 7176 0412 8

HEALTH AND SAFETY COMMISSION
Managing construction for health and safety. Approved Code of Practice L54
HSE, 1995, ISBN 0 7176 0792 5

HEALTH AND SAFETY COMMISSION
Safe use of lifting equipment. Approved Code of Practice
HSE Books, 1998

HEALTH AND SAFETY COMMISSION
Safe use of work equipment. Approved Code of Practice
HSE Books, 1998

HEALTH AND SAFETY COMMISSION
Work equipment. Guidance on Regulations. L22
HSE, 1992, ISBN 0 7176 0414 448

HEALTH AND SAFETY COMMISSION
Workplace health, safety and welfare. Approved Code of Practice L24
HMSO, 1992

HEALTH AND SAFETY EXECUTIVE
A guide to risk assessment requirements
HSE, 1996

HEALTH AND SAFETY EXECUTIVE
A guide to the Health and Safety at Work etc Act 1974. L1
HSE, 1990, ISBN 0 11 885555 7

HEALTH AND SAFETY EXECUTIVE
A guide to the Pressure Systems and Transportable Gas Containers Regulations 1989. HS(R)30
HSE, 1990, ISBN 0 11 885516 6

HEALTH AND SAFETY EXECUTIVE
A guide to the Reporting of Injuries, Diseases and Dangerous Occurrences Regulations 1995
HSE Books, 1996, ISBN 0 7176 1012 8

HEALTH AND SAFETY EXECUTIVE
Buying new machinery. INDG 271
HSE, 1998, ISBN 0 7176 1559 6

HEALTH AND SAFETY EXECUTIVE
Construction (Design and Management) Regulations 1994: The role of the client. Construction Sheet No 39
HSE, 1995

HEALTH AND SAFETY EXECUTIVE
Construction (Design and Management) Regulations 1994: The health and safety file. Construction Sheet No 44
HSE, 1995

HEALTH AND SAFETY EXECUTIVE
Five steps to risk assessment. INDG 163 (rev 1)
HSE, 5/98, ISBN 0 7176 1565 0

HEALTH AND SAFETY EXECUTIVE
Lifting gear standards. Guidance Note PM54
HSE, August 1985

HEALTH AND SAFETY EXECUTIVE
Health and safety in construction. HS(G)150
HSE Books, 1996, ISBN 0 7176 0806 9

HEALTH AND SAFETY EXECUTIVE
Memorandum of guidance on the Electricity at Work Regulations 1989.
Health and Safety Series Booklet HS(R)25
HSE, 1989, ISBN 0 11 883963 2

HEALTH AND SAFETY EXECUTIVE
Supplying new machinery. INDG 270
HSE, 1998, ISBN 0 7176 1560 X

HEALTH AND SAFETY EXECUTIVE
Using work equipment safely. INDG 229
HSE, 1998, ISBN 0 7176 1326 7

CLASSIFICATION RULES

DET NORSKE VERITAS
Design and classification of roll on/roll off ships
DNV, May 1980

LLOYD'S REGISTER OF SHIPPING
Code for lifting appliances in a marine environment
LRS, January 1987

LLOYD'S REGISTER OF SHIPPING
Rules and regulations for the classification of ships Part 7,
Chapter 6 Ship to shore ramps and linkspans
LRS, January 1993

LLOYD'S REGISTER OF SHIPPING
Rules and regulations for the classification of linkspans. Part 1. Regulations
Part 2. Manufacture, testing and certification of materials. Part 3. Construction, design
and testing requirements. Part 4. Engineering systems
LRS, 1998